PRACTICAL ENGLISH GRAMMAR

新编实用英语语法教程

主　编　曹姗姗
副主编　倪　媛　黄　娟
主　审　代小玲

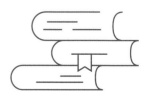

中国·武汉

图书在版编目(CIP)数据

新编实用英语语法教程/曹姗姗主编. —武汉:华中科技大学出版社,2022.6(2023.9 重印)
ISBN 978-7-5680-8229-7

Ⅰ.①新… Ⅱ.①曹… Ⅲ.①英语-语法-教材 Ⅳ.①H314

中国版本图书馆 CIP 数据核字(2022)第 077860 号

新编实用英语语法教程
Xinbian Shiyong Yingyu Yufa Jiaocheng

曹姗姗 主编

策划编辑:刘　平
责任编辑:刘　平
封面设计:廖亚萍
责任校对:张汇娟
责任监印:周治超

出版发行:华中科技大学出版社(中国·武汉)　　电话:(027)81321913
　　　　　武汉市东湖新技术开发区华工科技园　　邮编:430223
录　排:华中科技大学惠友文印部
印　刷:武汉开心印印刷有限公司
开　本:787mm×1092mm　1/16
印　张:16.25　插页:1
字　数:421 千字
版　次:2023 年 9 月第 1 版第 2 次印刷
定　价:48.00 元

本书若有印装质量问题,请向出版社营销中心调换
全国免费服务热线: 400-6679-118　竭诚为您服务
版权所有　侵权必究

前　　言

随着高职教育的发展，国家和社会对熟练掌握各类技能的技术应用型人才的要求越来越高。英语作为高职学生必备的一项基本技能，在学生就业及职场发展中的作用不言而喻。本书作为高等职业教育英语学科的重要教辅材料，对学生在英语学习过程中遇到的各种语法现象、规则、用法等进行了系统的梳理和介绍，并提供符合学生认知水平的例句和习题，帮助学生理解并掌握基础的语法知识点，提高英语运用能力和自学能力。

本书针对历年来公共英语教材中涵盖的重点语法内容和《高等职业教育专科英语课程标准》规定的高职高专英语课程语法范围，在编写上体现了如下几个特点。

一、条理性强。本书对高职高专英语教学中的语法项目，包括基本句型、句子成分、各种句法以及各类词法进行梳理、归纳，使各语法知识点概念清晰，重点显现，并配以浅显易懂的例句加以说明，让学生对语法有一个系统、完整的认识，从而提高使用的准确性。

二、针对性强。本书内容基于高职高专学生的真实英语水平，所选例句和习题贴合学生的认知水平和生活实际，使学生在学习过程中能触类旁通，学以致用。

三、操作性强。本书每一章后都附有大量的专项强化训练题，以便学生在掌握每一章节的理论基础上进行强化练习，学练结合，融会贯通。这部分的设计不仅给学生提供了大量的实际练习，而且让教师在教学中具有操作性。

参与本书编写的都是多年从事高职高专英语教学的教师，他们结合自己丰富的教学经验，对语法内容进行了深入分析、总结，使得本书在内容的选择、深度的把握上有着重点突出、难度适当、实用性强的特点。相信本书能为学生的课内外英语学习及教师的教学提供一定的帮助。

本书由曹姗姗老师担任主编，并全书统稿。其中，曹姗姗老师编写了第1、2、8章及其练习答案；倪媛老师编写了第3章及其练习答案；李晓莉老师编写了第4章及其练习答案；高明老师编写了第5章及其练习答案，以及附录部分；肖棠心老师编写了第6章及其练习答案；田恩泽老师编写了第7章及其练习答案；代小玲老师编写了第9章及其练习答案；黄娟老师编写了第10、11章及其练习答案。

由于编者水平所限，书中定有不足之处，望读者批评、指正。

编　者

2022 年 2 月

目　录

第1章　句子与句子成分 …………………………………………………………… (1)
　1.1　句子概说 …………………………………………………………………… (1)
　1.2　句子成分 …………………………………………………………………… (3)
　1.3　实战演练 ………………………………………………………………… (16)
　1.4　专项练习 ………………………………………………………………… (16)

第2章　动词的时态和语态 ……………………………………………………… (18)
　2.1　动词时态 ………………………………………………………………… (18)
　2.2　被动语态 ………………………………………………………………… (30)
　2.3　实战演练 ………………………………………………………………… (33)
　2.4　专项练习 ………………………………………………………………… (35)

第3章　虚拟语气 ………………………………………………………………… (40)
　3.1　语气 ……………………………………………………………………… (40)
　3.2　条件句 …………………………………………………………………… (41)
　3.3　名词性从句中的虚拟语气 ……………………………………………… (42)
　3.4　其他句型中的虚拟语气 ………………………………………………… (44)
　3.5　实战演练 ………………………………………………………………… (45)
　3.6　专项练习 ………………………………………………………………… (46)

第4章　非谓语动词 ……………………………………………………………… (50)
　4.1　动词不定式 ……………………………………………………………… (50)
　4.2　动名词 …………………………………………………………………… (54)
　4.3　分词 ……………………………………………………………………… (59)
　4.4　实战演练 ………………………………………………………………… (63)
　4.5　专项练习 ………………………………………………………………… (67)

第5章　名词性从句 ……………………………………………………………… (72)
　5.1　连接词 that 引导的名词性从句 ………………………………………… (72)
　5.2　whether/if 引导名词性从句 …………………………………………… (73)
　5.3　连接代词与连接副词引导的名词性从句 ……………………………… (74)
　5.4　实战演练 ………………………………………………………………… (76)
　5.5　专项练习 ………………………………………………………………… (77)

第6章　定语从句 ………………………………………………………………… (81)
　6.1　关系代词和关系副词引导的定语从句 ………………………………… (81)

6.2　限制性定语从句和非限制性定语从句 ……………………………… (84)
　　6.3　介词＋关系代词 ……………………………………………………… (86)
　　6.4　关系代词的选择 ……………………………………………………… (88)
　　6.5　定语从句与同位语从句的区别 ……………………………………… (90)
　　6.6　实战演练 ……………………………………………………………… (91)
　　6.7　专项练习 ……………………………………………………………… (92)
第7章　状语从句 ………………………………………………………………… (98)
　　7.1　时间状语从句 ………………………………………………………… (98)
　　7.2　地点状语从句 ………………………………………………………… (100)
　　7.3　条件状语从句 ………………………………………………………… (101)
　　7.4　让步状语从句 ………………………………………………………… (101)
　　7.5　原因状语从句 ………………………………………………………… (103)
　　7.6　目的状语从句 ………………………………………………………… (104)
　　7.7　结果状语从句 ………………………………………………………… (104)
　　7.8　方式状语从句 ………………………………………………………… (104)
　　7.9　比较状语从句 ………………………………………………………… (105)
　　7.10　实战演练 …………………………………………………………… (106)
　　7.11　专项练习 …………………………………………………………… (107)
第8章　一致关系 ………………………………………………………………… (110)
　　8.1　主谓一致 ……………………………………………………………… (110)
　　8.2　代词一致 ……………………………………………………………… (113)
　　8.3　实战演练 ……………………………………………………………… (114)
　　8.4　专项练习 ……………………………………………………………… (114)
第9章　倒装 ……………………………………………………………………… (117)
　　9.1　全部倒装 ……………………………………………………………… (117)
　　9.2　部分倒装 ……………………………………………………………… (119)
　　9.3　实战演练 ……………………………………………………………… (121)
　　9.4　专项练习 ……………………………………………………………… (122)
第10章　强调 …………………………………………………………………… (128)
　　10.1　位置强调 …………………………………………………………… (128)
　　10.2　词或词组强调 ……………………………………………………… (128)
　　10.3　句型强调 …………………………………………………………… (130)
　　10.4　实战演练 …………………………………………………………… (131)
　　10.5　专项练习 …………………………………………………………… (131)
第11章　构词法 ………………………………………………………………… (135)
　　11.1　派生法 ……………………………………………………………… (135)
　　11.2　转化法 ……………………………………………………………… (137)
　　11.3　合成法 ……………………………………………………………… (138)

- 11.4 截短法 ……………………………………………………………（139）
- 11.5 首字母缩略法 ……………………………………………………（139）
- 11.6 混合法 ……………………………………………………………（139）
- 11.7 实战演练 …………………………………………………………（140）
- 11.8 专项练习 …………………………………………………………（143）
- 附录 A 单词及专业词汇表（A 级）………………………………………（149）
- 附录 B "实战演练"参考答案 ………………………………………………（218）
- 附录 C "专项练习"参考答案 ………………………………………………（248）
- 参考书目 ……………………………………………………………………（252）

第1章　句子与句子成分

1.1　句子概说

1.1.1　基本句型

英语中有五种基本句型，而这五种基本句型主要由谓语动词的性质和特点决定。这里，S = 主语，V = 谓语，P = 表语，O = 宾语，Oi = 间接宾语，Od = 直接宾语，C = 宾语补足语。

1）主语—系动词—表语（SVP 主系表结构）

在这种结构中，V 是系动词（link *v.*），常见的系动词有 be, look, seem, appear, sound, feel, taste, smell, grow, get, become, turn 等。

　　Yangzhou is a beautiful city.
　　扬州是一座美丽的城市。（名词词组充当表语）
　　This idea sounds good.
　　这个主意听起来很好。（形容词充当表语）
　　The book is on English grammar.
　　这本书是英语语法书。（介词词组充当表语）

2）主语—谓语（SV 主谓结构）

这种结构中谓语动词为不及物动词，其后即使不带其他句子成分，意义也完整（当然也可带状语等修饰成分）。

　　He might have arrived.
　　他可能已经到了。
　　Leaves fall in autumn.
　　秋天树叶脱落。
　　This horse runs very fast.
　　这匹马跑得很快。

3）主语—谓语—宾语（SVO 主谓宾结构）

这种结构中谓语动词为及物动词，后须接宾语。

　　John likes music.
　　约翰喜欢音乐。（名词充当宾语）
　　They offered to help us.
　　他们给了我们帮助。（动词不定式充当宾语）

4）主语—谓语—间接宾语—直接宾语（SVOiOd 主谓双宾结构）

在这种结构中，谓语动词是带有双宾语的及物动词。常见的需带双宾语的动词有 give, ask, bring, offer, send, pay, lend, show, tell, buy, rob, warn 等。

He gave me a book/a book to me.

他给了我一本书。

He brought me a pen/a pen to me.

他给我带来了一支钢笔。

He offered me his seat/his seat to me.

他把他的座位让给了我。

注意下边动词改写后介词的变化：

Mother bought me a book/a book for me.

妈妈给我买了一本书。

He got me a chair/a chair for me.

他为我弄了一张椅子。

5）主语—谓语—宾语—补语（SVOC 主谓宾补结构）

在这种结构中，谓语动词是及物动词，其后须接宾语和宾语补足语（又称复合宾语）。常作宾语补足语的词有形容词、副词、介词短语、名词、不定式、现在分词和过去分词。常见的可接宾语补足语的动词有很多，哪些动词可以接哪几种形式作宾语，需根据动词的惯用法而定，不能一概而论。

Mary found this story interesting.

玛丽觉得这个故事有趣。（形容词充当宾补）

Mother asks me to study hard.

妈妈要求我努力学习。（动词不定式充当宾补）

1.1.2 句子结构

根据结构，英语的句子分为三种：简单句（Simple Sentence），并列句（Compound Sentence）和复合句（Complex Sentence）。换句话说，就句子结构而言，英语中的所有句子无非是上述三种句子中的一种。

1）简单句

简单句是指只有一个完整的主谓结构的句子。

The man arrived at the house.

那个男人到达了那栋房屋。（一个主语＋一个谓语）

The man arrived at the house and knocked at the door.

那个男人到达了那栋房屋，并敲了门。（一个主语＋两个谓语）

The man and the woman arrived at the house.

那个男人和女人到达了那栋房屋。（两个主语＋一个谓语）

The man and the woman arrived at the house and knocked at the door.

那个男人和女人到达了那栋房屋，并敲了门。（两个主语＋两个谓语）

2) 并列句

并列句是指具有两个完整的主谓结构的句子；两个主谓结构之间通常由并列连词或分号连接。常见的并列连词有 and，but，yet，for，as well as，either...or，both...and，neither...nor，not only...but also，whether...or，so 等，用来表达关联、选择、转折、否定、递进等关系。(注意：在英语中，通常不用逗号连接两个主谓结构)

I enjoy music and he is fond of playing guitar.

我喜欢音乐，而他喜欢弹奏吉他。(并列连词连接)

He sold his farm, so he had enough money for his trip.

他卖了他的农场，因此有足够的钱去旅游。

The coat was thin, but it was warm.

虽然这件大衣很薄，但是它保暖。

The man knocked at the door; no one answered.

那个男人敲了门，但是没人开门。(分号连接)

3) 复合句

复合句是指含有一个主句以及一个或几个从句的句子。从句通常由连接词引导。

When the man arrived at the house, he knocked at the door.

当那个男人到达那栋房屋时，他敲了敲门。(状语从句 + 主句)

I think that you are right.

我认为你是对的。(主句 + 宾语从句)

1.2 句子成分

构成句子的各个部分叫作句子成分。句子成分有主要成分和次要成分。主要成分有主语和谓语；次要成分有表语、宾语、定语、状语、补足语和同位语。句子的顺序一般是主语、谓语、宾语、宾语补足语，而表语、定语、状语的位置要根据情况而定。

1.2.1 主语

主语是一个句子所述说的主体，表示所说的是谁或是什么。它的位置一般在句首。可做主语的词类有名词、代词、数词、动名词、动词不定式及一些名词化的其他词类和从句。

1) 名词

A tree has fallen across the road.

一棵树倒下横卧在路上。

There is a desk and several chairs in the room.

房间里有一张桌子和几把椅子。

2) 代词

He fell off his horse and injured his back.

他从马上摔下来，背部受伤了。

Who likes to eat sea foods?

谁喜欢吃海鲜？

3）数词

Sixteen of them are for the plan; four are against it.

他们中 16 人赞成，4 人反对这个计划。

The second is yours.

第二个是你的。

4）动名词

Watching English TV news is a good way to learn English.

看英语电视新闻是一种学习英语的好方法。

Your going there won't help much.

你去了也帮不上多大的忙。

5）动词不定式

To play the piano well requires much practice.

要弹好钢琴，需勤加练习。

To obey the laws is everybody's duty.

遵守法律，人人有责。

It is necessary to master a foreign language.

掌握一门外语是有必要的。（it 作形式主语，真正的主语为后面的不定式）

6）名词化的其他词类

The deaf and dumb must be taken good care of.

聋哑人应受到良好的照顾。

A is the first letter of the English alphabet.

A 在英语字母表中排在第一个。

7）从句

What they said seems reasonable.

他们说的话似乎很有道理。

Whether he will come or not remains undecided.

他是否来还没有决定。

That he will refuse the offer is unlikely.

他不可能拒绝建议。

1.2.2 谓语

谓语说明主语所做的动作或具有的特征和状态。动词在句中作谓语，一般放在主语之后。谓语形式受主语限制，在数和人称上要与主语一致，表现出时态、语态和语气。

1）简单谓语

单纯由一个行为动词构成的谓语就是简单谓语。这个动词可以是单个动词，也可以是动词短语，也可以是其他动词词组。

I've heard him tell the same joke five times.

那个笑话我已经听他讲了五遍了。

Do you get along well with others in your office?

在办公室你与他人相处好吗？

He has fallen into bad habits.

他已经养成了一些坏习惯。

2）复合谓语

复合谓语都由两部分构成，主要有以下两类。

①由情态动词加动词原形和半助动词加不定式构成。

常用的情态动词有：may, can, must, will, shall, need, dare, ought to, used to 等。半助动词是在功能上介于主要动词和助动词之间的一种结构，常见的有：be able to, be certain to, be likely to, be willing to, be about to, be due to, be obliged to, be going to, be supposed to, had better, have to, be to 等。

You should see a doctor about this problem.

关于这毛病，你应该看医生。

When I was young, I used to swim every day.

当我年轻时，我通常每天游泳。

They are going to win the world cup.

他们将赢得世界杯。

You are certain to be happy with them.

与他们在一起你一定很高兴。

The flight is due to leave at 11：30.

这趟航班预计在十一点半起飞。

②由一个连系动词加表语构成复合谓语说明主语的特征、类属、状态、身份等。

You look tired.

你看起来疲惫。

The temperature continued very low.

气温依旧很低。

The leaves turned gold and red.

这些树叶变成了金红色。

1.2.3 表语

表语是用来说明主语的特征、状态和身份。它也可以说是一种主语补语。一般位于连系动词之后。表语可由名词、代词、数词、形容词、副词、不定式、动名词、分词、介词短语或从句表示。

1）名词

The wedding was that Sunday.

婚礼是在那个星期天举行的。

That sounds a good idea.

那听起来是个好主意。

When I heard my name mentioned, I was all ears.

我听见有人提到我的名字，就仔细听了。

2）代词

My suggestion is this.

我的建议是这样。

That hat is not mine; mine is over there.

那帽子不是我的，我的在那里。

3）数词

He was the first to arrive at the power station.

他是第一个到达电站的。

We are four altogether.

我们总共四人。

4）形容词

Fish and meat easily goes bad in hot weather.

鱼和肉在热天容易变坏。

They feel proud of what they have achieved.

他们为取得的成就而感到自豪。

5）副词

Time is up. Class is over.

时间到了，下课。

Prices of vegetables are usually up and down according to the weather.

蔬菜价格通常随气候变化而上下波动。

6）不定式

All I could do was to wait.

我只能等待。

Our task is to start a set of calculations at once.

我们的任务是马上开始一系列的计算。

The problem is how to finish the homework in such a short time.

问题是在这么短的时间里怎么完成家庭作业。

7）动名词

Complimenting is lying.

恭维就是说谎。

My favorite winter sport is skating.

冬天我最爱好的体育运动是溜冰。

Training students' short memory is not teaching reading.

训练学生的短期记忆力，并不是教阅读。

8）分词

I was so much surprised at it.

我对此事感到很惊讶。

The food is inviting.
食品很吸引人。
He got drunk on only two drinks.
他只喝了两杯就醉了。

9）介词短语

The show is from seven till ten.
演出时间为 7 点至 10 点。
The two boys are of the same height.
这两个男孩子的个子一样高。
This body remains at rest.
该物体仍处于静止状态。

10）从句

This is where I first met her.
这就是我初次与她会面的地方。
My suggestion is that we should go to the Great Wall instead of the Summer Palace.
我的建议是我们去长城，不去颐和园。

※补充：能作系动词的实义动词

表示变化的动词：
come, go, run, turn, get, become, keep, stay, make
感官动词：
feel, sound, smell, look, taste
似乎，好像：
seem, appear
Our dream has come true.
我们的梦想实现了。（come 后常加 easy, loose, natural 等）
He felt sick.
他病了。
Keep fit.
保重。（keep 作为系动词还常接 quiet, calm, cool, well, warm, silent, clean, dry）
The well ran dry.
这口井干枯了。
A thin person always seems to be taller than he really is.
一个瘦个子看起来比他的实际身高要高些。

1.2.4　宾语

宾语表示动作的对象或承受者，它一般位于及物动词和介词后面。宾语可分为直接宾语、间接宾语、复合宾语、介词宾语、同源宾语等。能作宾语的有名词、代词、数词、名词化形容词（或过去分词）、动词不定式、动名词短语、从句等。

1）直接宾语

　　直接宾语是指谓语动词所表示的动作的直接承受者或所导致的直接结果。

　　The waiter brought two coffees to the table.

　　侍者把两杯咖啡端到桌上。（名词）

　　It was too dark to see anything.

　　天太黑了，什么也看不见。（代词）

　　Five and five makes ten.

　　五加五等于十。（数词）

　　Robin Hood hated the rich and loved and protected the poor.

　　罗宾汉仇恨富人，热爱并保护穷人。（名词化形容词）

　　I want to cross out the unnecessary words.

　　我想删去不必要的词。（不定式短语）

　　Please excuse my being so late.

　　请原谅我来得这么晚。（动名词短语）

　　I think that he referred you to this dictionary.

　　我想他叫你查过这词典。（从句）

2）间接宾语

　　有些及物动词，如 give 等，需要两个宾语。往往一个指人，一个指物，指人的叫间接宾语，指物的叫直接宾语。间接宾语一般放在直接宾语之前。若要强调间接宾语，可以把间接宾语挪后，并在其前加上介词 to 或 for，根据动词决定。

　　He gave me some ink.

　　他给了我一点墨水。

　　I sent him a letter yesterday.

　　我昨天给他发了一封信。

　　Show your plan to him.

　　把你的计划给他看看。

　　She bought a new jacket for her husband.

　　她为她的丈夫买了一件新夹克。

　　He made a nice bookcase for his uncle.

　　他为叔叔做了一个漂亮的书柜。

　　通常可接双宾语的及物动词有 allow, bring, give, hand, offer, owe, lend, leave, cause, pass, pay, permit, promise, refuse, read, sell, send, show, take, teach, tell, wish, write, buy, choose, cook, fetch, get, make, order, paint, save, spare, sing 等。

3）同源宾语

　　英语中，有些不及物动词可以跟一个同源名词作宾语，这个名词就称为同源宾语。同源宾语有两种：一种是该名词与动词是同一个词根，意思也一样；另一种名词只是在意思上与动词相近。同源宾语前常带一个定语。

　　A. They began a good beginning.

他们有一个良好的开端。
The soldiers fought a brave fight.
战士们打得很勇敢。
The baby slept a sound sleep.
这婴儿睡得很香。
They lived a hard life before liberation.
解放前他们过着艰苦的生活。
The old man died a sudden death.
那位老人突然死了。
The boy dreamed a dreadful dream.
那男孩做了一个噩梦。

B. The boys ran a race in the park.
孩子们在公园里赛跑。
The wind blew a gale.
刮了一阵风。
They fought a good battle.
他们打了很好的一战。

4）介词宾语

介词宾语是指介词后面接的名词或相当于名词的词或短语。
Joans was hiding a smile with his hand.
琼斯用手掩饰他的笑。
The milk in the bottle went sour.
瓶子里的牛奶变酸了。
What prevented you from joining us last night?
昨天晚上是什么阻止了你和我们在一起？

5）复合宾语

复合宾语请参见"2.5 补足语"。

1.2.5　补足语

1）宾语补足语

英语中有些及物动词除要求有一个宾语之外，还要求一个补充说明宾语的成分，才能使句子的意义完整，这个成分叫作宾语补足语（object complement）。宾语和宾语补足语在逻辑上有着主谓关系，它们一起构成复合宾语。常见的能接复合宾语的动词有：

cause（引起，使得）	call（把……叫作……）
name（把……命名为……）	elect（选……为……）
find（发现……是……）	paint（把……漆成……）
ask（向……问……）	consider（认为……是……）
make（使……成为……）	get（让……，使得……）

have（让……，使得……） let（让……）
see（看见……） know（知道……）
start（使……开始……） hear（听见……）
allow（容许……，使……能……） want（想……）
keep（使……保持……） force（使……）
notice（注意……） watch（观看……）
think（认为……） permit（允许……）
prove（证明……是……） hold（认为……是……）
observe（注视……） …

They elected me captain of the team.

他们选我当队长。

We made her monitor of our class.

我们选她当我们班的班长。

We found everything there in good order.

我们发现那里的一切井井有条。

可以作宾语补足语的有名词、形容词、介词短语、动词不定式、分词等。

带有宾补的一般结构为：某些及物动词（如 make 等）+直接宾语（名词或代词）+宾语补足语。

（1）名词

We consider Mr. Wang a steel worker.

我们认为王先生是钢铁工人。

Everyone calls him Uncle Ben.

人人叫他本大叔。

（2）形容词

We consider the test very important.

我们认为这项试验很重要。

We must get something right.

我们必须搞清某事。

（3）动词不定式

They expect us to help them.

他们希望我们帮助他们。

We encourage him to go on with his experiment.

我们鼓励他继续做实验。

I should advise you not to miss the chance.

我劝你不要错过机会。

注意：在主动语态中，不定式在使役动词或感官动词后作宾语补足语时，通常不带 to。

Electricity makes the machine run.

电使机器转动。

All of us have seen a lifted body fall.

我们大家都见到过抛起的物体下落。

但是，在被动语态中，不定式作使役动词或感官动词的主语补足语时，一般不能省去 to。

The machine is made to run by electricity.

A lifted body has been seen to fall (by all of us).

这类及物动词有 make, have, let, see, hear, watch, notice, listen to, look at, observe 等。

(4) 分词

In our everyday life, we see things moving about on the ground or in the air. 在我们日常生活中，我们看见许多东西在地面和空中运动。

The newspaper article set me thinking.

报纸上的那篇文章使我陷入沉思。

I could feel my heart beating fast.

我可以感觉出自己的心跳得很快。

They found Wuhan greatly changed.

他们发现武汉变化很大。

At that time we were there and saw it done.

那时我们在那儿，并见到这件事做完。

注意：如果宾语和宾语补足语之间是主谓关系，宾补用现在分词；如果宾语和宾语补足语之间是动宾关系，宾补用过去分词。

(5) 介词短语

This makes it of great use.

这使它十分有用。

She found everything in the laboratory in good order.

她发现实验室内每件东西都放得井井有条。

(6) 由 as 引出的宾语补足语

I look upon him as my teacher.

我把他看成是我的老师。

The conclusion has been accepted as true.

这个结论已被公认为是正确的。

We consider machine parts as linked.

我们认为机器零件连接好了。

2) it 在复合宾语中的应用

宾语一般放在宾语补足语之前，但当复合宾语中的宾语是用不定式短语、动名词短语（结构较长）或从句表示时，往往可放在宾补之后（充当真正宾语），而用一个引导词 it（即形式宾语）来引导。

They thought it right to do this test.
他们原先想，做这项试验是对的。
We consider it useless learning a theory without practice.
我们认为学习理论而没有实践是无用的。
I must make it clear that I'm disappointed at your decision.
我得说清楚，我对你们的决定感到很失望。
如果上述结构变成被动语态，原宾语成为主语，原宾语补足语相应地变为主语补足语（subject complement）。
Some goods are left unsold.
有些货物剩下未出售。（分词做主语补足语）
She was elected director of public relations.
她被选为公关部主任。（名词短语做主语补足语）

1.2.6 定语

修饰名词或代词的词、短语或句子，称为定语。汉语中用"……的"表示。定语一般可由形容词、名词、代词、名词所有格、数词、不定式、动名词、分词（短语）、介词短语、副词或从句充当。单个词作定语时，通常放在被修饰的名词或代词的前面，称为前置定语；短语或从句作定语时，放在被修饰的名词或代词的后面，称为后置定语。

1）形容词

The little boy needs a blue pen.
小男孩需要一支蓝色的钢笔。
Tom is a handsome boy.
汤姆是个英俊的男孩。
Is there anything new in this book?
这本书里有新内容吗？
若形容词修饰 some, any, every, no 构成的复合不定代词时（如 something, nothing, anything 等），只能做后置定语。

2）名词

For instance, a steam engine can operate an oil pump.
例如，蒸汽机能带动一个油泵。
We expect him to come by the night train.
我们希望他乘夜间的火车回来。
There is only one ball pen in the pencil box.
这铅笔盒里只有一支圆珠笔。

3）代词

Give me another ten minutes and I'll finish it.
再给我十分钟，我就会完成。
I'm sorry my homework is late.

很抱歉我的作业迟交了。

4）名词所有格

His boy needs Tom's pen.

他的孩子需要汤姆的钢笔。

Some American tourists will visit the Children's Palace tomorrow.

一些美国游客明天要参观青少年宫。

5）数词

There are two boys in the room.

房间里有两个男孩。

You must review the first three chapters.

你必须复习一到三章。

6）不定式

The boy to write this letter needs a pen.

写这封信的男孩需要一支钢笔。

There is nothing to do today.

今天无事要做。

I won't go to the concert; I have an important letter to write.

音乐会我不去了，我还有一封很重要的信要写。

7）动名词

Living expenses are rising.

生活费用正在上涨。

The working conditions of miners are being further improved.

矿工们的工作条件正在得到进一步的改善。

8）分词（短语）

The smiling boy needs a pen bought by his mother.

那个微笑着的男孩需要一支他妈妈买的钢笔。

There are five boys left.

有五个留下的男孩。

There are still some mistakes in the corrected papers.

在改过的那一摞试卷中仍然存在一些错误。

The pen bought by her is made in China.

她买的笔是中国产的。

There is a long line waiting to get the new stamps.

一长排人等待购买新邮票。

Wang Meng is a writer loved by young people.

王蒙是一位受年轻人喜欢的作家。

9）介词短语

The boy in blue is Tom.

穿蓝色衣服的男孩是汤姆。

There are two boys of 9, and three of 10.

有两个9岁的，三个10岁的男孩。

I wonder whom the books on the shelf belong to.

我想知道书架上的书是谁的。

10）副词

少数副词（大部分是表示地点的副词）可以在句中做定语，一般是后置修饰，偶然也有前置修饰。

The boy there needs a pen.

那边的那个男孩需要一支钢笔。

The best boy here is Tom.

这里最棒的男孩是汤姆。

I am sorry I don't know the man over there.

很抱歉，我不认识那儿的那个人。

The above instructions will help you much when you do the following exercises.

上面的几点说明对你做下面这些练习很有帮助。

The then leaders paid little attention to the increase of production.

当时的领导不重视增产。

11）从句

The boy that you will know is Tom.

你将认识的男孩叫汤姆。

There are five boys who will play the game.

参加游戏的男孩有五个。

Those who help others are surely helped.

帮助别人的人一定也会得到帮助。

The boy who is reading needs the pen which you bought yesterday.

那个在阅读的男孩需要你昨天买的钢笔。

1.2.7 状语

状语是修饰动词、形容词、副词或整个句子的。它可以用来表示时间、地点、方式、原因、结果、条件、让步、比较、程度、目的、伴随情况等。常用来充当状语的有副词、介词短语、不定式、分词、名词、从句等。

1）副词（短语）

The boy needs a pen very much.

男孩非常需要一支钢笔。（程度状语）

The boy needs very much the pen bought by his mother.

男孩非常需要他母亲买的那支钢笔。（宾语较长则状语前置）

Factories and buildings are going up here and there.

到处建起工厂和楼房。（地点状语）

2）介词短语

In the classroom, the boy needs a pen.

在教室里，男孩需要一支钢笔。（地点状语）

Before his mother, Tom is always a boy.

在母亲面前，汤姆总是一个男孩子。（条件状语）

They managed to finish the job before Monday.

他们设法在星期一之前完成任务。（时间状语）

3）分词（短语）

The old man sat on the bench, enjoying the afternoon sun.

那位老人坐在长凳上，享受着下午的阳光。（伴随状态）

Having run for an hour, we were so tired.

跑了一个小时，我们都非常累。（时间状语）

Frightened, he sits there soundlessly.

（因为）受了惊吓，他无声地坐在那儿。（原因状语）

4）不定式

The boy needs a pen to do his homework.

男孩需要一支笔写家庭作业。（目的状语）

I arrived late only to find the train gone.

我晚到了，结果发现火车已经开了。（结果状语）

To make his dream come true, Tom becomes very interested in business.

为了实现梦想，汤姆变得对商业很感兴趣。（目的状语）

5）名词（短语）

We worked hard day and night.

我们夜以继日地努力工作。

He lived three miles away.

他住在离这三英里远的地方。

6）从句

I shall go there if it doesn't rain.

如果不下雨，我会去那儿。（条件状语从句）

As he was leaving the office, it started to rain.

当他离开办公室的时候，天开始下起雨来。（时间状语从句）

There is air all around us although we cannot see it.

虽然我们看不到空气，但我们周围的确存在着空气。（让步状语从句）

I am taller than he is.

我长得比他高。（比较状语从句）

1.3　实战演练

Analyze the following sentence structures, and point out whether they are simple sentences, compound sentences or complex sentences.

1. John behaves badly; nobody in the class likes him.
2. Everybody has a machine and we call it the brain.
3. Mrs. Brown got back home two hours later and found her husband waiting for her.
4. The doctor told Mr. Brown to stop smoking and he ignored the doctor's orders.
5. I asked John to show me the dictionary that he had bought the previous day.
6. I haven't got the dictionary at hand but I will show it to you later.
7. They said nothing about him because of his wife being there.
8. For most people, the left side of the brain deals with such things as logic, language, reasoning, number, and analysis, the so-called "academic" activities.
9. Sad stories are not very nice to read about, but if we think and talk about them, we may be able to prevent more accidents.
10. Most employers believe that those who look as if they care about themselves are more likely to care about their jobs.

1.4　专项练习

Fill in the following blanks with the proper forms of the words given in the brackets.

1. The program was implemented with great (efficient) _____ and speed.
2. All the workers in the factory are very (skill) _____ in doing their jobs.
3. It's hard to imagine life without (electric) _____ .
4. (serve) _____ the people well is our duty.
5. His (motivate) _____ for coming to China is to learn Chinese and travel around.
6. They were taught to (large) _____ photographs in Mr. Li's class.
7. With her knowledge and experience, she was surely (qualify) _____ for the work.
8. My friend and co-worker John (play) _____ basketball in his spare time.
9. It's very (thought) _____ and very kind of him to offer me a job in his school.
10. The pupils will get (confuse) _____ if they are made to learn too much.
11. Sleep, rest and (relax) _____ are the best remedies for many headaches.
12. My father (read) _____ your thesis all the afternoon.
13. His dream is not only to be a soldier but also (become) _____ a general in the future.
14. There were only a few (survive) _____ from the air-crash.
15. All factors must be taken into (considerate) _____ when we think over how to handle

the problem.

16. Without a passport, leaving the country is (possible) _____ .
17. Three-fourths of its surface of the earth (be) _____ sea.
18. Nothing at his college seemed (excite) _____ to him.
19. I don't think (anxious) _____ over your work is helpful.
20. We all like him because he has a great (sensitive) _____ of humor.
21. The English teacher became angry, because of her (absent) _____ from school for several days.
22. The (distant) _____ between the two cities is quite difficult to figure out.
23. He is such a (self) _____ man. You can't help but respect him.
24. To be frank, I like Mrs. Zhang's class most because she could speak English very (fluent) _____ .
25. There is a (child) _____ innocence between friends.
26. Lecturers must be very careful about their (express) _____ .
27. They decided not to go to the hometown because it was snowing (heavy) _____ .
28. It's (danger) _____ for children until 12 to ride the bicycle on the road.
29. Grandpa can walk (far) _____ than a young man.
30. The boy's father was so (thank) _____ that he taught him how to use a computer.
31. My sister has recently got a job as a (reception) _____ in a hotel.
32. Miss Cherry is a well-known singer. She showed (music) _____ tendencies from her early age.
33. The local government is trying to raise money to (modern) _____ the city's public transport systems.
34. If you want to get this job, you must first fill this (apply) _____ form.

第 2 章 动词的时态和语态

2.1 动词时态

英语中在不同时间和以不同方式发生的动作或状态要用谓语动词的不同形式来表示，这种表示动作或状态发生时间和方式的动词形式称作动词时态。时态由"时"和"态"构成。"时"主要有 4 种，即现在、过去、将来和过去将来；"态"也有 4 种，即一般、进行、完成和完成进行。将 4 个"时"和 4 个"态"组合在一起，就是时态的种类，共 16 种。（本章讲解 12 种常用时态）

	现在	过去	将来	过去将来
一般	do	did	will do shall do be going to do	would do
进行	be doing	was/were doing	will be doing	would be doing
完成	have done	had done	will have done	would have done
完成进行	have been doing	had been doing	will have been doing	would have been doing

2.1.1 一般现在时

一般现在时表示经常发生或习惯性的动作或状态，可表示主语的性格、特征、能力等。

1）一般现在时的构成（以 be 动词为例）

	单数	复数
第一人称	I am...	We are...
第二人称	You are...	You are...
第三人称	He/She/It is...	They are...

动词一般现在时第三人称单数动词变化规则如下。

① 直接在动词词尾加 s。

ask—asks work—works get—gets stay—stays

② 以字母 s, x, ch, sh 或 o 结尾的动词，在词尾加 es。

watch—watches wish—wishes fix—fixes do—does
go—goes pass—passes

③ 以"辅音字母加+y"结尾的动词，先变 y 为 i 再加 es。
try—tries study—studies cry—cries fly—flies
④ 不规则变化。
be—am/is/are have—has

2）一般现在时的句式

一般现在时在肯定、否定和一般疑问句中的形式如下表。

肯定	否定	一般疑问
I am...	I am not...	Am I...
He（She/It）is...	He（She/It）is not...	Is（he/she/it）...？
We（You/They）are...	We（You/They）are not...	Are we（you/they）...？
I（You）have...	I（You）have not...	Have I（you）...？
He（She/It）has...	He（She/It）has not...	Has he（she/it）...？
We（You/They）have...	We（You/They）have not...	Have we（you/they）...？
I（You）study...	I（You）do not study...	Do I（you）study...？
He（She/It）studies...	He（She/It）does not study...	Does he（she/it）study...？
We（You/They）study...	We（You/They）do not study...	Do we（you/they）study...？

3）一般现在时的基本用法

①表示经常或习惯性的动作，常与 often，usually，always，every，sometimes，at 等表示时间频度的时间状语连用。

He often goes swimming in summer.

夏天他经常去游泳。

I often have lunch in the canteen.

我中午常常在食堂吃饭。

It usually rains in summer at Wuhan.

武汉的夏天常常下雨。

They always go shopping at weekends.

她们周末总是去购物。

②表示客观真理、科学原理、自然现象等客观事实或格言、谚语等。

The sun rises in the east and sets in the west every day.

太阳每天东升西落。

Spring follows winter.

冬去春来。

The man who has never been to the Great Wall is not a real man.

不到长城非好汉。

③表示现在时刻的状态、能力、性格、个性。

All my family love football.

我全家人都喜欢足球。

My sister is always ready to help others.

我妹妹总喜欢帮助别人。

Li Ming writes good English but does not speak well.

李明的英语书面表达能力比口语好。

④在时间、条件或让步状语从句中表示将来的动作。

I will tell him the news when he comes back.

他回来后我会告诉他这个消息。

If you take the job, they will talk with you in great details.

如果你接受这份工作，他们会和你详谈。

Whether you believe it or not, it's true.

无论你是否相信，这都是真的。

⑤表示按计划或安排好的，或将要发生的动作，可用一般现在时表示将来，但只限于 start, begin, leave, come, arrive, return, take place 等动词。

Our order arrives tomorrow.

我们的订货明天到。

The train leaves at six tomorrow morning.

火车明早六点开。

He comes back tonight.

他今晚回来。

2.1.2 一般过去时

一般过去时表示过去某一时候或某一段时间所发生了的事情或存在的状态，常与过去时间 yesterday, this morning, just now, a moment ago, in May, last night/year/week, once upon a time, the other day, before, when clause, in the past 等连用。

1) 一般过去时的构成

①动词 be：第一人称单数和第三人称单数用 was，其余用 were。

②动词 have：一律用 had，没有人称和数的变化。

③动词 do：一律用过去时的形式 did，没有人称和数的变化。

④一般动词的过去式变化规则如下表。

情况	词尾变化	例词
一般情况	+ ed	worked, looked
以不发音 e 结尾的词	+ d	hoped, lived
以辅音字母 y 结尾的词	变 y 为 i + ed	studied, carried
以重读闭音节结尾而末尾只有一个辅音字母的词	双写最后的辅音字母 + ed（以 x 结尾的词直接加 - ed）	planned, stopped, mixed, fixed
以 ic 结尾的动词	变 ic 为 ick + ed	picnic—picnicked traffic—trafficked

续表

情况	词尾变化	例词
特殊情况	不规则	have—had are—were is/am—was do—did

2) 一般过去时的句式

①主语 + was/were + 名词/数词/形容词/副词/介词短语等

②主语 + 实义动词的过去式 + 其他

③主语 + could/might etc. + 动词原形 + 其他

3) 一般过去时的基本用法

①在确定的过去时间里所发生的动作或存在的状态。

Where did you go just now?

刚才你去哪了？

The last Olympic Games took place in London.

上一届奥运会在伦敦举行。

He went out an hour ago.

他一小时之前就出去了。

②表示在过去一段时间内经常性或习惯性的动作。

When I was a child, I often played football in the street.

我是个孩子的时候，常在马路上踢足球。

He smoked many cigarettes a day until he gave up.

他没有戒烟的那阵子，抽烟抽得可凶了。

③"used to + 动词原形"这一结构也可以表示过去反复或经常的动作。

Scarf used to take a walk after dinner.

斯卡夫过去常常晚饭后散步。

He used to take in a movie at weekends.

他以前周末常常看一场电影。

④wish, wonder, think, hope 等用过去时，表示试探性地询问、请求、建议等。

I thought you might have some.

我以为你想要一些。

2.1.3 一般将来时

一般将来时表示将来某一时刻的动作或状态，或将来某一段时间内经常的动作或状态，常常和表示将来的时间状语连用。

1) 一般将来时的构成

will/shall + 动词原形

2）一般将来时的肯定、否定和一般疑问句式

肯定	否定	一般疑问
主语 + will/shall + 动词原形	主语 + will/shall + not + 动词原形	Will/Shall + 主语 + 动词原形

3）一般将来时的基本用法

①表示将来发生的动作或存在的状态，常与一些表示将来的时间状语连用，如 tomorrow, next week, from now on, in the future 等。

We will have exercise tomorrow morning.
我们明天要做早操。
They shall go to Disneyland Parks next week.
他们下周要去迪斯尼乐园游玩。
Annie is going to be a great rocker in the future.
安妮将来会成为一个出色的摇滚乐手。

②"be going to + 动词原形"主要表示打算和预测。

We are not going to stay there long.
我们不准备在那里多待。（表示打算）
I'm afraid they're going to lose the game.
恐怕他们会输。（表示预测）
Look, it's going to rain.
瞧，要下雨了。（表示预见）

③"be to + 动词原形"表示按计划或安排即将要发生的动作，有时也表示命令、禁止或可能性。

He is to leave for Beijing tomorrow.
他决定明天去北京。
Tell him he's not to be back late.
告诉他不准迟回。
Sit down, everyone. The film is about to start.
大家坐好，电影马上就要开发始了。

2.1.4 过去将来时

相对过去某时间而言将要发生的动作或存在的状态，即过去的将来，常用于复合句中。

1）过去将来时的构成

would/should + 动词原形

2）过去将来时的肯定、否定和一般疑问句式

肯定	否定	一般疑问
主语 + be（was, were）going to + 动词原形	主语 + be（was, were）not going to + 动词原形	Be（Was, Were）+ 主语 + going to + 动词原形

3）过去将来时的基本用法

①当主句为过去时时，宾语从句常用过去将来时表示将要发生的事情。

Nobody knew what would happen after a hundred years.

没有人知道一百年之后将会发生什么事。

We didn't know whether she was going to speak at the meeting.

我们不知道她是否准备在会上发言。

②过去将来时也可以用"was/were to + 动词原形"或"was/were about to + 动词原形"这两种结构表示过去正要进行或计划要进行的动作。

She said she was about to have dinner in this restaurant.

她说要在这家餐厅吃晚餐。

She told me she was coming to see me.

她告诉我要来看我。

③ 特定场合的一般过去时可表示过去将来时，条件状语从句和时间状语从句中须用一般过去时代替过去将来时。

I didn't know when she would come, but when she came I would let you know.

我不知道她什么时候来，但她来了我会告诉你。

2.1.5 现在进行时

现在进行时表示现在或现阶段正在进行的动作。

1）现在进行时的构成

①am/is/are + 动词 ing 形式（现在分词）。

②现在分词的变化规则如下表。

情况	词尾变化	例词
一般情况	加 ing	wash—washing, read—reading, see—seeing
以不发音字母 e 结尾的动词	去 e, 加 ing	make—making, write—writing, use—using
以重读闭音节结尾且末尾又只有一个辅音字母的动词	双写末尾辅音字母，再加 ing	run—running, swim—swimming, put—putting
少数以 ie 结尾的动词	将词尾的 ie 变为 y, 再加 ing	tie—tying, lie—lying, die—dying

③现在进行时的肯定、否定和一般疑问句式。

肯定	否定	一般疑问
主语 + am/is/are + 现在分词	主语 + am/is/are + not + 现在分词	Am/Is/Are + 主语 + 现在分词

2）现在进行时的基本用法

①表示现在正在进行的动作和发生的事。

The students are doing the experiment.

学生们正在做实验。

He is brushing his teeth.

他正在刷牙。

We're far from home. What are our parents doing at the moment?

我们远离了家,我们的父母此刻在干什么呢?

②表示现阶段正发生的事,但此刻动作不一定正在进行。

Mr. Wang is teaching at Peking University.

王先生在北京大学教书。

We are learning how to assemble the engine these days.

我们目前在学习如何组装发动机。

③句中出现了Look！Listen！Can't you see? 等提示时,说明后面谓语动词的动作正在发生,该动词应用现在进行时。

Look！The plane is taking off at the airport.

看！飞机正从机场起飞。

Listen！Our English teacher is singing the popular English song.

听！我们的英语老师正在唱那首流行的英文歌曲。

3）现在进行时的特殊用法

①当其与always, forever, continually, constantly 等副词连用时,表示重复的动作,有着极大的感情色彩,表示不满或满意。

She is perpetually interfering in my affairs.

她老是干预我的事。（不满）

The students are making progress constantly.

学生们在不断进步。（满意）

②作为表语时,英语介词可以表示正在"进行"的动作。

He is at work.

他正在工作。

The house is on fire！

房子着火了！

The road is under construction.

路正在修。

2.1.6 过去进行时

过去进行时表示过去在某一时刻或某一段时间内正在发生或进行的动作或状态。

1）过去进行时的构成

was/were + 动词现在分词

2）过去进行时的肯定、否定和一般疑问句式

肯定	否定	一般疑问
主语 + was/were + doing	主语 + was/were not + doing	was/were + 主语 + doing

3）过去进行时的基本用法

①表示在过去某一时刻或某一段时间正在进行的动作，经常要用到表示过去的时间状语。

How can you ask again? I think you weren't listening at all when I presented the answer to you.

你怎能再问一遍？我认为当我在讲解答案时你根本没听。

I was doing my lessons when she came in.

她进门时我正在写作业。

②也可用一些表示瞬间动作的动词，如 go，come，start，leave 等来表示过去将要发生的动作；也可以与副词 always，constantly，continually，forever 等连用，表示某种感情色彩。

I was leaving for Wuhan that day.

我那天正好要去武汉。

She was coming later.

她随后就来。

Speaking of him, my mother was always praising him.

说起他时，我妈总是赞不绝口。

2.1.7 将来进行时

表示将来某时或某段时间正在发生的动作，常译为"将正在做某事"。

1）将来进行时的构成

shall/will + be + 现在分词

2）将来进行时的肯定、否定和一般疑问句式

肯定	否定	一般疑问
I（We）shall be traveling...	I（We）shall not be traveling...	Shall I（We）be traveling...？
You（They/He/She/It）will be traveling...	You（They/He/She/It）will not be traveling...	Will you（they/he/she/it）be traveling...？

3）将来进行时的基本用法

①表示将来某一时间正在进行的动作。

We shall be watching a film tomorrow evening.

明晚我们将正在看电影。

I will be traveling at France when you come next time.

你下次来时，我应该正在法国旅游。

②表示预料不久将要发生或势必要发生的动作。

You should be keeping healthy if you want to win the game next week.

要想赢得下周的比赛，你必须保持身体健康。

It will be getting very cold next week, just keep you warm.

下周将要降温了，你要时刻保暖。

③表示对将来的打算（区别于对将来的预测）。

My duties will be ending in July, and I'll be returning to Shanghai.

我的任务即将在七月底完成，那时我将返回上海。

2.1.8 现在完成时

现在完成时表示过去的动作或事件对现在造成的影响，动作可能已经结束，也可能会继续延续下去。

1）现在完成时的构成

主语 + has/have + 动词的过去分词

过去分词有规则动词的过去分词、不规则动词的过去分词两种形式，规则动词的过去分词在动词后加 ed，不规则动词的变化有其特定的形式，须一一记忆。

2）现在完成时的肯定、否定和一般疑问句式

肯定	否定	一般疑问
主语 + have/has + 动词的过去分词	主语 + have not/has not + 动词的过去分词	Have/Has + 主语 + 动词的过去分词

3）现在完成时的基本用法

①表示到目前为止已经发生或完成的动作，常与表示频度的时间状语连用，如 often, sometimes, ever, never, twice, on several occasion 等。

Judy has already finished the work.

朱迪已经完成了这项工作。

They have not bought the book yet.

他们还没有买那本书。

You have done what you need to do today.

你今天做了你该做的事情。

②强调过去发生的某一动作对现在造成的影响或结果，该动作到现在为止已经发生或完成。

I have ate at that restaurant.

我在那家餐厅吃过饭了。

I have returned the book to him yesterday.

我昨天已经将那本书还给他了。

Who has taken my bottle?

谁拿了我的瓶子？

③表示过去某一时间开始的动作一直延续到现在，并还将会延续下去，常与表示时间的词 for, since 引导的短语或 since 引导的从句连用。

I have been in the army for more than 5 years.

我在部队已经待了五年多了。

He has traveled to Japan for two weeks.

他已经去日本旅游了两个星期了。

I have had a cold since I moved to this city.

自从搬到这个城市以来我就开始患感冒了。

4）现在完成时的注意事项

① 现在完成时不能单独与准确时间状语连用（如表示过去的时间状语）。

He has joined the army yesterday morning.（错）

He joined the army yesterday morning.（对）

他昨天早上参军了。

②现在完成时往往同表示不确定的过去时间状语连用，如 already（肯定句中），yet（否定、疑问、句末），just，before，recently，still，lately，never 等。

He has already obtained a scholarship.

他已经获得了一份奖学金。

I haven't seen much of him recently（lately）.

最近我已经很长时间没有看到他了。

Have they found the missing child yet?

他们找到失踪的孩子了吗？

③现在完成时还可以用来表示过去的一个时间到现在这段时间内重复发生的动作。

We have had four texts this semester.

我们这学期进行了四次考试。

④在"This is（It is）the first（second）time that..."句型中，that 引导的从句要用现在完成时；在"It is（has been）...since..."结构中，since 引导的从句要用一般过去时。

This is the first time that Peter has experienced such a danger.

这是皮特第一次经历这种危险。

It has been a long time since I heard from you.

至上次收到你的来信已经好长时间了。

⑤对于某些表示状态的动词（如 seem 等），或因语义方面的原因，有时可能用一般现在时比现在完成时更合适。

It seems like years since we last met.

我们似乎几年没见面了。

Since when does the $36 plus $5 service charge come to $42?

从什么时候开始36元加5元的服务费等于42元了？

⑥现在完成时还往往可以同包括现在时间在内的时间状语连用，如 now, up to these few days/weeks/months/years，just，today，up to present，so far 等。

Up to the present everything has been successful.

目前为止一切顺利。

Man has now learned to release energy from the nucleus of the atom.

人类目前已经学会了从原子核中释放能量。

2.1.9 过去完成时

过去完成时表示过去某一时间或动作以前就已经完成的动作，即过去的过去，常用于复合句中。

1）过去完成时的构成

had + 过去分词构成

2）过去完成时的肯定、否定和一般疑问句式

肯定	否定	一般疑问
主语 + had + 动词过去分词	主语 + had + not + 动词过去分词	Had + 主语 + 动词过去分词

3）过去完成时的基本用法

①表示在过去某一时刻或动作之前已完成的动作（即过去的过去）。常用 by, before 等介词短语或一个时间状语从句来表示，也可以用一个表示过去的动作来表示，还可以通过上下文来表示。

When I woke up, it had stopped raining.
当我醒来时，雨已经停了。
By nine o'clock last night, we had got 200 pictures from the spaceship.
到昨晚九点钟，我们已经收到 200 张飞船发来的照片。
They had planted six hundred trees before last Wednesday.
在上周三之前他们已经种了 600 棵树了。

②表示由过去的某一时刻开始，一直延续到过去另一时间的动作或状态，常和 for, since 构成的时间状语连用。

I had been at the bus stop for 20 minutes when a bus finally came.
在公交站等了 20 分钟以后，终于来了一辆汽车。
I met Liu Yu in the street yesterday. We hadn't seen each other since he went to Beijing.
昨天在街上见到了刘宇。自从他去北京后我们就没见过了。
He went out as soon as the meeting was over.
开完会他就出去了。

③叙述过去发生的事情，在已叙述了过去发生的事情后，反过来追述或补述以前发生的动作时，常使用过去完成时。

Mr. Smith died yesterday. He had been a good friend of mine.
史密斯先生昨天去世了。他以前是我的好友。
I didn't know a thing about the verbs, for I had not studied my lesson.
我对动词一无所知，因为我没有好好学习功课。

④过去完成时还可用在 hardly...when..., no sooner...than..., It was the first (second, etc) time (that)... 等固定句型中。

Hardly had he begun to speak when the audience interrupted him.
他刚开始演讲，听众就打断了他。
No sooner had he arrived than he went away again.
他刚到就又走了。
It was the third time that he had been out of work that year.

这是他那一年第三次失业了。

2.1.10 将来完成时

将来完成时表示将来某一时间之前已经完成的动作。

1）将来完成时的构成

shall/will + have + 动词过去分词

2）将来完成时的肯定、否定和一般疑问句式

肯定	否定	一般疑问
主语 + shall + have + 动词过去分词	主语 + shall + not + have + 动词过去分词	Shall + 主语 + have + 动词过去分词

3）将来完成时的主要用法

①表示"将来完成",即表示到将来某个时间为止势必会完成或预计要完成的动作。

When we get there, she'll have gone to work.

我们到那里时她应该已经上班去了。

I expect you will have changed your mind by tomorrow.

我预料到明天你就会改变主意了。

②表示"持续",即表示某种状况将一直持续到说话人所提及的某一将来时间。

We will have been married a year on June 25th.

到6月25日我们俩结婚就满1年了。

By this time next week, I will have been working for this company for 24 years.

到下星期此刻,我就已经为该公司干了24年了。

③表示"推测",即表示根据某情况做出的推测。

That will have been Roland. He said he'd be back at 7.

准是罗兰。他说他7点钟回来。

There will have been a definite result before Friday.

星期五以前肯定会有结果。

2.1.11 现在完成进行时

现在完成进行时表示动作从过去某一时间开始一直持续到现在并可能延续下去,常译为"一直在做某事"。

1）现在完成进行时的构成

has/have + been + 现在分词

2）现在完成进行时的肯定、否定和一般疑问句式

肯定	否定	一般疑问
I (We/You/They) have been studying...	I (We/You/They) have not been studying...	Have I (we/you/they) been studying...?
He (She/It) has been studying...	He (She/It) has not been studying...	Has he (she/it) been studying...?

3）现在完成进行时的基本用法

①表示开始于过去的活动持续到现在，并且活动往往还没有结束，将继续持续下去。

I have been living in Wuhan for ten years.

我在武汉已经生活了十年。

She has been burning the midnight oil to prepare for GRE.

她最近在熬夜准备 GRE 考试。

Tom has been playing the online games for more than twenty hours.

汤姆玩网游已经超过二十个小时了。

②表示到目前为止的一段时间内重复发生的活动。

I have been telling you not to make trouble.

我一直劝你不要找麻烦。

The old man has been repairing cars for thirty years.

老人修车修了三十年了。

Jack has been practising Tai Chi for more than a year.

杰克练太极一年多了。

2.1.12 过去完成进行时

过去完成进行时表示动作从过去某一时间开始到过去一直在进行。

1）过去完成进行时的构成

had + been + 动词现在分词

2）过去完成进行时的肯定、否定和一般疑问句式

肯定	否定	一般疑问
I（You/He/She/It/We/They）had been reading...	I（You/He/She/It/We/They）had not been reading...	Had I（you/he/she/it/we/they）been reading...？

3）过去完成进行时的基本用法

过去完成进行时表示持续到过去某时的一个动作（可算是现在完成进行时的过去式）。

The ground was wet. It had been raining.

地是湿的，此前一直在下雨。

She was out of breath. She had been running.

她气喘吁吁，一直在跑来着。

He gave up smoking last year. He'd been smoking for twenty years.

去年他戒烟了。他抽烟已经二十年。

2.2 被动语态

语态是表示主谓之间关系的一种动词形式，有主动和被动两种语态。主动语态表示

主语是动作的执行者，被动语态表示主语是动作的对象或承受者。

All know the matter.

大伙都知道这事。（主动语态）

The matter is known by all.

这事大伙都知道。（被动语态）

2.2.1 被动语态的构成

be（有时态、人称和数的变化）+ 及物动词的过去分词。

被动语态的各种时态形式如下表所示。

	一　般　时	进　行　时	完　成　时
现在	*am* *is*　taken *are*	*am* *is*　being taken *are*	*have* *has*　been taken
过去	*was* 　　　taken *were*	*was* 　　　being taken *were*	had been taken...
将来	*shall* 　　　be taken... *will*		*shall* 　　　have been taken *will*
过去 将来	*should* 　　　　be taken *would*		*should* 　　　　have been taken *would*

2.2.2 被动语态的否定和一般疑问句式

将否定词 not 置于第一个助动词后构成被动语态的否定句；将主语后的第一个助动词置于句首构成被动语态的疑问句。

The city has been attacked.

这座城市遭到袭击了。

The city has not been attacked.

这座城市没有遭到袭击。

Has the city been attacked?

这座城市遭到袭击了吗？

2.2.3 被动语态的基本用法

①动作的执行者不明确，或是没必要指出动作的执行者是谁。

My car has been stolen.

我的车被偷了。（不知道是谁偷的）

The city was liberated in 1949.

这座城市是1949年解放的。（没提是谁解放的）

Computers are being used widely.

计算机正得到广泛使用。（没必要说谁在使用）

The order will be delivered next month.

这批货要在下月发送。(没必要提谁发送)

②当我们对动作或动作对象的兴趣比对动作执行者的兴趣更大(即强调或侧重动作的承受者)时。

The new building was finally completed.

新楼最终完工了。(关心新楼的完工,而不是关注谁干的)

We are required to hand in our plan at once.

要求我们马上上交计划。(强调动作的承受者,而不是动作的执行者)

Will you be invited to the dinner?

你是不是受邀请去吃饭?(此句关心的是被邀邀请的对象而不是邀请的执行者)

③出于委婉、礼貌方面的考虑,不想说出动作的执行者是谁。

Such behavior is generally considered to be impolite.

这种行为一般被认为是无礼的。

About the matter, much has been said but little had been done.

有关此事,说得多,做得少。

④在科技文献、正式布告和通知中,为了行文通顺,常用被动语态。

All the participants are required to present themselves at the meeting on time.

所有参加会议者应按时到会。(通知形式)

The professor was invited to the conference and gave a talk.

教授应邀出席了大会并做了报告。(为了行文的通顺)

2.2.4　带有情态动词的被动语态

带有情态动词的被动语态由情态动词 + be + 动词过去分词构成。

The delivery should be arrived before next Friday.

货应当在下周五前到达。

The exhibits cannot be touched.

展品不能触摸。

This material has to be used in the experiment.

实验中一定要使用这种材料。

2.2.5　带有双宾语的被动语态

在有双宾语的被动语态句中,主动语态中的直接宾语和间接宾语都可变为被动语态中的主语。如果主动语态中的直接宾语变为被动语态中的主语,要在间接宾语前加介词 to 或 for。

He gave me a piece of advice.

他给了我一个忠告。

I was given a piece of advice. / A piece of advice was given to me.

(他)给了我一个忠告。

Mike's father bought him a computer. / A computer was bought for Mike by his father. / Mike was bought a computer by his father.

迈克的父亲给他买了一台电脑。

2.2.6 某些主动语态里的谓语动词能表达被动语态的意义

①有些动词或动词短语以主动语态的形式出现，却含有被动的意义，这时就不能再用被动结构。

The civil right bill carried by large majority.

民权议案以大多数票通过。

With the development of science and technology, more and more plastic will come into use.

随着科技的发展，越来越多的塑料开始被使用。

②某些不及物动词后接副词的主动语态可表示被动意义。

某些不及物动词后加副词可表示被动意义，如 wash, write, sell, lock, clean 等。这些动词后常用的副词有 easily, well, badly, properly, quickly, smoothly 等。

This type of computers sells well.

这种电脑卖得很好。

The pen writes smoothly.

这支笔写起来很流畅。

The jacket washes easily.

这夹克很容易洗。

③某些动词后接动名词的主动语态能表示被动意义。

动词 want, deserve, need, require, be worth 等后接动名词的主动语态能表示被动意义。

The film is worth seeing.

这部电影值得一看。

My bike needs repairing.

我的自行车需要修理。

The plan requires changing.

计划需要修改。

2.3 实战演练

1. By the time you come to see me next month, I _____ my term paper.
   A. have completed   B. complete
   C. am completing   D. will have completed
2. This hospital, which (equip) _____ with modern facilities, is one of the best in the country.
3. In the past few years, traffic problems (become) _____ more and more serious.
4. For years, doctors _____ millions of patients' lives with the help of microscopes.
   A. have saved   B. will save   C. are saving   D. were saving

5. No one can deny that we (make) _____ tremendous progress in the past twenty years.
6. The people injured in the accident (send) _____ to the nearest hospital for treatment last night.
7. By the end of next month, we (find) _____ a good solution to the technical problem.
8. Ever since I arrived here, I _____ in the dormitory because it is cheaper.
   A. lived   B. was living   C. had been living   D. have been living
9. The policemen (tell) _____ not to take any action until they received further order.
10. The father wants to know why his son (question) _____ by the police last week.
11. He _____ in this company since he graduated from Andong Technical College ten years ago.
    A. worked   B. has been working
    C. had worked   D. was working
12. By the end of this year, the factory (produce) _____ 20 000 cell phones.
13. All the members of the club were present when the Chairman (elect) _____ last week.
14. Though he _____ well prepared before the job interview, he failed to answer some important questions.
    A. will be   B. would be   C. has been   D. had been
15. Before the flight takes off, all passengers (ask) _____ to fasten their seat belts.
16. We surely (find) _____ a good solution to the technical problems in the near future.
17. The car _____ by the side of the road and the driver tried to repair it.
    A. breaks down   B. was breaking down
    C. has broken down   D. broke down
18. As a rule, readers (not allow) _____ to take dictionaries out of the reading room.
19. By the end of last year, nearly a million cars (produce) _____ in that auto factory.
20. By the time you get to Shanghai tomorrow, I _____ for Chongqing.
    A. am leaving   B. will leave   C. shall have left   D. had left
21. The villagers told us that a new bridge (build) _____ across the river in a year.
22. This time next week I'll be in vacation. Probably I _____ in a beautiful beach.
    A. am lying   B. have lain   C. will be lying   D. will have lain
23. Jim told me he (join) _____ the army two years before.
24. Linda feels exhausted because she _____ so many visitors today.
    A. has been having   B. had been having
    C. was having   D. had had
25. Most students (take) _____ sixty credits by the time they graduate.
26. Most of the people who are visiting Britain _____ about the food and weather there.
    A. are always to complain   B. have always complained
    C. always complain   D. will always complain

27. The cause of the accident may never (discover) _____ in spite of the effort of the police.
28. He was told that the stranger (wait) _____ for him for 2 hours.
29. The police promised that they (try) _____ their best to look into the matter.
30. The students _____ their papers by the end of this month.
    A. have finished   B. will be finishing
    C. will have finished   D. have been finished

2.4 专项练习

1. We hoped that by the end of the year we _____ the job.
   A. had finished   B. finished
   C. would have finished   D. will finish
2. By the end of 2007, Henry _____ more than a thousand foreign stamps.
   A. was collecting   B. would collect
   C. had collected   D. would be collecting
3. — "You haven't got the dictionary for me yet."
   — "I know, and I _____ to get it for the last two weeks."
   A. had tried   B. will be trying
   C. have been trying   D. will have been trying
4. By next week John _____ a month without smoking a cigarette.
   A. has gone   B. will have gone   C. will go   D. has been going
5. I don't swim now, but I _____ when I was a child.
   A. used to   B. used to it   C. used to do D. used to doing it
6. You _____ to a party to be given at the Workers' Club.
   A. invited   B. will invited   C. invite   D. are invited
7. Automatic machines can only do the jobs, they _____ to do.
   A. have asked   B. ask   C. have been asked   D. will ask
8. Because the chief speaker is unable to come tomorrow, the meeting _____ postponed.
   A. has   B. is being   C. has been   D. will have been
9. We congratulated them on the victory they _____.
   A. had won   B. have won   C. won   D. win
10. The bus came after I _____ for about half an hour.
    A. had been waiting   B. had been waited
    C. have waited   D. was waiting
11. He _____ of how he can do more for the people.
    A. will always think   B. is always thinking
    C. has always thought   D. does always think

12. We _____ each other since I left Shanghai.
    A. haven't seen   B. don't see   C. hadn't seen   D. didn't see
13. Tom _____ into the room when no one _____.
    A. slipped; was looking   B. had slipped; looked
    C. slipped; had looked   D. was slipping; looked
14. This is the best dinner that I _____.
    A. enjoyed   B. have enjoyed   C. had enjoyed   D. enjoy
15. How long _____ the concert _____?
    A. has; been lasted   B. did; last   C. will; be lasted   D. was; lasted
16. I'll return the book to the library as soon as I _____ it.
    A. will finish   B. am going to finish
    C. finished   D. have finished
17. —Have you telephoned the hospital?
    —Yes, a doctor _____.
    A. has sent for   B. has been sent for
    C. was sent for   D. was sent
18. —What did you do yesterday, Bob?
    —Well, I _____ to see a friend of mine. But in the end I _____ at home doing nothing at all.
    A. went; stayed   B. was going; stayed
    C. had gone; was staying   D. would go; had stayed
19. —Where have you been?
    —I _____ to an evening party.
    A. have been invited   B. have invited
    C. was invited   D. am invited
20. While Mary _____ a bath, her husband _____ TV.
    A. was having; was watching   B. has; was watching
    C. was taking; had   D. had; watched
21. I _____ to come over to see you last night, but someone called and I couldn't get away.
    A. was hoped   B. hoped   C. has hoped   D. had hoped
22. My brother _____ the army for five years. He devotes most of his sparetime to teaching himself advanced physics.
    A. has joined   B. joined   C. has been in   D. had been in
23. The children _____ many times not to play with fire.
    A. hasn't told   B. are being told   C. have told   D. have been told
24. I don't want to go home, because a lot of work _____ yet.
    A. hasn't finished   B. hasn't been finished
    C. has been finished   D. haven't finished

25. —Will he finish the job soon?
    —Yes, he _____ it by next Friday.
    A. shall finish   B. finishes
    C. has finished   D. will have finished

26. What _____ you _____ this time tomorrow?
    A. will; do   B. will; have doing
    C. will; be done   D. will; be doing

27. Mr. Peter was chosen director of the department store last June and _____ in charge ever since.
    A. was   B. has been   C. had been   D. is

28. _____ continuous development of all forms of education in China since 1987.
    A. It has   B. There was   C. There is   D. There has been

29. Every time I came here, he _____ me something important.
    A. will tell B. is going to tell   C. tells   D. told

30. —What were you doing when Anna phoned you?
    —I had just finished my work and _____ to take a bath.
    A. had started   B. to start   C. have started   D. was starting

31. This medicine _____ you feel better. Please take it three times a day.
    A. makes   B. is making   C. made   D. will make

32. Mr. Green hasn't come to work since last week. Where do you think he _____?
    A. is going   B. has been   C. has gone   D. went

33. Mary entered the office, _____ at her desk and began to type the letter.
    A. sit   B. sat   C. seating   D. seated

34. She _____ on this essay for twenty minutes but she has written only a hundred words.
    A. has worked B. worked   C. has been working D. will have worked

35. It is reported some villagers living in the forest _____ two days ago.
    A. was disappeared   B. has disappeared
    C. disappeared   D. have been disappeared

36. Many new universities _____ in our country in recent years.
    A. will be set up   B. were set up
    C. are to be set up   D. have been set up

37. The vegetables didn't taste very good. They _____ for too long.
    A. were cooked   B. have been cooked
    C. should have been cooked   D. had been cooked

38. The whole city is like a big construction site. Many tall buildings _____.
    A. have been built   B. are being built
    C. are going to be built   D. are building

39. —Is Paul playing both soccer and tennis for the school?

—Yes, he _____ . But now he has given up playing tennis.

A. is B. has C. was D. had

40. —Put these glasses away before they _____ .

— OK. I'll put them in the cupboard.

A. have broken B. are breaking C. get broken D. will be broken

41. —Did you come to the museum by bike yesterday?

—No. Two meters of snow fell during the night. As a result, several main roads _____ .

A. covered snow B. had been closed C. were blocked D. covered with snow

42. —_____ my dictionary?

—Yes. I put it in your desk just now.

A. Do you see B. Have you seen C. Did you see D. Had you seen

43. —When did he go to America?

—Oh, he _____ there since half a year ago.

A. went B. has been C. has gone D. was

44. You _____ things about. Look, what a mess in your room!

A. always throw B. have always thrown

C. are always throwing D. have always been throwing

45. —Look! Someone has spilt coffee on the carpet.

—Well, it _____ me.

A. isn't B. wasn't C. hasn't been D. hadn't been

46. —Hello, Jim. I _____ to see you today, Jone said you _____ ill.

—Oh, I am OK.

A. don't expect; were B. haven't expected; are

C. am not expecting; are D. didn't expect; were

47. —Look! How long _____ like this?

—Three weeks! It is usual here that rain _____ without stopping these days of the year.

A. has it rained; pours B. has it been raining; pours

C. is it raining; is pouring D. does it rain; pours

48. Our team was ahead during the first half, but we _____ in the last ten minutes.

A. had lost B. would lose C. were losing D. lost

49. You needn't hurry her; she _____ it by the time you are ready.

A. will have finished B. will finish

C. will be finishing D. has finished

50. By the time you get to the airport, she _____ for New Zealand.

A. would be leaving B. has already left

C. has been leaving D. will have left

51. —Who is the old man talking with our teacher?

—I don't know. I _____ him before.

A. was never seeing B. had never seen
C. never saw D. wouldn't see

52. —Tom came back home the day before yesterday.
    —Really? Where _____ at all?
    A. had he been B. has he been C. had he gone D. has he gone

53. After everybody _____, the concert began.
    A. was seated B. seated C. is seated D. was sat

54. —Can I help you, Madam?
    —No, thanks. I _____.
    A. have just looked around B. just look around
    C. am just looking around D. just looked around

55. —Has Tommy finished his job yet?
    —I have no idea of it; he _____ it this morning.
    A. was doing B. had been doing C. has done D. did

56. —Have you heard from Janet recently?
    —No, but I _____ her over Christmas.
    A. saw B. will be seeing C. have seen D. have been seeing

57. —The telephone is ringing.
    —I _____ answer it.
    A. will B. am going to C. am to D. am about to

58. —What do you think of my composition?
    —It _____ well _____ a few spelling mistakes.
    A. reads; except for B. read; besides
    C. is read; except for D. is read; besides

59. In 1960, this was the longest bridge that _____.
    A. was ever built B. had ever built
    C. have ever been built D. had ever been built

60. —Isn't it hard to drive downtown to work?
    —Yes, that's why I _____ to work by train.
    A. have been going B. have gone
    C. was going D. will have gone

第 3 章 虚 拟 语 气

3.1 语气

语气（Mood）是英语中谓语动词的变化形式，用来表示说话人的意图和态度。英语中的语气分为四种：陈述语气（Indicative Mood）、疑问语气（Interrogative Mood）、祈使语气（Imperative Mood）、虚拟语气（Subjunctive Mood）。

陈述语气陈述事实或提出想法，有肯定和否定形式。英语中的句子大部分是陈述语气。

Iraq is an Asian country.（肯定句）
伊拉克是亚洲国家。
The US and British armies did not start the Second Gulf War until March 20, 2003.（否定句）
美英联军直到2003年3月20日才发动第二次海湾战争。
疑问语气主要用来提问。
Who was it that they want to help?
他们想要帮忙的人到底是谁呀？
Have you ever been to Japan?
你去过日本吗？
祈使语气表示说话人向听者发布命令、提出要求，或进行劝告、警告、威胁等。祈使语气通常用于面对面直接交流，故一般情况下主语不出现，但必要时也可以出现。祈使语气的动词形式为原形动词。
Please come over here.
请到这边来。
Be quiet, children.
孩子们，安静点。
Watch your steps!
当心！（走路）
Never be late again!
再也不要迟到了。
Let me out!
让我出去！

虚拟语气用来表示假设，表示所说的不一定是事实，或与事实相反，或仅是主观愿望，难以实现。虚拟语气通过谓语动词的特殊形式来表示。

I wish I were you.

我要是你就好了。（与事实相反，因为我永远也不可能是你；这里不能用"I was"）

If he were/was here, he would help us.

如果他在这儿，他会帮我们的。（事实上他现在不在这里）

If only I had taken your advice.

我要是采纳了你的意见就好了！（事实上我当时并没有采纳你的意见）

比较：If he doesn't hurry up, he will miss the bus.

如果他不快点，就会错过公交车。（并非虚拟语气，因为这种情况基本是事实）

If he is free, he will ask me to tell stories.

如果他有空，就会要求我讲故事。（并非虚拟语气，因为这种情况基本是事实）

3.2 条件句

包含条件从句的句子就叫条件句。条件句可分为两类，一类为真实条件句，是可能实现的；一类为非真实条件句，是假想的情况，这类条件句中谓语动词就需要用虚拟语气。

If you eat junk food, you will put on weight.

如果吃垃圾食品，你就会变胖。（真实条件句，因为这种情况很可能会发生）

If I were you, I would start over.

如果我是你，我会重新开始。（非真实条件句，因为这种情况不可能发生，要用虚拟语气）

If there were/was no air, we couldn't live.

如果没有空气，我们就不能生存。（非真实条件句，因为实际情况是现在有空气，我们能生存，所以要用虚拟语气）

非真实条件句的虚拟语气时态见下表。

非真实条件	从句	主句
与现在事实相反	动词用过去式	should/would/could/might + 动词原形
与过去事实相反	had + 过去分词	should/would/could/might + have + 过去分词
与将来事实相反，或 将来不太可能发生	a. 动词用过去式 b. were to + 动词原形 c. should + 动词原形	should/would/could/might + 动词原形

注：在 If I were you 这样的句子中，were 不能改成 was，但在第三人称单数后用 was 也可以。

If I were you, I would consider the suggestion.

如果我是你，就会考虑这个建议。（与现在事实相反）

If Helen were /was here, how nice it would be!

海伦要是在这里就好了！（与现在事实相反）

If he had had enough money at that time, he could have bought the computer.

如果当时有足够的钱，他可能就买下了那台电脑。（与过去事实相反）

If the sun were to rise in the west, I would lend you the money.

要我借钱给你，除非太阳从西边出来。（与将来事实相反）

3.2.1 错综时间条件句中的虚拟语气

所谓错综时间条件句，即条件从句谓语与主句谓语所指时间不一致，如从句谓语表示过去，而主句谓语表示现在或将来，此时应根据具体的语境，对时态做相应的调整。

If we had not got everything ready yesterday, we would be having a terrible time now.

要是我们昨天没把一切准备好，今天可就糟透了。（从句表示与过去事实相反的假设，主句则表示与现在事实相反）

If they had not worked hard in past years, the project could not be going so smoothly now.

要不是他们过去多年努力工作，这项工程现在不可能进行得如此顺利。（从句表示与过去事实相反，主句则表示与现在事实相反）

If he were leaving/to leave, you would have heard about it.

如果他真要走，你早就听到消息了。（从句表示与将来事实相反，主句表示与过去事实相反）

3.2.2 省略if的倒装句中的虚拟语气

在非真实条件句中，从句有时可以省略连词if，而将谓语中的be动词或助动词等移到主语之前，构成倒装。

Had it not been for the captain, the ship would have sunk.

要不是因为船长，这艘船早沉了。（从句正常结构为If it had not been for the captain）

Were they here, they should agree with me.

要是他们在这里，他们会赞成我的。（从句的正常结构为If they were here）

3.2.3 含蓄条件句中的虚拟语气

有些条件句中的条件从句不表示出来，只暗含在短语或上下文中，这种句子叫含蓄条件句。常见的表示含蓄条件的词有but for, without, otherwise等。

Without water, there would be no life on the earth.

如果没有水，地球上就没有生命。（without的隐含条件为If there were no water）

But for your help, we couldn't have succeeded in the experiment.

要不是你帮我们，实验不会成功。（but for的隐含条件为If you hadn't helped us）

3.3 名词性从句中的虚拟语气

3.3.1 主语从句中的虚拟语气

在表示建议、要求、命令的主语从句中，从句谓语动词一律用"should + 动词原

形"构成。(should 可以省略) 此类结构常见的有:

It is (was) important/necessary/advisable/possible/ insistent/best/better that…

It is (was) a pity/shame/suggestion/proposal/request that…

It is (was) desired/decided/ordered/suggested...

It is necessary that he (should) be sent there at once.

有必要马上派他去那里。

It is important that we (should) speak politely.

我们说话要礼貌,这很重要。

3.3.2 宾语从句中的虚拟语气

在 suggest, order, demand, propose, request, desire, beg, advise, insist, require 等表示命令、建议、请求的动词后接宾语从句时,从句的谓语用"should + 动词原形"。(should 可以省略)

I suggested that he (should) not go there alone.

我建议他不要单独去那儿。

The manager required that the money (should) be used for advertising their new products.

经理要求用这笔钱为他们的新产品做广告。

3.3.3 wish 后宾语从句中的虚拟语气

在动词 wish 后的宾语从句中,谓语动词须用虚拟语气,表示与事实相反或不大可能实现的愿望,通常有以下三种形式。

①对过去未实现的愿望或未发生的事表示遗憾。从句谓语用相当于过去完成时的形式。

I wish she had been here yesterday.

我真希望她昨天在这里。(实际不在)

He wishes he had got the job last year.

他真希望去年得到了那份工作。(实际没得到)

② 表示与现在事实相反的愿望。从句谓语为过去时。

I wish I knew how to use the new computer.

我真希望会用这台新电脑。(实际不会用)

The girl wishes she flied in the sky.

这女孩希望能在空中飞翔。(实际不可能)

③表示将来没有把握或不太可能实现的愿望。从句谓语结构为"would /could/might + 动词原形"。

We all wish the scientist could come to our college to give us a lecture.

我们都希望那位科学家能来我们学院做一次讲座。(可能性不大)

I wish you would go with us tomorrow.

要是你明天同我们一起去就好了。(可能性不大)

3.4 其他句型中的虚拟语气

3.4.1 if only 引导的虚拟语气

在 if only 引导的句子中，虚拟语气结构与 wish 后的宾语从句虚拟语气结构基本相同，表示"但愿……""要是……就好了"的意思。

If only I could help you.

我要是能帮助你就好了。（实际帮不了）

If only she had started earlier, she would not have missed the flight.

她要是早点动身就好了，那样就不会错过航班。（实际已经错过了）

3.4.2 as if/as though 引导的方式状语从句中的虚拟语气

①表示与现在事实相反的情况或对现在的情况表示怀疑，从句谓语动词为过去式。

It seems as if it were spring.

现在好像是春天了。（实际现在并不是春天）

You look as if you knew the truth.

你看起来好像知道真相似的。（说话者表示怀疑，认为很可能你并不知道真相）

②表示对过去事实的假设，从句谓语动词为过去完成式。

He talked with her as if he had known her for a long time.

他同她交谈，仿佛认识她很长时间似的。（实际是初次见面）

Fancy you sitting there as if nothing had happened.

瞧你坐在那儿，好像没事似的。（实际发生了很严重的事）

3.4.3 lest 引导的目的状语从句中的虚拟语气

在 lest（以免）引导的目的状语从句中，从句的谓语结构为"should+动词原形"。（should 可省略）

We dare not play jokes on him lest he (should) become angry.

我们不敢和他开玩笑，怕他生气。

I was in mortal fear lest he (should) see me.

我非常害怕他会看见我。

3.4.4 It's (high, about) time that 引导的定语从句中的虚拟语气

在 It's (high, about) time that 引导的定语从句中，that 引导的从句谓语动词多用过去式，从句表示："早该……"。

It is (high) time that we started.

我们早该出发了。

It is (high) time that they stopped making such products.

他们早该停止生产这种产品了。

3.4.5 would rather, would just as soon 等引导的宾语从句中的虚拟语气

would rather, would just as soon 等短语表示"但愿、宁愿、宁可"等意思，其后的宾语从句中谓语部分要用虚拟结构，即用过去时表示与现在事实相反，用过去完成时表

示与过去事实相反。

I would rather he were here.

我宁愿他现在在这里。

The young man would just as soon he had given his life to the girl.

那个年轻人宁愿那时为那女孩献出了生命。

3.5 实战演练

1. If I (be) _____ you, I wouldn't miss the job interview tomorrow morning.
2. It is high time that the manager (pay) _____ more attention to the services for the customers.
3. It is required that anyone applying for a driver's license _____ a set of tests.
   A. take   B. took   C. takes   C. will take
4. If he had taken his lawyer's advice, he (save) _____ himself a great deal of trouble.
5. The representative of the company demanded that part of the agreement _____ revised.
   A. will be   B. is   C. to be   D. be
6. The boy passed the final exams. But if he had spent more time on them, the results (be) _____ much better.
7. It is most desirable that he _____ for the information by himself with a few clicks online.
   A. search   B. searched   C. has searched   D. will search
8. _____ he was seriously ill, I would not have told him the truth.
   A. If I knew   B. If I know   C. Had I known   D. Did I know
9. We could not have fulfilled the task in time if it _____ for their help.
   A. was not   B. is not   C. had not been   D. has not been
10. The ATM has been out of service for a few days. It should _____ last we.
    A. fix   B. be fixed   C. have fixed   D. have been fixed
11. _____ last Friday, he would have got to Paris.
    A. Would he leave   B. Had he left
    C. If he is to leave   D. If he was leaving
12. I think it's high time we _____ strict measures to stop pollution.
    A. will take   B. take   C. took   D. have taken
13. The manager of the company insisted that all staff members _____ the new safety rules.
    A. would observe B. observe   C. observed   D. will observe
14. I could have called you yesterday, but I _____ your telephone number.
    A. didn't have   B. won't have   C. hadn't had   D. wouldn't have
15. Tom might not have made such a serious mistake if he _____ your advice.
    A. followed   B. follows   C. had followed   D. has followed

16. _____ I had a problem, I would talk with someone online to seek help.
    A. As if   B. Just as   C. Every time   D. So far
17. Every Monday morning when I am in my small office, I wish I _____ in a multinational company.
    A. were working   B. have worked   C. am to work   D. work
18. If he _____ my advice at that time, he would have got the job he applied for.
    A. took   B. takes   C. had taken   D. has taken
19. If we _____ more time and money, we could have visited many more places.
    A. have   B. had had   C. have had   D. could have
20. If Jack _____ the real situation, he would have made a different plan.
    A. knows   B. knew   C. will know   D. had known

3.6 专项练习

1. It is necessary that he _____ in time to attend the conference.
   A. came   B. come   C. comes   D. will come
2. The picture exhibition bored me to death, I wish I _____ to it.
   A. did not go   B. had not gone
   C. have not gone   D. should not have gone
3. I'd rather _____ those important papers with you.
   A. you didn't take   B. your not taking
   C. that you won't take   D. please don't you take
4. Your advice that she _____ till next month is reasonable.
   A. wait   B. will wait   C. waits   D. would wait
5. If I had a bike, I _____ it to you yesterday.
   A. would lend   B. had lent   C. lent   D. would have lent
6. John obviously does not know what has happened, otherwise he _____ such a stupid remark.
   A. doesn't make   B. wouldn't have made
   C. wouldn't make   D. didn't make
7. Without your help, we _____ so much.
   A. didn't achieve   B. will not achieve
   C. would not have achieved   D. don't achieve
8. Had she been given some information, she _____ the questions.
   A. can answer   B. can have answered
   C. could answer   D. could have answered
9. If you had others do your homework, you _____ them eat your lunch.
   A. should have to have   B. had better to have

C. might as well have D. ought to have

10. It's essential that these application forms _____ back as early as possible.
    A. must be sent   B. will be sent   C. are sent   D. be sent

11. The teacher demanded that the exam _____ before eleven.
    A. must finish   B. would be finished
    C. be finished   D. must be finished

12. He felt lonely and sad as if the whole world _____ against him.
    A. turns   B. has turned   C. had turned   D. is turning

13. How I wish I _____ him yesterday.
    A. meet   B. met   C. have met   D. had met

14. I'm sorry I'm so busy now. I wish I _____ with you.
    A. can go   B. could go   C. had gone   D. have gone

15. The doctor suggested that my father _____ smoking.
    A. should give up   B. gave up   C. gives up   D. would give up

16. If I were you, I _____ ask the teacher for advice.
    A. will   B. would   C. shall   D. am going to

17. If it _____ fine yesterday, I would have gone there.
    A. were   B. was   C. had been   D. should be

18. Without the leadership of the Party, there _____ a new China.
    A. would not   B. would not have been
    C. is not   D. won't

19. It's time we _____ to the meeting.
    A. go   B. shall go   C. went   D. are going

20. You talk as if you _____ there.
    A. were really   B. has really been
    C. had really been   D. would really be

21. It is suggested that the work _____ at once.
    A. would start   B. should start
    C. would be started   D. should be started

22. He insisted that he _____ no help.
    A. would need   B. needed   C. need   D. needs

23. We are working hard so that we _____ our country into a powerful state.
    A. will build   B. build   C. shall build   D. could build

24. You didn't let me drive. If we _____ in turn, you _____ so tired.
    A. drove; didn't get   B. drove; wouldn't get
    C. were driving; wouldn't get   D. had driven; wouldn't have got

25. It's very important that everybody _____ carefully.
    A. listened   B. listens   C. listen   D. listening

26. I don't want to do the shopping. I'd rather somebody else _____ it.
    A. do B. to do C. did D. done
27. They are very kind to me. They treat me _____ their own son.
    A. like I am B. as if I am C. as if I was D. as if I were
28. If it _____ warmer, I wouldn't mind going to the beach with you.
    A. is B. has been C. were D. had been
29. I don't know what I'd have done, _____ to make that decision.
    A. could I B. had I had C. have had D. did I have
30. We must stop now. It's time we _____ home.
    A. have gone B. are going C. were going D. will go
31. I would have come to see you, had it been possible, but I _____ so busy then.
    A. had been B. were C. was D. would be
32. Ten minutes earlier, _____ we could have caught the last train.
    A. or B. but C. and D. so
33. The local government stopped several small factories, otherwise, the beautiful river _____ .
    A. will be polluted
    B. would be polluted
    C. was polluted
    D. would have been polluted
34. _____ you were coming today, I'd have met you at the airport.
    A. I had known
    B. Had I known
    C. Have I known
    D. I have known
35. _____ today he would get there by Friday.
    A. Would leave
    B. Was he leaving
    C. Were he to leave
    D. If he leaves
36. If you had taken your medicine yesterday, you _____ well now.
    A. had been B. were C. would be D. should have been
37. Frankly speaking, I'd rather you _____ anything about it for the time being.
    A. have done B. haven't done C. don't do D. didn't do
38. It's necessary _____ the dictionary immediately.
    A. that he will return
    B. that he returned
    C. that he return
    D. that he has to return
39. He must have had an accident, or he _____ then.
    A. would have been there
    B. had to be there
    C. should be there
    D. would be there
40. You don't have to be in such a hurry. I would rather you _____ on business first.
    A. would go B. will go C. went D. have gone
41. _____ the English examination I would have gone to the concert last Sunday.
    A. In spite of B. But for C. Because of D. As for

42. To be frank, I'd rather you _____ in the case.
    A. will not be involved   B. not involved
    C. not to be involved   D. were not involved

43. He _____ another career but, at that time, he didn't have enough money to attend graduate school.
    A. might have chosen   B. might choose
    C. had to choose   D. must have chosen

44. It was essential that the application forms _____ back before the deadline.
    A. must be sent   B. would be sent   C. be sent   D. were sent

45. She didn't tell anybody where she would go lest her husband _____ her.
    A. find   B. finds   C. had found D. would find

46. The physicists propose that our attention _____ towards the use of special methods of thinking and acting.
    A. would be directed   B. is directed
    C. directs   D. should be directed

47. Tom was too tired, _____, he would have gone on with the experiment.
    A. but   B. however   C. otherwise D. therefore

48. Supposing the weather _____ bad, would you go?
    A. is   B. will be   C. were   D. be

49. He _____ the job well, but he _____ so careless.
    A. hadn't done; had been   B. could have done; was
    C. could do; was   D. had done; had been

50. _____ he come, the problem would be settled.
    A. Would   B. Should   C. Shall   D. If

第 4 章　非谓语动词

在英语中，不能用作句子谓语，但可以担任其他语法功能的动词，叫作非谓语动词（Non-finite Verbs）。非谓语动词有三种：动词不定式、动名词和分词（现在分词和过去分词）。

4.1　动词不定式（Infinitive）

4.1.1　动词不定式的功能

动词不定式是一种非谓语动词形式。它由"to + 动词原形"构成，动词不定式可以带宾语或状语，构成不定式短语（如：to answer the question, to study hard, to study English hard 等）。动词不定式可以作主语、表语、宾语、定语、状语和宾语或主语的补语。

1）作主语

To master a foreign language is very important.

掌握一门外语是非常重要的。

To solve the problem is not easy.

解决这个问题不容易。

不定式短语作主语时，可用 it 作形式主语，而真正主语——动词不定式放在句子后面，保持句子平衡。上面的例句可用如下形式：

It is very important to master a foreign language.

It is not easy to solve the problem.

2）作表语

Her wish is to become a doctor.

她的愿望就是成为一名医生。

My suggestion is to give up smoking.

我的建议是戒烟。

3）作宾语

常接不定式作宾语的动词有：want（想要），ask（要求），hope（希望），wish（希望），expect（期望），refuse（拒绝），learn（学会），decide（决定），agree（同意），promise（许诺），plan（计划），offer（提出），manage（设法），prepare（准备），fail（未能），afford（担负得起），arrange（安排），attempt（试图），tend（倾向于），pretend（假装），intend（企图），claim（声称），long（渴望），determine（决定）等。

He intended to change his job.

他想换工作。

She managed to accomplish her work in time.

她设法及时完成了工作。

不定式短语作宾语，后面有宾语补足语时，往往把不定式宾语放在宾语补足语后，而用 it 作形式宾语。

The workers think it necessary to increase productivity.

工人们认为提高生产率是必要的。

We found it impossible to get everything ready in advance.

我们发现提前做好一切准备是不可能的。

4）作宾语（或主语）的补足语

在主动语态句中作宾语补足语的成分，在被动语态句中则作主语补足语。

The manager asked him to work out a plan.

经理要他制定一个计划。（宾语补足语）

He was asked to work out a plan.

（主语补足语）

［注］在感官动词 see，watch，look（at），hear，listen（to），feel，notice，observe 等和使役动词 make，let，have 等词后的宾语补足语中，不定式不带 to，但以上动词若为被动语态时，作主语补足语的不定式则要加上 to。

I saw her enter the classroom.

我看见她走进了教室。

She was seen to enter the classroom.

有人看见她走进了教室。

I heard her lock the door.

我听见她锁门了。

He was often heard to sing this song.

人们常常听见她唱这首歌。

5）作定语

She is the first one to come to the office.

她是第一个到办公室的人。

I have a meeting to attend.

我有一个会议要参加。

［注］作定语的不定式如果是不及物动词，不定式后面必须有相应的介词。

This is the earth for us to live on.

这是我们居住的地球。

She is looking for a room to live in.

她正在找一个住的房间。

He has nothing to worry about.

他没有什么值得发愁的事。

但是，不定式所修饰的名词如果是 time，place 或 way，不定式后面的介词习惯上要省去。

The old man had no money and no place to live.

这位老人没有钱和住的地方。

6）作状语（表目的、原因和结果）

To improve his spoken English, he often talks to foreigners in English.

(= In order to improve his spoken English, he often talks to foreigners in English.)

(= He often talks to foreigners in English so as to improve his spoken English.)

为了提高口语，他常常用英语和外国人交谈。（目的）

I am very glad to meet you.

见到你我很高兴。（原因）

He woke up only to find himself lying on a bed in a hospital.

他醒来结果发现他自己躺在病床上。（结果）

不定式作表语形容词的状语，和句中主语构成逻辑上的动宾关系时，不定式多用主动形式。

The novel is difficult to understand. (to understand the novel).

这部小说难以理解。

"too＋形容词或副词＋不定式"作状语，一般表示否定的结果。

It's too dark for us to see anything.

天太黑了我们什么也看不见。

7）不定式与疑问词 what，which，who，when，how，why 等连用，在句中起名词作用，可作主语、表语、宾语等

Where to have the meeting hasn't been decided yet.

在哪里开会还没有决定。(Where to have the meeting 作主语)

My question is how to organize the work.

我的问题是如何组织这项工作。(how to organize the work 作表语)

There were so many good books that I didn't know which to choose.

有这么多好书以至于我不知道选哪一本。(which to choose 作动词 know 的宾语)

4.1.2　动词不定式的逻辑主语

有时，所表达的意义需要不定式有一个逻辑主语。就用"for＋名词（或代词宾格）＋不定式"的结构，其中"for＋名词（或代词宾格）"作不定式的逻辑主语。

It is possible for us to realize our hopes.

我们实现希望是可能的。

I found an interesting book for my son to read.

我找到了一本我儿子看的有趣的书。

有时，在表示人物性格、特点等的形容词的后面，用 of 引出不定式的逻辑主语。

It was very thoughtful of you to make all the necessary arrangements for us.

你们考虑得真周到，为我们做好了一切必要的安排。

It is wise of her to do that.

他那样做是明智的。

4.1.3 不定式的否定式"not + to do"

He pretended not to see me.

他假装没看见我。

It would be wrong not to take that problem into consideration.

不把那个问题考虑在内是错误的。

4.1.4 不定式的时态和语态

不定式的时态和语态如下表所示。

时态 \ 语态	主　动	被　动
一般式	to do	to be done
进行式	to be doing	/
完成式	to have done	to have been done

1) 动词不定式的时态

①不定式的一般式表示的动作与句中谓语动词的动作同时（或几乎同时）发生，或发生在其后。

I saw her go out.

我看见她出去了。

I promise not to be late again.

我保证不再迟到。

②不定式进行时所表示的动作与谓语动词的动作同时发生。

I am very glad to be working with you in the same office.

我很高兴与你在同一个办公室工作。

They seem to be getting along quite well.

他们好像相处得很好。

③不定式的完成时所表示的动作发生在谓语动词之前。

I'm sorry to have kept you waiting.

我很抱歉让你久等了。

He is said to have written a letter to his mother.

据说他已给他母亲写了信。

2) 动词不定式的语态

当不定式的逻辑主语是动词不定式所表示的动作的执行者时，用主动语态。是动作的承受者时，用被动语态。

He agreed to work in the countryside.

他同意到农村工作。

He agreed to be sent to work in the countryside.

他同意被派到农村工作。

It is impossible for the task to be finished in an hour.

在一小时之内完成这项任务是不可能的。

4.1.5 使用不带 to 的不定式的几种句型

1）在口语中，以 why 开头的简短疑问句中

Why not go out for a walk?

为什么不出去散散步呢？

2）在 had better, rather than 等习惯用法中

It's cold outside. You'd better stay at home.

外面很冷，你最好待在家里。

Rather than take a bus, he would prefer to go home on foot.

他宁愿步行回家也不乘公共汽车。

3）在 do nothing/anything/everything but（except）结构中

but（except）后接不带 to 的不定式，即动词原形。

We could do nothing but wait.

我们只有等。

He will do anything but study.

除了学习外，他什么都愿干。

但是如果谓语动词不是"do nothing/anything/everything"，那么 but（except）后应接带 to 的不定式。

We have no choice but to stay here.

我们别无选择，只有待在这里。

The doctor told him nothing but to stay at home and have a good rest.

医生除了让他待在家好好休息，其他没有说什么。

4.2 动名词（Gerund）

4.2.1 动名词的功能

动名词由"动词+ing"构成；具有动词的特征，它可有自己的宾语、状语，动名词可以带宾语或状语构成动名词短语；具有名词性质，在句中动名词或动名词短语可作主语、表语、宾语和定语。

1）作主语

Making friends with her is no easy thing.

与她交朋友不是件容易的事情。

Seeing is believing.

百闻不如一见。

[注] 也可用 it 作形式主语。

It's no easy thing making friends with her.

与她交朋友不是件容易的事情。

It's no use (no good, useless) arguing with him.

与他争论没用（没好处）。

［注］动名词和不定式都可以作主语，动名词作主语表示一般或抽象的多次行为，不定式作主语往往表示具体的或一次性的动作。

Walking is a good form of exercise for both young and old.

对年轻人和老年人来说，散步是一种好的锻炼形式。

To finish the work is my task for today.

我今天的任务就是完成这项工作。

2）作表语

My favorite sport is playing basketball.

我最喜爱的运动是打篮球。

Our work is serving the people.

我们的工作是为人民服务。

3）作宾语

常见的只能跟动名词作宾语的动词和动词短语有：finish（完成），enjoy（喜欢），mind（介意），avoid（避免），miss（错过），suggest（建议），appreciate（欣赏，喜欢），consider（考虑），delay（耽搁），escape（逃避），admit（承认），deny（否认），practice（练习），excuse（原谅），keep（使……保持着某一状态），mention（提到），include（包括），imagine（想象），risk（冒……危险），resist（抵抗，反抗），be accustomed to（习惯），be used to（现在习惯于），can't stand（受不住，不能容忍），can't help（禁不住），feel like（想，欲），give up（放弃），put off（推迟），devote to（专心于，致力于），look forward to（盼望），end up（结束，告终）等。

Our teacher suggested going to the reading-room after class.

我们老师建议下课后去阅览室。（动词宾语）

We have to prevent the air from being polluted.

我们必须阻止空气被污染。（介词宾语）

［注］在动词 advise, allow, forbid（禁止），permit（允许）等后，如果没有人称宾语，后跟动名词；如果有人称宾语则后跟不定式。

They don't allow fishing here.

他们不准在这儿钓鱼。

They don't allow people to fish here.

他们不准人们在这儿钓鱼。

4）作定语

动名词作定语通常表示目的和用途。

Is there a swimming pool in your school? (a pool for swimming)

你们学校有游泳池吗？

You'd better make a studying plan. (a plan for studying)

你最好制定一个学习计划。

4.2.2 动名词的逻辑主语

动名词的逻辑主语与句子的主语通常是一致的，但也有不一致的情况。如果动名词的逻辑主语与句子的主语不一致时，则要用复合结构。动名词的复合结构有两种形式：

a. 物主代词所有格（或代词宾格）+动名词；

b. 名词所有格（或普通格）+动名词。

在句子开头必须用物主代词所有格或名词所有格+动名词的形式。

①His coming made me very happy.

他的到来使我很高兴。

（His coming 是"物主代词所有格+动名词"构成的动名词复合结构，作主语）

不可说：Him coming made me very happy.

（Him coming 是"物主代词宾格+动名词"构成的动名词复合结构，不能作主语，只能作宾语）

②Xiao Wang's coming made me very happy.

小王的到来使我很高兴。

（Xiao Wang's coming 是"名词所有格+动名词"构成的动名词复合结构，作主语）

不可说：Xiao Wang coming made me very happy.

（Xiao Wang coming 是"名词普通格+动名词"构成的动名词复合结构，不能作主语，只能作宾语）

③We look forward to his coming.

我们盼望他的到来。

或者说：We look forward to him coming.

④We look forward to Xiao Wang's coming.

我们盼望小王的到来。

或者说：We look forward to Xiao Wang coming.

（动名词的复合结构作宾语时，两种形式都可以用）

4.2.3 动名词的否定式

动名词的否定式为"not + doing"。

We regret not having taken your advice.

我们懊悔没有接受您的建议。

4.2.4 动名词的时态和语态

动名词的时态和语态如下表所示。

时态 \ 语态	主　动	被　动
一般式	doing	being done
完成式	having done	having been done

1) 动名词的时态

①如果动名词的动作没有明确地表示出时间是与谓语动词同时发生或在谓语动作之前发生，用动名词的一般式。

Facing your weak points is very necessary.

正视你的缺点是非常必要的。

He is very interested in playing football.

他对足球很感兴趣。

②如果动名词的动作发生在谓语动词所表示的动作之前，通常用动名词的完成时态。

I was criticized for not having finished my work in time.

我由于没有按时完成工作而受到批评。

She was praised for having made a great contribution to her hometown.

她由于为她的家乡做出了巨大的贡献而受到表扬。

2) 动名词的语态

当动名词的逻辑主语是动名词所表示动作的承受者时，动名词用被动语态。动名词完成式的被动语态一般避免使用。

He didn't mind being left at home.

把他留在家里他并不在意。

We did it without being asked.

我们是主动做的那件事。

4.2.5 其他跟动名词的结构

①There is no + v-ing（动名词作主语）

There is no joking about that matter.

那事开不得玩笑。

There is no denying that great changes have taken place in China.

不容否认，中国发生了巨大的变化。

②be busy (in) + v-ing

We are busy (in) preparing for the exam.

我们正忙于准备考试。

③be worth + v-ing（动名词表示被动含义）

The book is worth reading.

这本书值得一读。

④ have difficulty/trouble/problem/a good time/a wonderful time/a hard time/fun (in) + v-ing

We had difficulty (in) finding this bookstore.

我们好不容易才找到这家书店。

Do you have any problem (in) doing this experiment?

做这个实验有什么困难吗?

⑤spend time（in）+ v-ing

He spent two hours finishing his task.

他花了两个小时完成任务。

⑥It is no use/good/need + v-ing

It is no use crying.

哭没有用。

⑦go + v-ing

go + fishing/boating/camping/hunting/skating/skiing/shopping/swimming/picnicking/bowling/golfing/bathing

⑧How/What about + v-ing

How/What about going out for a walk after dinner?

晚饭后出去散步如何？

⑨No + v-ing

No smoking.

不准抽烟！

4.2.6 可接动名词或不定式的动词比较

①某些动词后既可跟动名词也可跟不定式作宾语，但有明显的语义差异。

如：remember to do（记住要做某事），remember doing（记得曾做过某事）；forget to do（忘记要做某事），forget doing（忘记曾做过某事）；stop to do（停下来去做另一件事），stop doing（停止正在做的事情）；try to do（设法做某事），try doing（试着做某事）；regret to do（因要做某事而感到不安），regret doing（因做了某事感到后悔）；mean to do（打算做某事），mean doing（意味着）；go on to do（做完某件事接着做另一件事），go on doing（继续做某事）；can't help（to）do（不能帮助做）；can't help doing（忍不住做）等。

I remembered giving you the book this morning.

我记得今天早上把书还给了你。

You must remember to give her the book tomorrow.

你必须记着明天把书给她。

He forgot doing this thing.

他忘记曾做过这件事。

He forgot to do this thing.

他忘记去做这件事。

Stop reading.

不要读了。

He stopped to read this book.

他停下来读这本书。

We tried to get there before noon.

我们尽力在中午之前到达那里。

He tried using another method.
他试着使用另外一种方法。
I mean to accomplish the task.
我打算完成这项任务。
Missing the bus means waiting for another hour.
误了这趟汽车意味着再等一个小时。
When we heard the funny story, we can't help laughing.
当我们听到这个有趣的故事，我们忍不住笑起来。
I can't help clean the bedroom, for I am very busy now.
我不能帮助打扫寝室，因为我现在很忙。
②在 want，need，require（都取"需要"之意）等动词后，尽管表示的是被动含义，却用动名词的主动形式（或不定式的被动式）。
The machine wants repairing（to be repaired）.
这台机器需要修理。
The window needs（requires）cleaning（to be cleaned）.
窗户需要清洗。

4.3 分词（participles）

4.3.1 分词的功能

分词分为现在分词（v-ing）和过去分词（v-ed）。一般来说，现在分词表示的意义是主动的，进行的；过去分词表示的意义是被动的，完成的。分词主要起形容词和副词的作用，在句中担任定语、表语、宾语或主语的补足语和状语等。

1）作定语

分词短语作定语时一般应放在被修饰的词之后；单个分词作定语时，一般放在所修饰的词之前。分词作定语，其逻辑主语就是分词所修饰的中心词。

a developing country
发展中国家
a developed country
发达国家
The boy sitting next to me is called John.
坐在我旁边的男孩叫约翰。
Have you read the book written by Lu Xun?
你看过鲁迅所写的书吗？
①动名词与现在分词作定语时的区别。
动名词作定语时要放在所修饰词的前面，动名词通常表示目的或用途。现在分词作定语时，与被修饰的词之间有逻辑上的主谓关系。
a sleeping boy（= the boy who is sleeping）

（熟睡的男孩）（现在分词）

a sleeping car（ = the car for sleeping）

（卧车）（动名词）

②现在分词、过去分词、不定式作定语的区别。

不定式作定语表示将要发生的动作，现在分词作定语表示正在进行的动作，过去分词作定语表示已经发生的动作。他们的逻辑主语就是他们所修饰的中心词，如果表示主动、进行就用 doing；如果表示被动、进行就用 being done；如果表示主动、将要发生就用 to do；如果表示被动、将要发生就用 to be done；如果表示被动、完成就用 done。

The person giving us a report is Professor Wang.

(= The person who is giving us a report is Professor Wang.)

正在给我们做报告的人是王教授。

The person to give us a report tomorrow is Professor Wang.

(= The person who will give us a report tomorrow is Professor Wang.)

明天要给我们做报告的人是王教授。

The question being discussed at the meeting is quite important.

(= The question which is being discussed at the meeting is quite important.)

会上正在讨论的问题是十分重要的。

The question to be discussed at the meeting is quite important.

(= The question which will be discussed at the meeting is quite important.)

会上要讨论的问题是十分重要的。

The question discussed at the meeting is quite important.

(= The question which was discussed at the meeting is quite important.)

会上所讨论的问题是十分重要的。

2）作表语

①分词作表语，其逻辑主语就是句子的主语。现在分词作表语表示主语的特征；过去分词作表语表示主语的状态。

The story is very interesting.

这个故事非常有趣。

She was interested in the story.

她对这个故事感兴趣。

②动名词与现在分词作表语时的区别：动名词也可以作表语，它作表语时，相当于名词。它可以和主语互换位置，意思和语法上都保持正确。现在分词作表语时起形容词作用，不可与主语互换位置。

My job is teaching（ = Teaching is my job）.

我的工作是教书。（动名词）

My job is boring.

我的工作很乏味。（现在分词）

3）作宾语（或主语）补足语

常用于表示感觉、心理状态动词后，如：see，hear，feel，notice，find，watch 等；用于表示"使役"意义的动词后，如：keep，get，leave，make。

The students saw the teacher entering the classroom.
学生们看见老师正走进教室。（宾补）
The teacher was seen entering the classroom. （主补）
I am very glad to see the work well done.
看到这事做得这样好，我十分高兴。（宾补）
He had his car repaired.
他请人把他的车修了。（宾补）
He had water running while brushing his teeth.
刷牙的时候，他让水不停地流着。（宾补）

①分词作宾语补足语时，其逻辑主语就是宾语，如果宾语与后面的非谓语动词是主动的逻辑关系，并表示动作正在发生或处于某状态时，用现在分词；如果是被动关系就用过去分词。

②在 see，hear，watch，feel，observe，listen to，notice 等感官动词后，既可以用现在分词作宾语补足语，也可以用不带 to 的不定式作宾语补足语，但两者的含义是有差别的：用现在分词，表示动作正在发生；用不定式表示动作发生的全过程。

I sat there and watched boys playing football.
我坐在那里看男孩子们踢足球。
I watched boys play football and leave.
我看见男孩子们踢了足球，离开了。

4）作状语

分词或分词短语作状语时，可表示时间、原因、条件、结果、方式或伴随情况等，其逻辑主语一般是句子的主语，如果二者是主动关系，就用现在分词；反之，被动关系，就用过去分词。分词或分词短语作时间状语或条件状语时，可以带上连接词 when，while，if 等。

（While）Walking along the street, I saw the bus on fire.
我在街上散步时看见公汽着火了。（时间）
Attracted by the beauty of nature, he decided to spend another two hours in the park.
由于被公园里的自然美景吸引住了，他决定在公园里再待两个小时。（原因）
（If）Given another chance, he will do it better.
如果再给他一次机会，他会把它做得更好。（条件）
His wife died, leaving him with his two children.
他的妻子死了，留下他和他的两个孩子。（结果）
He stood there reading a newspaper.
他站在那里看报纸。（伴随）

[注] 不定式、分词作状语的区别：

不定式可作目的、原因、结果状语。不定式放在句首时，一般作目的状语。作原因、结果状语时，往往位于句末。

分词可以作时间、条件、原因、方式、结果等状语，不作目的状语。时间、条件、原因状语通常位于句首，方式、结果状语通常位于句末。

  To catch the train, we hurried through our work.
  为了赶火车，我们匆匆干完了工作。
  Not knowing how to do it, I asked him for help.
  不知道如何去做这事，我向他寻求帮助。
  Compared with developed countries, developing countries still have a long way to go.
  与发达国家相比，发展中国家还有很长的路要走。

4.3.2 分词独立结构

  分词或分词短语作状语时，其逻辑主语必须与句子的主语一致。如果与句子的主语不一致时，就必须带上自己的逻辑主语，即：名词或代词＋现在分词或过去分词，这种结构叫分词独立结构。它往往在句中作时间、条件、原因、方式等状语，分词的逻辑主语就是它前面的名词或代词。如果代词为人称代词时，应用主格；如果前面的名词或代词与后面的非谓语动词是主动的逻辑关系，就用"名词或代词＋现在分词"；如果是被动关系就用"名词或代词＋过去分词"结构。

  Homework finished, he went out to play.
  家庭作业完成后，他出去玩。
  (Homework finished 为"名词＋过去分词"构成的分词独立主格结构，作时间状语。homework 是 finish 的逻辑主语，二者为被动关系，故用 finished。)
  Weather permitting, we will go out for a picnic.
  如果天气允许的话，我们将出去野餐。
  (Weather permitting 为"名词＋现在分词"构成的分词独立主格结构，作条件状语。Weather 是 permit 的逻辑主语，二者为主动关系，故用 permitting。)
  Mr. Wang falling ill, I took his class instead.
  由于王先生病了，所以我给他代课。
  (Mr. Wang falling ill 为分词独立主格结构，表原因，在句中作原因状语。)
  He walked into the classroom, a book held in his hand, his eyes looking at his students.
  他手里拿着一本书，眼睛看着学生们，走进了教室。
  (a book held in his hand, his eyes looking at his students 是两个分词独立主格结构，作伴随状语。)

4.3.3 分词的时态和语态

  现在分词有时态和语态的变化。现在分词有一般式和完成式，有主动语态和被动语态，见下表。

语态 时态	主　动	被　动
一般式	doing（主动，与谓语动词所表示动作同时发生）	being done（被动，与谓语动词所表示动作同时发生）
完成式	having done（主动，在谓语动词所示的动作之前发生）	having been done（被动，在谓语动词所表示的动作之前发生）

Walking in the street, I met Sally.

当我在街上走的时候,我遇见了莎莉。

(主动,与谓语所表示的动作同时发生)

The house being built is our library.

正在修建的房子是我们的图书馆。

(被动,与谓语所表示的动作同时发生)

Having finished my homework, I went out.

完成家庭作业后,我出去了。

(主动,在谓语动词所表示动作之前发生)

Having been criticized by his parents, he gave up smoking.

挨了父母亲的批评之后,他戒烟了。

(被动,在谓语动词所表示的动作之前发生)

过去分词表示在谓语动词之前发生的动作,本身有被动的含义,只有一般式没有完成式。

4.4 实战演练

1. They still have some problems _____ in designing the new energy vehicles.
   A. overcome   B. overcoming   C. to overcome   D. overcomes
2. Sometimes _____ a business can feel like a tough decision to make, no matter how good your idea is.
   A. starting   B. being started   C. start   D. to be started
3. It is not (surprise) _____ that this new style of handbag is mainly purchased by young women.
4. A completely new idea (deal) _____ with air pollution in big cities attracted much public attention.
5. All our spare parts are guaranteed if you have your car _____ with us each year.
   A. serviced   B. be servicing   C. to service   D. serving
6. The course comes in three books of case studies, _____ a variety of business activities in different parts of the world.
   A. being covered   B. covering   C. cover   D. covered
7. He asked the applicant to have her cell phone (turn) _____ off during the interview.
8. Young volunteers enjoy (help) _____ the senior citizens in their everyday life.
9. We've agreed (transfer) _____ part of our business to a new owner.
10. Medical accidents _____ by drugs have attracted much attention in that country.
    A. causing   B. to be caused   C. be caused   D. caused
11. The sales department of a company is engaged in _____ the products and making profits.
    A. selling   B. sell   C. being sold   D. having sold

12. There may be a need for retraining if you expect employees _____ new technology.
    A. using   B. use   C. to use   D. used
13. A survey suggests that nearly one in six children has difficulty _____ to talk.
    A. to learn   B. learning   C. learn   D. learnt
14. Among the major products (import) _____ by Malaysia were iron and steel, and medical instruments.
15. While (study) _____ at college, he got to know the professor and learned a lot from him.
16. _____ great losses in the financial crisis, the company closed down last year.
    A. Being suffered   B. To suffer   C. Having suffered   D. Suffered
17. The company is offering a five percent discount to customers as a way _____ its online sales.
    A. promoting   B. promoted   C. to promote   D. promotes
18. I am told that Mr. Smith has refused (work) _____ in the Human Resources Department.
19. Consumers have become less interested in 3D TV at home, partly because of (have) _____ to wear special glasses.
20. According to a report (publish) _____ yesterday, an increasing number of young people are involved in community activities.
21. Greatly (encourage) _____ by his friends, Jack has signed up for the singing competition.
22. Before the age of the Internet, we used to _____ our holidays through travel agents.
    A. book   B. having booked   C. booking   D. have booked
23. Generally, it takes courage for an aged person _____ a new life in a strange country.
    A. beginning   B. began   C. to begin   D. to have begun
24. These scientists are interested in (find) _____ out how short-term memory becomes long-term memory.
25. The sales manager asks his men every week (inform) _____ him of everything concerning sales.
26. I am very sorry _____ you such a lot of trouble by the delayed shipment.
    A. caused   B. causing   C. to have caused   D. to be caused
27. If you turn to the right at the corner, you'll find a path _____ to the historical building.
    A. lead   B. leading   C. to lead   D. leads
28. Only after they had performed hundreds of experiments did they succeed in (solve) _____ the problem.
29. The human resources department, as well as the other departments, will have its budget _____ to $2 million this year.
    A. to reduce   B. reduce   C. reduced   D. reducing

30. Miss Smith's assistant enjoys _____ for her although she treats him very strictly.
    A. work   B. working   C. to work   D. worked
31. Companies are legally required (keep) _____ record of all their financial transactions.
32. Before (apply) _____ for a working holiday visa, you should read the information on the United Kingdom Working Holiday page.
33. At the meeting I made some proposals, but no one seemed to be (interest) _____ in them.
34. The proposal _____ at the meeting now is of great importance to our department.
    A. being discussed   B. to be discussed
    C. having discussed   D. discussing
35. According to the survey (conduct) _____ recently, 52% of American business people booked their business travel online last year.
36. It was reported that the (injure) _____ people were taken to the hospital immediately after the accident.
37. The bank refused (accept) _____ my application for the loan because they were not convinced by my business plan.
38. She didn't know _____ to express her ideas in English clearly in public.
    A. which   B. why   C. what   D. how
39. _____ in the company for three years, Mark has become experienced in business negotiation.
    A. Having worked   B. Have been working
    C. Have worked   D. Worked
40. Employees are not allowed (make) _____ personal phone calls in the office.
41. The shop assistant priced the goods before (put) _____ them on the shelf.
42. I shall appreciate your effort in (correct) _____ this error in my bank account as soon as possible.
43. Measures should be taken to avoid the negative effect (bring) _____ about by unfair competition.
44. I think that the Great Wall is worth _____ hundreds of miles to visit.
    A. to travel   B. traveled   C. traveling   D. travel
45. _____ by the failure of the project, the manager could hardly say a word.
    A. To be shocked   B. Be shocked   C. Shocked   D. Shocking
46. The auto industry spend large amount of money on marketing campaigns _____ young adult customers.
    A. attract   B. to attract   C. attracted   D. attracts
47. We must keep the manager (inform) _____ of the advertising campaign.
48. The university graduate is confident of (win) _____ the post as the assistant to the managing director.

49. With such a short time (leave) _____, it's impossible for us to finish this complicated experiment.

50. I don't regret _____ her what I thought about her proposal, even if it upset her.
    A. tell   B. to tell   C. told   D. telling

51. _____ that I wasn't going to get much chance for promotion, I soon became bored with my work.
    A. To realize   B. Realizing   C. Being realized D. Realized

52. Scientists should be kept _____ of the latest developments in their research areas.
    A. inform   B. informing   C. informed   D. to inform

53. It was in his childhood that he read most of the books (write) _____ by Mark Twain.

54. Mr. Smith considered (sell) _____ his car and his house before moving to Beijing.

55. The lecture was so (bore) _____ that many of the students in the classroom fell asleep.

56. With the help of the police, the woman finally found her (lose) _____ child after a sleepless night.

57. _____ up at the clock on the wall, the secretary found it was already midnight.
    A. Looking   B. Look   C. To look   D. Looked

58. The first textbook _____ for teaching English as a foreign language came out in the 16th century.
    A. writing   B. written   C. to write   D. to be written

59. Believe it or not, when first (introduce) _____ to Europe, tomato was thought to be poisonous.

60. I remember (see) _____ you somewhere before, but I can't tell the exact place.

61. I don't think it necessary (discuss) _____ the matter with him before the problem is settled.

62. It's my great honor _____ to give a speech at the opening ceremony.
    A. to invite   B. inviting   C. having invited D. to be invited

63. I was almost asleep last night when I suddenly heard someone _____ at the door.
    A. be knocking   B. knocking   C. to knock   D. having knocked

64. The conference _____ in Beijing next week is bound to be a great success.
    A. holding   B. being held   C. to hold   D. to be held

65. The engineers spent the whole night (work) _____ on the new device.

66. The research group has submitted a report, (suggest) _____ reforms to be made.

67. When (ask) _____ about the advertising campaign of the new product, the manager said it was a great success.

68. _____ to find the proper job, he decided to give up job-hunting in this city.
    A. Failed   B. Being failed   C. To fail   D. Having failed

69. The proposal _____, we'll have to make another decision about when to start the project.
    A. accepted   B. accepting   C. to accept   D. be accepted

70. The policeman kept his eyes _____ on the screen of the computer to identify the criminal's footprint.
    A. fixed   B. fixing   C. being fixed   D. to fix
71. The nurse told the visitors (not speak) _____ so loudly as to disturb the patients.
72. (impress) _____ by the young man's good qualifications, they offered him a job in their firm.
73. We all felt excited when China succeeded in (launch) _____ its first manned spaceship.
74. We regret to inform you that we no longer manufacture the product you are (interest) _____ in.
75. The tall building (complete) _____ last month is our new classroom building.
76. _____ that Bob had got promoted, his friends came to congratulate him.
    A. Heard   B. Having heard   C. Hear   D. To hear
77. The children (play) _____ the violin over there will go on the stage next week.

4.5 专项练习

Ⅰ. Fill in each blank with the proper form of the word given in the brackets.

1. (read) _____ newspapers every day is his habit.
2. It is typical of him (offer) _____ to take hard jobs.
3. It is an honor for me (invite) _____ to give a speech here.
4. It is no good (study) _____ without thinking.
5. My hobby is (collect) _____ stamps.
6. My suggestion is (operate) _____ on the patient immediately.
7. The cartoon (amuse) _____ the children. The children were (amuse) _____ . The story was (amuse) _____ .
8. He suggests (hold) _____ a class meeting next Friday.
9. They are considering (set) _____ up some schools for poor children.
10. They consider it necessary (set) _____ up some schools for poor children.
11. All things (consider) _____ , it's a good plan.
12. He pretended (study) _____ hard when the teacher came in.
13. She claimed (treat) _____ badly there.
14. She doesn't enjoy (make) _____ fun of others. She doesn't enjoy (make) _____ fun of by others.
15. I used to (live) _____ in the countryside. But now I am used to (live) _____ in big cities.
16. Would you mind my (smoke) _____ ?
17. Would you mind not (invite) _____ to the birthday party.

18. I didn't mean (do) _____ morning exercises.
19. Doing morning exercises means (get) _____ up early.
20. I remember (see) _____ him once.
21. This is an important letter. Please remember (post) _____ it for me.
22. We spend half an hour (read) _____ English textbooks every morning.
23. They had difficulty (finish) _____ the work in two days.
24. We could do nothing but (admit) _____ to our teacher that we were wrong.
25. We had no choice but (admit) _____ to our teacher that we were wrong.
26. The farm tool needs (repair) _____ right away.
27. We didn't need (repair) _____ the farm tool right away.
28. The teacher spoke loudly in class so that he could make himself (hear) _____ by the students.
29. The teacher spoke loudly in class so that he could make the students (hear) _____ him clearly.
30. Frank doesn't have to be made (learn) _____. He always works hard.
31. When I walked past the playground, I saw some students (play) _____ basketball.
32. We often see them (play) _____ basketball on the playground.
33. Christmas is coming. You'd better have your house (decorate) _____.
34. Christmas is coming. You'd better have your children (decorate) _____ your house.
35. Christmas is coming. I have a lot of housework (do) _____.
36. We found the path (cover) _____ with snow.
37. I heard the song (sing) _____ next door when doing my homework.
38. We'll keep you (inform) _____ if we grant you an interview.
39. The police had a hard time keeping the traffic (move) _____.
40. He is said (translate) _____ the novel into English.
41. The novel is said (translate) _____ into English.
42. She had to walk home with her bike (steal) _____.
43. They pretended to be working hard all night with their lights (burn) _____.
44. (improve) _____ his spoken English, he practices speaking every day.
45. (study) _____ hard and you will make great progress in your Chinese learning.
46. (study) _____ hard, you will make great progress in your Chinese learning.
47. (see) _____ from the top of the mountain, our city looks more beautiful.
48. (see) _____ from the top of the mountain, we can see our beautiful city.
49. I am sorry (give) _____ you so much trouble.
50. We were excited (hear) _____ the news that our team won the game.
51. We are glad (invite) _____ to the opening ceremony.
52. They hurried to the classroom only (find) _____ nobody there.
53. (not complete) _____ the project, they have to stay there for another two months.

54. He stood there, (look) _____ out of the window.
55. It (be) _____ a hot day, we went swimming.
56. It (be) _____ a hot day, so we went swimming.
57. The first thing (do) _____ is to find a place (live) _____.
58. The library (build) _____ last year is an eight-story building.
59. The library (build) _____ next year will be an eight-story building.
60. The library (build) _____ now is an eight-story building.

Ⅱ. Choose the correct answer from the four choices marked A, B, C and D.

1. I always go this way to avoid _____ by Mr. Smith.
   A. seeing   B. being seen   C. to see   D. to be seen
2. I look forward to _____ you.
   A. hear from   B. hearing from   C. hear of   D. hearing of
3. It is not unusual in England _____ a conversation by talking about the weather.
   A. begin   B. to begin   C. began   D. begins
4. I would appreciate _____ it a secret.
   A. your keeping   B. you to keep   C. you keep   D. you kept
5. Please remain _____ and keep your seat belts _____.
   A. seat...fasten   B. seated...fastening
   C. seating...fastened   D. seated...fastened
6. It took ten minutes _____ that she had spelled my name incorrectly.
   A. for her to realize   B. her to realize
   C. her realizing   D. for she to realize
7. I am going to the department store. Do you have anything _____?
   A. bought   B. buying   C. to buy   D. to be buying
8. I am planning to go to England if I'm lucky enough _____ to Oxford University.
   A. to admit   B. to be admitted   C. to have admitted   D. to be admitting
9. This new type of lap-top, originally _____ by only a few, is rapidly becoming available to many people.
   A. to be used   B. to use   C. used   D. using
10. She was lucky to escape _____ to prison.
    A. being sent   B. sending   C. to send   D. to be sent
11. The online world is increasingly merging with the "real" world, _____ nearly every side of life.
    A. to influence   B. influenced   C. influences   D. influencing
12. This question is very difficult. I don't know _____ to answer it.
    A. what   B. why   C. how   D. which

13. My brother likes _____ but he doesn't like _____ this afternoon.
    A. playing football... to play football   B. to play football... playing football
    C. playing football... to playing football D. play football... playing football
14. The food is unfit for eating unless _____.
    A. heat   B. heating   C. heated   D. is heated
15. _____ that you like the gift, it is polite to write a thank-you letter to the sender.
    A. To show   B. Showing   C. Showed   D. To have shown
16. I apologized to you for _____ you in time.
    A. not my contacting   B. my not contacting
    C. my contacting not   D. for me not to contact
17. _____ in remote villages, some of them have never seen a train.
    A. Bring up   B. To bring up   C. Bringing up   D. Brought up
18. There were thirty people _____ in the car accident.
    A. injured   B. to injure   C. injuring   D. to be injured
19. _____ another chance, he will do it much better.
    A. Give   B. Giving   C. Given   D. To give
20. He spent much time _____ the grammatical mistakes in my writing.
    A. correcting   B. to correct   C. correct   D. corrected
21. He was heard _____ such a word before.
    A. say   B. to say   C. saying   D. said
22. I felt _____ at the sight of the big dog.
    A. frighten   B. frightened   C. frightening   D. to frighten
23. This equipment is said _____ already.
    A. to test   B. to be tested   C. to be testing   D. to have been tested
24. When he came in, I happened _____ my dinner.
    A. to be having   B. to have   C. to have had   D. to be had
25. Don't you think _____ better to stay here waiting for the bus?
    A. much   B. it   C. that   D. more
26. He is very glad of his son's _____ the job.
    A. give   B. to give   C. giving   D. being given
27. The question now _____ at the meeting is very important.
    A. being discussed B. is discussed   C. discussed   D. discussing
28. _____ the meaning of the word, he stopped _____ a dictionary.
    A. Not knowing; consulting   B. Knowing not; consulting
    C. Not knowing; to consult   D. Not known, to consult
29. The class meeting _____ this evening is of great importance.
    A. to be held   B. to hold   C. holding   D. held

30. _____ a fine day, we went fishing.
    A. Being   B. It being   C. To be   D. It was
31. She felt so frightened that she could do nothing but _____ when she saw a snake.
    A. run away   B. to run away   C. ran away   D. running away
32. The bedroom is so dirty that it needs _____ badly.
    A. clean   B. to clean   C. cleaning   D. being cleaned
33. She regrets _____ my advice.
    A. not take   B. not to take   C. not having taken   D. not taken
34. The little boy wants to go out to find some children _____ .
    A. to play   B. to play with   C. who to play   D. whom to play with
35. Because of my _____ English, I can't make myself _____ .
    A. broken... understood
    B. broken... understand
    C. break... understood
    D. breaking... understanding
36. _____ , we will do it again.
    A. If time will permit
    B. Time permitting
    C. If time permitted
    D. Time permits
37. Here is a notice _____ people not to litter the beach.
    A. to warn   B. warns   C. warned   D. warning
38. While doing my homework, _____ .
    A. the telephone rang
    B. the telephone rings
    C. I heard the telephone ring
    D. I heard the telephone rings
39. _____ the news, she had a pleased look on her face.
    A. Hear   B. Hears   C. To hear   D. Having heard
40. We want the school _____ as soon as possible.
    A. to set up   B. to be set up   C. being set up   D. to have been set up

第 5 章　名词性从句

在句子中起名词作用的各种从句，统称为名词性从句。名词性从句的功能相当于名词词组，它在复合句中能担任主语、宾语、表语、同位语、介词宾语等。因此根据它在句中不同的语法功能，名词性从句又可分别称为主语从句、宾语从句、表语从句和同位语从句。

引导名词性从句的连接词可分为三类：
1）连接词：that, whether, if（不充当从句的任何成分）
2）连接代词：what, whatever, who, whoever, whom, whose, which, whichever
3）连接副词：when, where, how, why

5.1　连接词 that 引导的名词性从句

5.1.1　that 引导主语从句（连接词 that 不可省略）

如果主语从句很长，往往将它移至整个复合句的最后。该从句原来所在的位置由 it 替代，it 被称为形式主语。

That she was chosen made us very happy.
她被选上了，我们很高兴。
It's a pity that you should have to leave.
你非走不可真是件憾事。
It is evident/clear/obvious that she is telling a lie.
很显然，她在撒谎。
It is a pity that you didn't meet him.
你没有遇见他，真是遗憾。
It is reported that forty people lost their lives in this flood.
据报道，有四十个人在这次洪灾中丧生。
It does not seem likely that they will be here in time.
他们似乎不可能及时赶到这儿。

5.1.2　that 引导表语从句

The problem is that I don't have much experience in this kind of work.
问题是我在这方面没有多少经验。
The reason why he didn't come was that he had to take care of his sick mother at home.
他没来，是因为他不得不在家中照顾生病的母亲。

5.1.3 that 引导宾语从句

连接词 that 引导的从句作宾语时，that 可以省略。

Everyone can see (that) the driver is not to blame.

人人都明白司机没有责任。

在有宾语补足语的句子中，作宾语的 that 从句要移至句尾，其原来的位置由 it 替代。

We must make it known to the public that trash collectors do very important work.

清洁工人做着非常重要的工作，我们必须让公众明白这点。

5.1.4 that 引导同位语从句

that 从句有时跟在某些名词的后面，对前面的名词做进一步的说明。

that 从句与其前面的名词应为同一内容，只是更加详细具体，这样的 that 从句就叫同位语从句。能跟同位语从句的名词通常是抽象名词，常见的有 fact, news, idea, thought, question, reply, report, remark, answer, hope, belief, doubt, suggestion, conclusion, promise, possibility, order, decision, problem, discovery, certainty, explanation, opinion, evidence 等。引导词 that 不能省略。

We heard the news that our team had won.

我们听到消息说我们队赢了。

The fact that he has not been seen recently disturbs everyone in his office.

近来谁也没有见过他，这一情况令办公室所有的人不安。

The old lady expressed her hope that she would visit the town one day.

老太太表达了她想有一天来参观这城镇的愿望。

He still went there despite the fact that he would risk his life.

尽管有生命危险，他还是去了那儿。

5.2 whether/if 引导名词性从句

5.2.1 whether 引导主语从句

whether 引导的从句作主语，whether 和 if 不能互换；whether 引导的主语从句也可以放在句尾，原来的位置由形式主语 it 替代。

Whether the plane will arrive on time is not clear.

飞机是否会准时到达，谁也不知道。

—It isn't clear whether the plane will arrive on time (or not).

Whether he will come does not matter.

他来不来，无关紧要。

—It does not matter whether he comes (or not).

5.2.2 whether 引导表语从句

whether 引导的从句作表语，不可用 if 替换。

The question is whether we can finish the task today.

问题是我们能不能今天完成任务。
The point is whether we should lend him the money.
问题在于我们是否应该借钱给他。
The question remains whether they will be able to help us.
问题是他们是否能帮助我们。

5.2.3　whether/if 引导宾语从句

在宾语从句中，whether 和 if 可以互换。
He didn't know whether (if) his partner would continue to invest.
他不知道他的合伙人是否会继续投资。
Let us know whether/if you can finish the article before Friday.
请让我们知道你是否能在星期五以前把文章写完。
但是，在以下情形中，不可用 if，只能用 whether 引导宾语从句：
No one can predict whether it will rain or not.
谁也不能预料天是否会下雨。（whether 后有 or not 时）
I worry about whether he can pass through the crisis of his illness.
我担心他是否能度过疾病的危险期。（whether 引导的从句作介词的宾语时）
Success depends on whether we make enough effort.
是否成功，这要看我们是否付出足够的努力。

5.2.4　whether 引导同位语从句

whether 引导的从句做同位语，不可用 if 替换。
I have no idea whether he will agree to join our team.
我不清楚他会不会同意加入我们队。

5.3　连接代词与连接副词引导的名词性从句

5.3.1　引导主语从句

How the book will sell depends on its author.
书销售如何取决于作者本人。
Who damaged the computer is still unknown.
谁弄坏了电脑，还不清楚。
When and where the meeting will be held is not yet fixed.
会议将在何时何地召开，还没有确定下来。
How the thief managed to open the safe is being investigated now.
小偷是如何打开保险柜的，这点正在调查中。
What he said is true.
他所说的情况属实。
这类 wh-系列的连接词引导的主语从句通常也可以放在句末，用 it 做形式主语。
How long the meeting will last is unclear.

—It is unclear how long the meeting will last.

不清楚会议将持续多长时间。

What he says about my work does not matter.

—It doesn't matter what he says about my work.

他如何评论我的工作都不重要。

When they are going to get married remains unknown.

—It remains unknown when they are going to get married.

他们何时结婚还不清楚。

5.3.2 引导表语从句

The problem is how we should break the tragic news to her.

问题是我们该如何把这个悲剧性的消息告诉她。

He is running a fever. That is why he is absent from class today.

他正在发高烧，这就是他今天缺席的原因。

China is no longer what it used to be ten years ago.

中国不再是十年前的中国了。

My question is who will take over president of the Foundation.

我的问题是谁将接任该基金会主席的职位。

5.3.3 引导宾语从句

Tell me who is in charge here.

告诉我这里谁负责。

Everyone is guessing who Tom is going to marry.

人人都在猜测汤姆会与谁结婚。

I cannot make sense of what he said.

我不能明白他所说的话。

In one's own home one can do what one likes.

在自己家里可以随心所欲。

whatever, whoever, whichever 所引导的从句，无论作主语、宾语还是表语，都有强调之意。

Whoever breaks the law will be punished.

无论是谁犯了法，都必定受到惩罚。

I will give this book to whoever wants it.

谁要这本书，我就把它给谁。

He wrote down whatever his teachers taught in class.

他记下老师在上课时教的所有东西。

Take whichever shirt you like best.

你最喜欢哪件衬衫就拿哪件吧。

以上所有例句都表明，在所有的名词性从句中，主语与谓语不可颠倒，即从句应是陈述语序。

I wonder what her name is and where she comes from.

我不知道她叫什么名字，来自哪里。

I don't know what the matter is with him today.

我不懂他今天是怎么回事。

5.3.4 引导同位语从句

I have no idea when he will return.

我不知道他什么时候回来。

No one can explain the question why he will go.

没人能解释他为什么要去。

Then arising the question where we could get the machine we needed.

那么问题是我们到哪里弄到所需要的机器。

5.4 实战演练

1. I don't doubt _____ the stock market will recover from the economic crisis.
   A. if B. what C. that D. which
2. News came from the sales manager _____ the new product had been selling well in the local market for three months.
   A. whose B. what C. which D. that
3. There is no evidence _____ oil price will come down in the near future.
   A. which B. that C. where D. as
4. What do you think of his suggestion _____ we all attend the meeting?
   A. which B. whether C. that D. what
5. She didn't know _____ to express her ideas clearly when she was invited to speak at a meeting.
   A. where B. why C. what D. how
6. We were all excited at the news _____ our annual sales had more than doubled.
   A. which B. that C. it D. what
7. There are so many dresses there that I really don't know _____ to choose.
   A. whether B. when C. which D. why
8. He wanted to know _____ child it was on the grass.
   A. that B. whose C. what D. whom
9. He got a message from Miss Zhang _____ Professor Wang couldn't see him the following day.
   A. which B. whom C. that D. what
10. _____ breaks the law will be punished sooner or late.
    A. Who B. Someone C. Anyone D. Whoever

11. The news _____ the Chinese football team had won the match excited all of us.
    A. that   B. which   C. what   D. as
12. _____ woke me up was a loud cry from someone in the next room.
    A. How   B. That   C. What   D. Which
13. There is no evidence _____ he was on the site of the murder.
    A. where   B. that   C. which   D. how
14. We investigated other companies in the market to discover _____ they handled complaints from their customers.
    A. that   B. how   C. what   D. where
15. Please feel free to tell us _____ you think about our program so that we can benefit from your views and experience.
    A. what   B. that   C. if   D. lest

5.5 专项练习

1. _____ he says, I'm going.
   A. Whatever   B. Whether   C. That   D. If
2. Energy is _____ makes things work.
   A. what   B. something   C. anything   D. that
3. Information has been received _____ more middle school graduates will be admitted into universities.
   A. while   B. that   C. when   D. as
4. This is _____ the Shenzhou V Spaceship landed.
   A. there   B. in which   C. where   D. when
5. They are all wondering _____ .
   A. where he has gone   B. where did he go
   C. which place has he gone   D. where has he gone
6. _____ do you think will give us a talk?
   A. Which   B. What   C. Who   D. Whom
7. _____ the accident happened is still a complete mystery.
   A. What   B. That   C. How   D. Which
8. _____ appeared to me that he enjoyed the film very much.
   A. What   B. It   C. All that   D. That
9. _____ he will go to work in a mountain village is uncertain.
   A. What   B. That   C. Whether   D. If
10. I don't know _____ they will do with this old machine.
    A. how   B. what   C. that   D. when

11. My father was sure _____ I would overcome my fears.
    A. that   B. what   C. as   D. which
12. It happened _____ John wasn't there that day.
    A. if   B. how   C. why   D. that
13. One of the main reasons why men have gone into female-dominated fields is _____ jobs are available in these fields.
    A. because   B. why   C. that   D. for
14. _____ it is expensive or not is the crucial question.
    A. That   B. Whether   C. Which   D. How
15. _____ is the richest men in this town.
    A. Whom do you think   B. Who do you think
    C. Do you think who   D. Who you think
16. It was not clear _____ the burglar entered the room.
    A. what   B. where   C. how   D. which
17. The reason why he did not come to the meeting was _____ he was ill.
    A. because   B. because of   C. that   D. which
18. I don't doubt _____ they will be here.
    A. that   B. whether   C. if   D. when
19. _____ we need more practice is quite clear.
    A. What   B. /   C. That   D. When
20. _____ this material can be used in our factory has not been studied yet.
    A. Which   B. What   C. That   D. Whether
21. _____ will take part in the physics contest will be announced at this meeting.
    A. Who   B. Whom   C. Which   D. That
22. _____ the 2016 Olympic Games will be held in New York is not known yet.
    A. Whenever   B. If   C. Whether   D. That
23. _____ knows the truth about it will tell you.
    A. Who that   B. That   C. Whoever   D. That who
24. I doubt _____ we will pass the exam.
    A. whether   B. that   C. what   D. /
25. _____ he will start off to Shanghai isn't known to us.
    A. That   B. Which   C. Because   D. When
26. He couldn't remember _____ .
    A. what was the formulae   B. what the formulae was
    C. what were the formulae   D. what the formulae were
27. If you had told us earlier _____ he was, we could have introduced him at the party.
    A. whom   B. whoever   C. who   D. which

28. He will tell us _____ he thinks of our arrangement.
    A. what   B. that   C. which   D. whether
29. _____ one is ignorant of the law is not accepted as an excuse for breaking the law.
    A. Which   B. Whether   C. That   D. When
30. I doubt _____ he will lend you the book.
    A. that   B. which   C. when   D. whether
31. The music was terrible. That's _____ they left the party.
    A. how   B. why   C. what   D. because
32. _____ some mammals come to live in the sea is not known.
    A. How   B. Since   C. If   D. Which
33. Do you know _____?
    A. when does the movie start   B. if does the movie start
    C. what time the movie starts   D. what time starts the movie
34. I have made it clear _____ I will never go back on my word.
    A. when   B. where   C. that   D. however
35. I will give my books to _____ needs them.
    A. who   B. whoever   C. that   D. whom
36. _____ a good thing that they didn't catch you.
    A. That's   B. There's   C. It's   D. What's
37. _____ a table spoonful of soil can tell us so much about the structure an dearly history of the moon.
    A. Remarkably   B. It is remarkable that
    C. Quite remarkably   D. It is remarkable fact that
38. He worked too hard. That is _____ is wrong with him.
    A. that which   B. what   C. the what   D. the thing what
39. "What is that building?" "_____ the garden equipment is stored."
    A. There is in which   B. The building that
    C. That's where   D. That's the building which
40. One reason why women live longer than men after retirement is _____ women can continue to do something they are used to doing.
    A. that   B. why   C. because   D. what
41. Do you remember where _____ my watch?
    A. had I put   B. I had put   C. had put I   D. put I
42. "When are your parents going to Florida?" "They haven't decided when _____."
    A. they are going   B. they do go   C. are they going   D. do they go
43. Ask him how much _____ before you make the decision.
    A. did it cost   B. it costs   C. it was costed D. it costed

44. He wondered _____ .
    A. what will be his wife's reaction   B. what would his wife's reaction be
    C. how would be his wife's reaction   D. what his wife's reaction would be
45. There is also a fat lady who asked Alex _____ he wanted something to eat.
    A. what   B. that   C. if   D. which
46. "What did the teacher say to you just now?" "She asked me _____ ."
    A. whether or not I finished my work   B. did I finish my work or not
    C. is my work finished or not   D. if or not I have finished my work
47. She was surprised _____ .
    A. how simple was his problem   B. how was his problem simple
    C. how his problem was simple   D. how simple his problem was
48. _____ he did was quite wrong, yet he would never admit it.
    A. What   B. That   C. If   D. Which
49. He didn't live up to _____ had been expected of him.
    A. which   B. what   C. all what   D. that
50. He was delighted at _____ .
    A. how the airline had been efficient   B. how had the airline been efficient
    C. how efficient had been the airline   D. how efficient the airline had been

第6章 定语从句

在复合句（包括主句和从句）中，用来修饰主句中某一名词或代词的从句叫作定语从句，它所修饰的名词或代词叫作先行词。定语从句一般跟在先行词的后面，由关系词（关系代词或关系副词）引出。

关系代词有：who, whom, whose, that, which 等。
关系副词有：when, where, why 等。

This is the machine that/which they made last month.
　　　　　先行词　　　　　定语从句
这就是他们上个月生产的机器。

Beijing is the place where (in which) I was born. 北京是我的出生地。
　　　　　先行词　　　　　定语从句

6.1 关系代词和关系副词引导的定语从句

关系代词和关系副词既起连接作用，引导定语从句，修饰主句中的某个名词或代词，同时又充当定语从句中的某种成分。

6.1.1 关系代词引导的定语从句

1) who 用来指人，在定语从句中作主语或宾语

Where is the man who I saw this morning?
今天早上我看见的那个人在哪？（作动词 saw 的宾语）
Mr Smith is the teacher who the students like best.
史密斯是学生们最喜爱的一位老师。（作动词 like 的宾语）
No visitors who come to Beijing would fail to see the Great Wall.
到北京去的游客没有哪一个不去看长城。（作主语）
Do you know anyone who can speak Spanish?
你认识会讲西班牙语的人吗？（作主语）

2) whom 用来指人，在定语从句中作宾语

The young man whom the teachers loved best was killed in the accident.
老师们深爱的那个年轻人在这次事故中丧生了。（作动词 love 的宾语）
The little girl whom her parents left alone in the room was crying terribly.
那个被（她的）父母独自留在家里的小女孩正在大哭。（作动词 left 的宾语）

3) which 用来指物，在定语从句中作主语、宾语或表语

Where is the book which I bought this morning?

我今天早晨买的那本书在哪儿？（指物，作动词 bought 的宾语）

The story which was very interesting made all the students laugh.

这个十分有趣的故事使得所有学生都笑了。（指物，作主语）

4）that 用来指人或物，在定语从句中作主语、宾语或表语

The boy that we saw yesterday was Tom's brother.

我们昨天看见的那个男孩是汤姆的弟弟。（指人，作动词 saw 的宾语）

The man that is talking to my father is our headmaster.

正和我父亲谈话的那个人是我们的校长。（指人，作主语）

The car that my uncle had just bought was destroyed in the earthquake.

我叔叔刚买的那辆车在地震中毁坏了。（指物，作动词 bought 的宾语）

It sounded like a train that was going under my house.

那听起来就像一列火车正从我的屋下驶过。（指物，作主语）

注意：当关系代词 who, whom, which, that 在从句中作宾语时，常可以省略。

The boy (whom) his parents love very much likes asking questions.

那个受到他父母疼爱的男孩喜欢问问题。

The book (which) you gave me yesterday is very interesting.

你昨天给我的那本书非常有趣。

5）whose 用来指人或物，在定语从句中作定语

①在由关系代词 whose 引导的定语从句中，关系代词 whose 作"……的"解，它是关系代词 who, which 的所有格，在定语从句中作定语，修饰从句的主语或宾语（动词的宾语或介词的宾语）。

The child whose mother died in the fire is now an engineer in our company.

他母亲在大火中丧生的那个孩子现在是我们公司的工程师。

I know someone else whose father works here.

我还认识另外一个人，他的父亲在这里工作。

There are some students whose questions I can't answer.

这里有一些学生，他们的问题我回答不上。

Are you the gentleman whose umbrella I borrowed?

你就是那位我借过你的伞的先生吗？

The gentleman, with whose daughter I worked, looked down upon women.

我曾和那位先生的女儿一块儿工作过，他瞧不起妇女。

Mr Green, in whose factory I worked, is a very kind man.

格林先生是一位好人，我曾在他的工厂工作过。

②关系代词 whose 通常用来指人，表示"某人的"，但也可以指物，表示"某物的"。

He is living in a house whose windows are painted white.

他住在一座窗户漆成白色的房子里。

The engineers enjoy working in the company, whose boss is Mr Little.

工程师们都喜欢在这家公司工作，公司的老板是利特尔先生。
They also raise deer whose horns provide valuable medicine.
他们也养鹿，鹿角可以作为昂贵的药材。
The car whose color is black was bought seven years ago.
那辆黑色的小汽车是七年前买的。
③whose 指具体事物或抽象概念时，能与名词 + of which 结构互换，但以前者更为普遍。
I saw a house, whose windows are broken.
I saw a house, the windows of which are broken.
我看见一幢房子，它的窗户破了。
I saw some trees, whose leaves were black with disease.
I saw some trees, the leaves of which were black with disease.
我看见了一些树，它们的树叶因病而发黑。
Yesterday I bought a magazine, whose cover is very beautiful.
Yesterday I bought a magazine, the cover of which is very beautiful.
昨天我买了一本杂志，它的封面十分漂亮。
④在正式文体中，whose 与它所修饰的名词也可以被 of which + 名词短语所取代。
He mentioned a book, whose title has slipped my memory.
He mentioned a book, of which the title has slipped my memory.
我忘了他提到的那本书的名字了。
It's a kind of game, whose purpose is to try to put the ball into a "basket".
It's a kind of game, of which the purpose is to try to put the ball into a "basket".
那是一种比赛，目的是要尽力把球投入到一个"篮子"里。

6.1.2 关系副词引导的定语从句

1) when 指时间，在定语从句中作时间状语

I still remember that day when I first saw the Great Wall.
我仍记得第一次看见长城的那个日子。
I will never forget those days when I worked in the countryside.
我永远忘不了我在乡村工作过的那些日子。
The date when he joined the Party was July 1, 1992.
他入党的日期是 1992 年 7 月 1 日。
Can you still remember that evening when we met for the first time?
你还记得我们第一次见面的那个晚上吗？
October 1, 1949 was the day when the People's Republic of China was founded.
1949 年 10 月 1 日是中华人民共和国成立的日子。

2) where 指地点，在定语从句中作地点状语

The factory where his father works was set up by twelve families in the village.
他父亲工作的那家工厂是村里十二家人办起来的。

Can you show me the house where Shakespeare lived?
你能带我看看莎士比亚曾住过的那座房子吗？

Chengdu is the city where I was born.
成都是我出生的城市。

I hope to see you again in the small town where we first met each other five years ago.
我希望能在五年前我们初次见面的那个小城镇再次见到你。

3）why 指原因，在定语从句中作原因状语

I don't know the reason why the boys wear their hair long.
我不知道这些男孩子为什么要留长发。

The reason why he came to school late this morning was that he met the traffic jam.
他今天早晨上学迟到的原因是堵车了。

I don't know the reason why he didn't tell it to his father.
我不明白为什么他没有把这件事告诉他父亲。

4）由"介词+关系代词"引导，在定语从句中作状语

由于关系副词在定语从句中相当于"介词+名词"如：when = on/in/during the day，where = in/at/on the place，why = for the reason，因此 when, where 和 why 可以用"介词+which"代替。

That is the day when (= on which) he did the experiments.
那就是他做实验的那一天。

That is the house where (= in which) he lived ten years ago.
那就是他十年前住过的房子。

That is the reason why (= for which) he is leaving very soon.
那就是他为什么要马上离开的原因。

注意：这种"介词+关系代词"中介词的选择取决于 which 所指的名词与介词的搭配关系，或者取决于定语从句中动词词组与介词的搭配关系。

This is the farm where (= on which) I worked three years ago.
这就是我三年前工作过的农场。

He can't forget that year when (= in which) he was taken to Beijing.
他忘不了他被带到北京去的那一年。

6.2 限制性定语从句和非限制性定语从句

定语从句就其与先行词的关系可分为限制性定语从句和非限制性定语从句。

6.2.1 限制性定语从句

①限制性定语从句是先行词在意义上不可缺少的定语，它与先行词有着不可分割的联系，缺少了它，作为先行词的名词（词组）便不能明确地表示其所指的对象。

The man who spoke at the meeting was Dr Brown.
在会上发言的那个人是布朗先生。

Here is the boy who broke the window.

这就是打破窗户的男孩。

②限制性定语从句在口语中前后没有停顿，在书写中通常不用逗号。

The man who stole Mr Green's wallet has been caught.

偷格林先生钱夹的那个人被抓住了。

The chair (which) I sat in was a broken one.

我坐的那张椅子是坏的。

She came on the day when he left.

她在他离开的那天来了。

6.2.2 非限制性定语从句

①非限制性定语从句和它的先行词之间只有比较松散的联系，它不是先行词不可缺少的组成部分，而仅仅是对先行词提供一些补充说明。因此，如果省略了一个非限制性定语从句，并不影响先行词所指的意义。

My cousin, who is an engineer, went to Europe last week.

我的表兄上周去了欧洲，他是一位工程师。

Tom has two sisters, who are both nurses.

汤姆有两个姐姐，她们都是护士。

Three days later he arrived at the village, where he was to stay for a month.

三天后，他达到了那个村庄，并将在那里待上一个月。

②非限制性定语从句在口语中有停顿，在书写中通常用逗号隔开。非限制性定语从句的引导词通常是 who, whom, whose, which 等词，引导非限制性定语从句的关系代词不能省略。关系副词 where 和 when 也能引导非限制性定语从句。that 和 why 一般不用于引导非限制性定语从句。

The Chairman, who spoke first, sat on my right.

主席坐在我的右边，他首先发了言。

His sister, whom you met at my house, married my brother.

他的妹妹和我哥哥结婚了，你在我家见过她。

The girl, whose name I didn't know at that time, gave me a friendly smile.

那个女孩对我友好地笑了笑，当时我并不知道她的名字。

Yesterday he bought two books, which were written by a Chinese writer.

昨天他买了两本书，都是由一位中国作家写的。

I'm seeing the manager tomorrow, when he will be back from New York.

明天我将见经理，那时他将从纽约回来。

I advise you to go to Hainan Island, where you can see many plants you can't find in the north.

我建议你去海南岛，在那儿你能看到许多在北方看不见的植物。

③在英语译为汉语时，限制性定语从句常译为定语；而非限制性定语从句，就其意义而言，在从句中有时相当于一个并列句，所以通常译为一个并列句。

The time when man can walk in space has come.

人类能够在太空中行走的时代已经来到了。

I told the story to Tom, who later did it to his brother.

(= I told the story to Tom, and he later told it to his brother.)

我把这个故事讲给了汤姆听，随后他又告诉给了他哥哥。

We visited the historical museum last Sunday, where everyone was deeply moved.

(= We visited the historical museum last Sunday, and everyone was deeply moved there.)

我们上星期天参观了历史博物馆，大家在那里都深受感动。

He likes reading, which I am glad to hear.

(= He likes reading, and I am glad to hear that.)

他喜欢读书，听见这事我很高兴。

④as 和 which 都能引导非限制性定语从句，其用法有相同之处，也有不同之处。as 和 which 都可以指代主句中的一部分或整个句子，有时可以互换。

She is fond of sports, which/as we all know.

我们都知道，她喜欢体育。

Tom married Mary, as/which was natural.

汤姆和玛丽结婚了，这很自然。

但在下列情况下 as 和 which 不能互换。

a. as 引导的非限制性定语从句位于句首时，不能用 which-从句代替。

As was natural, she married a handsome young man.

很自然，她和一位英俊的年轻人结婚了。

b. 在 the same...as, such...as, so/as...as 句型中不能用 which。

I had the same experience as you had.

我有与你同样的经历。

Some people have no doubt that their cat understands as many words as a dog does.

一些人对于自己的猫能懂得和狗同样多的话深信不疑。

6.3　介词 + 关系代词

6.3.1　"介词 + whom/which" 引导的定语从句

由 "介词 + whom" 引导的定语从句修饰表示人的先行词时，不能用 who 或 that 来代替 whom。由 "介词 + which" 引导的定语从句修饰表示物的先行词时，不能用 that 来代替 which。whom 和 which 在介词后都不能省略。

The person to whom you should write is your father.

你应该给他写信的那个人是你的父亲。

Do you know the person for whom he'd like to do everything is not his own son but you?

你知道吗？那个他愿意为之做一切的人不是他自己的儿子而是你？

James is a man for whom I have the greatest respect.
詹姆斯是我最敬佩的人。
The house in which you are living now belongs to David.
你现在住的那个房子是大卫的。
The drawer in which the letters are kept is locked.
装信的那个抽屉是锁着的。
注意：①由"介词+关系代词"引导的定语从句多用于正式文体中。能够这样用的关系代词主要是which，其次是whom。与关系代词搭配的介词也可以是短语介词。
I am now talking about the school in front of which there is a supermarket.
我现在谈到的是前面有一家超市的那座学校。
The bed from under which the cat climbed out is Tom's.
猫从下面爬出来的那张床是汤姆的。
②在"介词+关系代词"引导的定语从句中，介词的选择受到一定的制约，或与前面名词词组搭配有关，或与后面动词词组搭配有关。
The speed at which the light travels is 300 000 kilometers per second.（at the speed）
光的转播速度是每秒300 000公里。
Do you believe that the material of which the clothes are made is paper?（be made of）
你相信制作这种衣服的材料是纸吗？
The purpose for which we spend much time talking to the foreigners every day is to practice our spoken English.（for the purpose）
我们每天花大量时间与外国人交谈的目的就是要练习口语。
③非限制性定语从句的介词不能后置。
He was drunk and in great rage, at which moment I decided to go home.
他喝醉了并很生气，这时我决定回家。

6.3.2　在非限制性定语从句中，名词\代词+of+which\whom表示整体与部分的关系

The workers, some of whom stayed for four years, came from different countries.
那些工人来自不同的国家，他们中有些人在这儿已经有四年了。
There are 65 students in our class, most of whom are League members.
我班有65个学生，其中大部分是团员。
The man acted in many films, many of which he wrote and directed himself.
那个人演过很多的电影，其中许多是他自编自导的。
We met two foreigners in Mount Tai, both of whom came from America.
我们在泰山遇到两个外国人，他们俩都来自美国。
We all know the portable electric systems, all of which use batteries as power.
我们知道便携式电子系统都是以蓄电池为电源的。
There are 110 elements found in nature, most of which are metals.
在自然界中发现了110种元素，其中大部分是金属。

6.4 关系代词的选择

6.4.1 在定语从句中，只能用关系代词 which 的几种情况
①当关系代词前有介词时。
This is the lab in which we often do experiments.
这是我们常做试验的那个试验室。
②用在非限制性定语从句中。
All the books there, which have beautiful pictures in them, were written by him.
他写的所有的书，里面都有许多漂亮的图画。
③当其引导的定语从句修饰前面整个句子时。
The sun heats the earth, which makes it possible for plants to grow.
太阳使地球变暖，这使得植物生长成为可能。
④一个句子中若有两个定语从句，一个用 that 引导，另一个宜用 which 引导。
At the station I bought some magazines that might help me to kill the time on the train and which could pass on to others when I shed them.
在车站我买了一些杂志，那些杂志可以帮助我在火车上打发时间，也可供别人消遣。

6.4.2 在定语从句中，只能用关系代词 that 的几种情况
①先行词被序数词或形容词最高级修饰时。
This is the first book of the kind that was on sale in our city.
这是在我市出售的第一本这样的书。
This is the best Science Museum that we have ever visited.
这是我们曾参观的最好的科学博物馆。
This is the best novel that was written by Jane Austin.
这是简·奥斯汀写得最好的一部小说。
The most important thing that I want to say is that we must trust ourselves.
我想说的最重要的一件事情就是我们必须相信自己。
②先行词为 all, everything, nothing, something, anything, little, much, a lot 等不定代词时或先行词被 all, every, no, some, any, little, much, something, anything, nothing 等不定代词修饰时。
All that you have to do is to have a good rest.
你不得不做的事情是好好休息一下。
Everything that must be done has been done.
该做的一切都已经做了。
All that glitters is not gold.
发光的并非都是金子。
Is there anything else that you want to say to me?

你还有别的话对我说吗?

There is nothing that I can't do.

没有我做不到的事。

There is little that I can do to make up for the lost time.

我不能补回浪费的时间。

Put away all the books that are on the desks.

把桌上所有的书收好。

③先行词被 the only, the very, the last 等词修饰时。

The only language that is easy to learn is the mother tongue.

容易学的唯一的语言就是母语。

She is the only person that I can trust.

她是我唯一可以信赖的人。

She is the very person that we're looking for.

她正是我们在寻找的那个人。

④先行词是个既指人又指物的并列名词词组时。

They're now talking of the men and the books that interest them.

他们现在正在谈论让他们感兴趣的人和书。

We talked about the people and the things that we remembered far into the night.

我们谈论我们记得的那些人与事情,一直谈到深夜。

⑤先行词是疑问代词 who 时。

Who that has such a house does not love it?

拥有这样一栋房子,有谁不喜欢呢?

6.4.3　在定语从句中,只能用关系代词 who 的几种情况

①当 those 作为先行词指人时。

Those who are Party members should go first.

是党员的先去。

Those who want to see the film put up your hands.

想要看那部影片的人举起手。

②当先行词为 one, the one（s）, anyone 时。

The man you have to talk with is the one who knows me well.

你不得不与他谈话的人对我很了解。

③当先行词是代词 I, you, he, they 等时。

He who plays with fire gets burned.

玩火者必自焚。

He who does not reach the Great Wall is not a true man.

不到长城非好汉。

6.4.4　先行词是 way 的情况

先行词是 way 时,定语从句可用 in which 引导,也可用 that 代替 in which,也可

省略。

The way (in which/that) you look at problems is wrong.
你看问题的方法不对。

6.5 定语从句与同位语从句的区别

定语从句与同位语从句都可以由 that 引导，也可以由 when，where 和 why 引导，但有区别。

6.5.1 that 引导的定语从句与同位语从句

引导词 that 在定语从句中是关系代词，它在从句中充当一定成分——主语或宾语，有具体词义，作宾语时还可以省略。that 在同位语从句中是连词，只起连接作用，在从句中不充当句子成分，并且没有具体词义，that 不可省略。

I doubt the truth of the news (that/which) she revealed to me this morning.
我怀疑她今早透露给我的消息是真实的。(that/which 引导定语从句，在从句中充当动词 reveal 的宾语。)

The news that he will leave for Shanghai is true.
他将要去上海的消息是真的。(that 引导同位语从句)

I'll keep the promise that/which I made two years ago.
我将履行两年前许下的诺言。(that/which 引导定语从句，在从句中充当动词 made 的宾语)

I'll keep a promise that I will write to you as soon as I get to Beijing.
我会守诺，一到北京就给你写信。(that 引导同位语从句)

6.5.2 when，where 和 why 引导的定语从句与同位语从句

when，where 和 why 既可以引导定语从句，也可以引导同位语从句，它们的共同点是在这两种从句中都充当状语。但是，定语从句前有相应的先行词（分别为表示时间、地点和原因状语的名词）。而同位语从句前，没有相应的名词。

I still remember the day when (＝on which) I first came to Beijing.
我仍记得我第一次来北京的那一天。(定语从句)

I have no idea when she will be back.
我不知道她何时才会回来。(同位语从句)

This is the house where (＝in which) I lived two years ago.
这幢房子是我两年前住的那一幢。(定语从句)

He raised the question where we would go.
他提出这个问题，我们去哪儿。(同位语从句)

I didn't know the reason why (＝for which) he didn't come yesterday.
我不知道他昨天为什么没有来。(定语从句)

He solved the problem why it couldn't work.
他解决了机器不能运转的毛病。(同位语从句)

6.6 实战演练

1. I tried to get out of the business _____ I found impossible to carry on.
   A. why   B. which   C. what   D. where
2. Once more I have to leave Beijing, _____ I have been living for eight years.
   A. that   B. where   C. which   D. as
3. This book is designed for the learners _____ native languages are not English.
   A. whose   B. which   C. who   D. what
4. She got to know the young man very well _____ she had worked for so long.
   A. to whom   B. in whom   C. whom   D. with whom
5. The hotel _____ during the vacation was rather poorly managed.
   A. as I stayed B. where I stayed C. which I stayed D. what I stayed
6. This is the microscope _____ which we have had so much trouble.
   A. at   B. from   C. of   D. with
7. _____ is often the case, one third of the workers have over-fulfilled the production plan.
   A. What   B. This   C. That   D. As
8. Mr. Jones, _____ life was once very hard, is now very successful in his business.
   A. of him   B. his   C. whose   D. by whom
9. Our department has a large collection of books, _____ are in English.
   A. many of which B. many of them C. many ones   D. their many
10. Immigrants have to adapt themselves culturally and physically to the new surroundings _____ they have moved.
    A. on which   B. by which   C. into which   D. from which
11. Jack said the construction of the subway would be completed in October, _____ is a great surprise to us.
    A. this   B. what   C. that   D. which
12. The manager said that there were two reasons _____ our sales dropped sharply last year.
    A. because   B. since   C. why   D. while
13. In fact, there are different reasons _____ people are working long hours.
    A. where   B. which   C. why   D. how
14. Broadband connections are widely available now, _____ makes online shopping much easier.
    A. what   B. whatever   C. who   D. which
15. In addition to economic considerations, there are other reasons _____ people work long hours.
    A. what   B. why   C. when   D. where

16. We take great pride in our campus, _____ is one of the most beautiful university settings in the country.

    A. where   B. which   C. what   D. when

6.7 专项练习

1. The earthquake _____ happened in 1906 destroyed a great part of San Francisco.
    A. who   B. it   C. when   D. which

2. The number of people _____ lost homes reached as many as 10 000.
    A. whom   B. who   C. which   D. what

3. She is one of the students _____ the Great Wall several times.
    A. who has gone to   B. who have gone to
    C. who has been to   D. who have been to

4. All _____ I want _____ have a good sleep.
    A. which, are to   B. which, is to   C. that, are to   D. that, is to

5. You are the only person _____ can help me.
    A. that   B. /   C. which   D. whom

6. I will never forget the days _____ I spend together with my friends in the countryside.
    A. when   B. who   C. that   D. whom

7. What do you call a person _____ writes novels?
    A. whom   B. /   C. who   D. which

8. Have you anything in mind _____ you'd like to do tomorrow evening?
    A. that   B. which   C. when   D. where

9. _____ produced _____ you eat and wear?
    A. Which, all   B. Who, all that   C. Who, that all   D. Whom, all

10. Is this the book _____?
    A. you are looking for   B. that you are looking for it
    C. which you are looking for it   D. at which you are looking

11. Where is the shop _____ I can buy fruit?
    A. that   B. which   C. in which   D. /

12. China is a country _____ has a long history.
    A. which   B. it   C. /   D. whom

13. This is the house, _____ the window _____ last night.
    A. whose, was broken   B. to which, broken
    C. whose, broken   D. of which, was broken

14. The hospital _____ I used to work in is a supermarket now.
    A. in which   B. where   C. that   D. whose

15. This is the place _____ I visited two years ago.
    A. in which   B. where   C. with which   D. that
16. The person _____ I share the room is a young teacher fresh from college.
    A. with who   B. with whom   C. who   D. whom
17. After living in Paris for fifty years, he returned to the small town _____ he grew up as a child.
    A. which   B. where   C. that   D. when
18. Is this the shop _____ sells children's clothing?
    A. where   B. when   C. that   D. who
19. Gone are the days _____ my heart was young and gay.
    A. when   B. that   C. which   D. for which
20. Is that the reason _____ you aren't fond of sports?
    A. which   B. why   C. when   D. where
21. Is that the supermarket _____ you bought the bicycle?
    A. that   B. where   C. which   D. when
22. The reason _____ he didn't go to school yesterday was _____ he was ill.
    A. that, why   B. that, what   C. why, that   D. why, what
23. I still remember the sitting-room _____ my brother and I used to sit in the evening.
    A. which   B. that   C. what   D. where
24. Is this the museum _____ they visited last month?
    A. in which   B. where   C. that   D. when
25. I also enjoyed the evenings _____ we spent together.
    A. /   B. when   C. where   D. why
26. A child _____ parents are dead is called an orphan.
    A. which   B. whose   C. that   D. his
27. His parents wouldn't let him marry anyone _____ family was poor.
    A. whose   B. of whom   C. of whose   D. whom
28. The doctor _____ is leaving for Africa next month.
    A. the nurse is talking to him   B. whom the nurse is talking
    C. the nurse is talking to   D. who the nurse is talking
29. He has two sons, _____ have turned scientists.
    A. both of them   B. both of whom C. both of which   D. they both
30. Last month I bought a shirt, _____ is black.
    A. its color   B. the color of the shirt
    C. the color of which   D. of whose color
31. I know a lady _____ husband is a painter.
    A. who   B. whom   C. that   D. whose

32. The small town _____ isn't shown on this map.
    A. I come from it   B. I come from
    C. that I come   D. from that I come

33. That's a word _____ meaning escapes me.
    A. whose   B. which   C. what   D. that

34. The weather turned out to be very good, _____ was more than we could expect.
    A. what   B. which   C. that   D. it

35. She told us the good news, _____ caused great excitement.
    A. which   B. that   C. when   D. where

36. Watch everything _____ the teacher will do.
    A. which   B. it   C. that   D. what

37. His father is an engineer, _____ makes him very proud.
    A. that   B. which   C. who   D. what

38. _____, computers are widely used.
    A. Which is known to all   B. It is know that
    C. We all know   D. As is known to all

39. A dictionary is a book _____ one can find out the meaning of words.
    A. which   B. what   C. in which D. that

40. He is not such a man _____ you described.
    A. that   B. as   C. who   D. whom

41. They have three daughters, _____ work in the same factory.
    A. all of them   B. all of who   C. all of whom   D. all of which

42. She _____ has a good ear for music often takes part in concerts.
    A. /   B. which   C. that   D. who

43. Last week I visited the house _____ I used to live in my forties.
    A. where   B. which   C. that   D. in that

44. The stories about the famous scientists, _____ this is one example, are well written.
    A. in which   B. about which   C. on which   D. of which

45. I didn't like the way _____ he spoke to us a bit.
    A. by that   B. in that   C. which   D. that

46. I'll never forget the days _____ we spent together in Lushan last summer.
    A. when   B. during that   C. that   D. of which

47. I am interested in _____.
    A. all you have told me to   B. all that you have told me
    C. that you have told me   D. which you have told me

48. Who _____ knows him would believe him?
    A. whom   B. that   C. which   D. who

49. Listen to Mary and the recorder _____ are singing in the next room.
    A. who   B. which   C. that   D. who and which
50. _____ is quite natural, a beginner can't read the books written in English very quickly.
    A. Which   B. As   C. What   D. That
51. Such idioms _____ he's learned _____ used nowadays.
    A. that, are widely   B. as, is wide
    C. that, is wide   D. as, are widely
52. Mr Smith, _____ everyone loves, will attend our meeting tomorrow.
    A. whom   B. that   C. which   D. /
53. The lady heard a terrible noise in her uncle's room, _____ brought her heart into her mouth.
    A. it   B. which   C. that   D. this
54. The stadiums, _____ were already fully, were surrounded by a lot of football fans who had no tickets.
    A. most of which   B. most of all   C. most of them   D. which most
55. The telephone directory, _____ I paid 50 dollars, was missing.
    A. which   B. that   C. for which   D. to which
56. Her hand was stuck out of the second storey window, _____ she could pick the apples on the trees.
    A. there   B. from where   C. in which   D. from which
57. There is a rocket motor _____ the direction of the satellite can be changed.
    A. with which B. by which   C. by that   D. with that
58. Sunday is the day _____ people go to church in England.
    A. that   B. on which   C. for which   D. at which
59. The goals _____ he had fought all his life no longer seemed important to him.
    A. after which   B. at which   C. for which   D. to which
60. There are nine planets in the solar system, _____ are larger than our earth.
    A. some of that   B. some of which   C. some of whose   D. some of them
61. He spoke confidently, _____ impressed me most.
    A. so that   B. it   C. that   D. which
62. He took down a square green bottle, _____ he poured into a dish.
    A. its content   B. which content
    C. the content of which   D. the content of that
63. The advanced worker was the person _____.
    A. in whose honor the prize was given   B. whom the prize was given for him
    C. for him the prize was given   D. whose honor the prize was given
64. This test is for students _____ native language is not English.
    A. that   B. of which   C. whose   D. which

65. The size of the audience, _____ we had expected, was a thousand.
    A. whom   B. as   C. who   D. that
66. It was raining, _____ was a pity.
    A. what   B. that   C. the which   D. which
67. By using both ears one can tell the direction _____ a sound comes.
    A. in which   B. from which C. beyond which D. with which
68. The train was crowded and I had to get into a carriage _____ there were already seven other people.
    A. when   B. where   C. which   D. that
69. All _____ is a continuous supply of fuel oil.
    A. what is needed   B. the thing is needed
    C. that is needed   D. for their needs
70. The buildings _____ of bricks last longer than those of mud.
    A. which   B. which they are made
    C. which are made   D. are made
71. May the fourth is the day _____ we Chinese people will never forget.
    A. which   B. when   C. on which   D. about which
72. I painted two pictures, _____ .
    A. one of that I was not satisfied   B. one of that I was not satisfied with
    C. one of which I was not satisfied   D. one of which I was not satisfied with
73. July the first is the day _____ the Chinese Communist Party was founded.
    A. which   B. when   C. that   D. on that
74. The news _____ he had landed on the moon spread all over the school campus.
    A. which   B. that   C. what   D. as
75. We need a chairman _____ everyone has confidence.
    A. whom   B. in whom   C. who   D. in who
76. There was not a hut in the village _____ he had not brought food and comfort.
    A. which   B. in which   C. to which   D. that
77. _____ is known to the world, Mark Twain is a great American writer.
    A. That   B. It   C. Which   D. As
78. The residents, _____ had been damaged by the flood, were given help by the Red Cross.
    A. all whose homes   B. all theirs homes
    C. whose homes   D. all of their homes
79. Children should read such books _____ will make them better and wiser.
    A. which   B. what   C. as   D. that
80. Have you bought the same dictionary _____ I referred to yesterday?
    A. as   B. that   C. which   D. of which

81. "Then about Tolstoy's great novels."

"Who _____ has read his great novels can forget their fascination?"

  A. who   B. that   C. which   D. whomever

82. Men and horses _____ were killed there were innumerable.

  A. who   B. which   C. that   D. whom

83. The thing _____ Jane was not sure was that she failed in her physics exam.

  A. that   B. which   C. in which   D. about which

84. The question _____ he should confess it or not trouble him greatly.

  A. that   B. whether   C. if   D. because of

85. He got a message from Mr. Johnson _____ the manager could not see him that afternoon.

  A. who   B. whom   C. which   D. that

第 7 章 状 语 从 句

在复合句中起状语作用的从句叫状语从句。状语从句通常由从属连词或起连词作用的词组引导。每一种状语从句都有各自的引导词。状语从句的位置可以在主句之前，通常用逗号与主句隔开，也可以在主句之后。根据它们的含义，状语从句可分为时间、地点、原因、目的、结果、条件、方式、比较、让步等九类。

7.1 时间状语从句（Adverbial Clause of Time）

在句中起时间状语作用的从句叫时间状语从句，通常由下列几组词引导。

7.1.1　when（ever），while，as，after，before，since 引导的时间状语从句

When I visit London, I like to travel by bus.
我参观伦敦时，喜欢坐公共汽车旅游。
Whenever we met with difficulties, they would come to our help.
无论何时我们遇到困难，他们都会伸出援手。
Work while you work; play while you play.
该工作时就工作，该玩时就玩。
The telephone rang just as I entered the room.
正当我走进房间，电话铃响了。
I arrived at the airport after the guests had gone.
客人们走了之后，我到了机场。
It will be a long time before we finish the dictionary.
我们要完成这词典，还要很长时间。
Since the new technology was adopted, productivity has greatly increased.
自从采用了新技术，生产力大大提高了。

1）when，while 和 as 引导的时间状语从句
①when 引导的从句表示的时间可以是连续的，也可以是瞬时的，而 while 和 as 引导的从句表示的时间一般都是连续性的。
I got a real shock when I opened the box.
（瞬时动作）我打开盒子时吓了一大跳。
As/When/While I was walking down the street I noticed a police car in front of the bank.
（连续动作）我顺着街道往前走时，发现有一辆警车停在银行门前。
②when 从句表示的动作可以发生在主句谓语动词之前或之后，或与其同时发生，

而 while 和 as 从句表示的动作一般都是与主句谓语动词同时发生。

When plants died and decayed, they formed organic materials.

植物死亡并腐烂后，便形成有机物。（不可用 while 或 as）

I saw Peter as I was getting off the bus.

我下车的时候看见了彼得。

They arrived while we were having dinner.

他们来的时候我们正在吃饭。

③当主句和从句描述的是两个同时进行的延续动作（时间或情况）时，都用进行时或一般时。

While Jim read, Sam sang.

吉姆读书时，山姆在唱歌。

He was taking a bath while I was preparing dinner.

我准备晚饭的时候，他在洗澡。

④as 可以用来表示两种正在发展或变化的情况。

As he grew older, she became more pessimistic.

她年龄越大，变得越悲观。

As time passed, things seemed to get worse.

随着时间的推移，事情变得越来越糟。

2）since 引导的时间状语从句

since 引导的从句，其谓语动词可以是延续性的动词，也可以是瞬时动词。在一般情况下，从句的谓语动词用一般过去时，主句的谓语动词用现在完成时。译为"自从……"；但在 It is + 时间段 + since 从句的句型中，主句多用一般现在时。译为："(自从) ……有多长时间了"。

I have been in Beijing since you left.

自从你离开，我一直在北京。

Where have you been since I saw you last time?

自从我上次见到你，你一直在哪里？

It is six years since she graduated from the university.

自从她大学毕业已有六年的时间了。

7.1.2 until, till 引导的时间状语从句

两个词的意思相近，后者通常用于口语中。当用于肯定句时，表示："主句的动作或状态延续到从句所表示的时间为止"，动作必须是延续性的。

We should continue the struggle until our object is reached.

我们应该继续斗争，直到实现我们的目标。

Please wait till the rain stops.

请等到雨停吧。

当用于否定句时，表示："直到……才"。

People do not know the value of health until they lose it.

人们直到失去健康才知道它的价值。
I will not stop shouting till you let me go.
直到你让我走，我才会停止喊叫。

7.1.3 by the time 引导的时间状语从句

by the time 的意思为："到……时候"。当它引起时间状语从句时一定要注意时态的变化；在一般情况下，如果从句的谓语动词用一般过去时，主句的谓语动词用过去完成时；如果从句的谓语动词用一般现在时，主句的谓语动词用将来完成时。

By the time you came back, I had finished this book.
到你回来时，我已经写完这本书了。
By the time you come here tomorrow, I will have finished this work.
你明天来这儿的时候，我将已经完成此工作了。

7.1.4 once, each time, every time, the moment, as soon as, immediately (that), no sooner...than 引导的时间状语从句

once, each time, every time 的意思分别为："一旦""每次，每当"。其他的短语都表示："一……就……""刚……就……"。

Once the drug is found to be effective, it will be produced in great quantities.
一旦发现这药有效，就会大批生产。
She was frightened each time she saw that ugly man.
每次看到那个丑男人，她都很怕。
I'll contact you the moment I arrive in Shanghai.
我一到上海，就跟你联系。
I got in touch with him immediately I received his letter.
我一收到他的信，就跟他联系上了。
She had no sooner heard the news than she cried.
她一听到这消息就哭了。
如果把 no sooner 置于句首，就要用倒装结构。
No sooner had she heard the news than she cried.
注意：在以 as soon as, when, after 等引导的时间状语从句中，或以 if, unless 等引导的条件状语从句中，通常用一般现在时代替一般将来时。
I'll call you as soon as he comes back.
他一回来我就给你打电话。
I believe she'll succeed if she does her best.
我相信她如果尽全力就会成功。

7.2 地点状语从句（Adverbial Clause of Place）

地点状语从句通常由 where, wherever 引导。
I found my books where I had left them.

我在上次放书的地方找到了我的书。
Make marks where you have questions.
在有问题的地方做个记号。
Wherever John happens to be, he can make himself at home.
无论到哪里，约翰总是毫不拘束。
Wherever you find high wages, you will generally find high prices.
有高薪的地方，通常物价也很高。

7.3 条件状语从句（Adverbial Clause of Condition）

条件状语从句是表示前提或条件的状语从句，通常由下列几组词引导。

7.3.1 if, unless 引导的条件状语从句

unless 在意义上相当于 if not，因此，if 引导的否定句可用 unless 引导的肯定句所取代。

The engine will not run efficiently if the correct fuel is not used.
——The engine will not run efficiently unless the correct fuel is used.
如果没有使用合适的燃料，引擎就无法运作。
We will be late if we don't hurry.
——We will be late unless we hurry.
再不快点，我们就晚了。

7.3.2 provided/providing (that), as/so long as, in case, on condition that, supposing 引导的条件状语从句

这些词语的意思分别为："在……条件下""只要""万一""在……条件下，倘若""假设，假如"。

Provided/providing (that) he wins the support of that group, he can win the election.
只要赢得那个团体的支持，他就能赢得大选。
You can go out, as/so long as you promise to be back before eleven.
你可以出去，只要你保证十一点之前回来。
You had better take an umbrella in case it rains.
你最好带把伞，以防下雨。
He says he'll accept your offer on condition that you are sincere.
他说他会接受你的条件，条件是你必须诚心诚意。
Supposing the plane doesn't arrive on time, we'll have to postpone the meeting.
假如飞机没有按时抵达，我们就得推迟会议。

7.4 让步状语从句（Adverbial Clause of Concession）

让步状语从句通常由下列几组词引导。

7.4.1　though, although, ever if, even though, whether, while 引导的让步状语从句

这些引导词分别表示："虽然，尽管""即使""无论是……还是……""虽然，而"。though, although 不与 but 连用，可与 yet, still 连用。

Although/though the traffic held us up, yet we got to the airport on time.
尽管路上堵车了，我们还是按时到达了机场。

They were able to find a room even though they didn't have a reservation.
尽管没有预定，他们还是找到了一个房间。

Even if it rains tomorrow, I will start off.
即使明天下雨，我还是要出发。

Whether he drives or takes the train, he must be there on time.
无论是开车还是乘火车，他都必须按时到达。

While I like the color of the hat, I don't like its shape.
我虽然喜欢这帽子的颜色，可是不喜欢他的样式。

7.4.2　as 引导的让步状语从句

在正式语体或文学作品中，为了强调让步的意义，可用 as 引导让步从句。这时从句要用倒装结构，通常是把表语置于句首。如果提前的表语是名词，则不用冠词。

Rich as he is, I don't envy him.
尽管他很有钱，我也不嫉妒他。

Much as I should like to see you, I am afraid you may find it hard to come in this hot weather.
虽然我很想见你，但恐怕你会觉得这么热的天过来会很困难。

Try as she may, she never succeeds.
尽管她很努力，但是她从未成功。

Child as he was, he had to help support the family.
虽然他还是一个孩子，但是他得帮助维持这个家庭。

7.4.3　wh- + ever 引导的让步状语从句

这类结构的含义通常为："不论……，无论……"

Keep calm, whatever happens.
无论发生什么，都要保持镇静。

Does British foreign policy remain the same whichever party is in power?
不论哪个政党执政，英国的对外政策都保持不变吗？

Whoever else was responsible, it was not that man.
不论是谁负责，总之不是那个人。

Whenever it rains, this road is flooded.
每逢下雨，这路就被淹了。

Wherever he may be, he must be found.
不论他在哪儿，都必须找到他。

However hard he tried, he just could not remove the rock.
不论怎么用力，他也没法移动那块岩石。

7.4.4 no matter + wh-words 引导的让步状语从句

在口语中常用"no matter + wh-"来代替"wh- + ever"。

No matter what I did (= Whatever I did), no one paid any attention.
无论我做什么，没人会注意。

No matter when he comes (= Whenever he comes), we will wait for him.
不论他什么时候来，我们都会等他。

No matter how cold it is (= However cold it is), he keeps on jogging.
不论天多冷，他都坚持慢跑。

7.5 原因状语从句（Adverbial Clause of Cause）

原因状语从句一般由 because, as, since, for, seeing that, now that, considering that 等引导。

7.5.1 because, since, as 引导的原因状语从句

because 语气最强，表示必然的因果关系，用来说明人所不知的原因，回答 why 提出的问题，整个句子的重点在从句上；当原因是显而易见的或已为人们所知，就用 since 或 as（as 的原因语势最弱），整个句子的重点在主句上。

I didn't go because I was ill.
我因为生病没有去。

Since/As the weather is so bad, we have to put off our trip.
天气不好，我们只能推迟旅行。

7.5.2 for 引导的原因状语从句

for 是并列连词，因此不能出现在句首，它后面的句子是补充说明前句的内容；由 because 引导的从句如果放在句末，且前面有逗号，则可以用 for 来代替；但如果不是说明直接原因，而是多种情况加以推断，就只能用 for。

He is absent today, because/for he is ill.
他今天缺席是因为他病了。

He must be ill, for he is absent today.
他一定是病了，因为他今天缺席了。

It must be dawn now, for the birds are singing.
现在一定是黎明了，因为鸟儿在歌唱。

7.5.3 seeing that, now that, considering that 等引导的原因状语从句

Now that we all agree on this plan, let's carry it out.
既然我们大家都赞成这个计划，那就执行这个计划吧。

Considering that he is only a beginner, he speaks English very well.
考虑到他只是个初学者，他英语说得是很不错的。

7.6 目的状语从句（Adverbial Clause of Purpose）

表示目的状语从句可以由 so that, in order that, lest, for fear that, in case 等词引导。

7.6.1 so that, in order that 引导的目的状语从句

在 so that, in order that 引导的目的状语从句中，必须用情态动词（如 can, could, will, would, should, may 等）。

You must speak louder so that/in order that you can be heard by everyone.
你必须讲大声点，以便所有的人都能听见。

7.6.2 lest, for fear that, in case 引导的目的状语从句

在 lest, for fear that, in case 引导的目的状语从句中，这三个连词（词组）的意思是"以防，以免"。lest 从句一般要用虚拟语气，形式为"should + 动词原形"或只用动词原形。for fear that 从句和 in case 从句一般用虚拟语气，但有时也可以用陈述语气。

He wrote the name down for fear that（lest）he should forget it.
他把名字写下，以防忘记。
Take an umbrella with you in case it should rain（rains）.
带上雨伞，以防下雨。

7.7 结果状语从句（Adverbial Clause of Result）

结果状语从句常由 so...that 或 such...that 引导，掌握这两个句型，首先要了解 so 和 such 与其后的搭配规律。such 是形容词，修饰名词或名词词组，so 是副词，只能修饰形容词和副词。so 还可与表示数量的形容词 many, few, much, little 连用，形成固定搭配。

They are such young boys that they can't go to school.
——The boys are so young that they can't go to school.
他们太小还不能上学。
It is such bad weather that we have to stay indoors.
天气如此糟糕，我们只好待在室内。
He drives so carefully that he has never had an accident.
他驾驶很谨慎，从没有出过车祸。
He has so many friends that we all envy him.
他有这么多的朋友，以至于我们都羡慕他。

7.8 方式状语从句（Adverbial Clause of Manner）

方式状语从句通常由 as,（just）as...so..., as if, as though 引导。

7.8.1 as 引导的方式状语从句

as 引导的方式状语从句通常位于主句后，但在（just）as...so... 结构中位于句

首，这时 as 从句带有比喻的含义，意思是"正如……""就像"，多用于正式文体。
Always treat others as you would like them to treat you.
你希望人家怎样待你，你就要怎样待人。
As water is to fish, so air is to man.
我们离不开空气，犹如鱼儿离不开水。
Just as we sweep out our rooms, so we should sweep backward ideas from our minds.
正如打扫房屋一样，我们也要扫除我们头脑中落后的东西。

7.8.2　as if, as though 引导的方式状语从句

as if, as though 引出的状语从句谓语多用虚拟语气，表示与事实相反；有时也用陈述语气，表示所说情况是事实或实现的可能性较大。意思是"仿佛……似的""好像……似的"。

They completely ignore these facts as if (as though) they had never existed.
他们完全不理睬这些事实，好像它们不存在一样。（与事实相反，虚拟语气）
He looks as if (as though) he had been hit by lightning.
他看上去就像被闪电击中了似的。（与事实相反，虚拟语气）
It looks as if the weather may pick up very soon.
看起来天气很快就要转晴了。（实现的可能性较大，陈述语气）
说明：as if/as though 也可以引导一个分词短语、不定式短语或动词短语。
He stared at me as if seeing me for the first time.
他盯着我看，好像第一次见到我一样。
He cleared his throat as if to say something.
他清了清嗓子，好像要说什么一样。

7.9　比较状语从句（Adverbial Clause of Comparison）

通常由 than, as...as, not so...as, not so much as, the same as 等引导。为了避免重复，从句中有些成分可以省略，而把相比的部分突出来，因此，这类从句多数看来都是不完整的。

This text is a little (bit) more difficult than the other one.
这篇课文比另一篇课文难一点。
She has made far greater progress this term than she did last term.
本学期他比上学期取得了较大的进步。
Nothing is as/so precious as health.
没有什么比健康更珍贵。
Petrol is twice as expensive as it was a few years ago.
石油的价格是几年前的两倍。
Please send me your photos as soon as possible.
请尽快把你的照片寄给我。

Actually, the busier he is, the happier he feels.
实际上，他越忙，就越感到高兴。

7.10　实战演练

1. Please note that I will be away from Boston next week, _____ you want call me and discuss things.
   A. in case   B. unless   C. until   D. so that
2. I'll ask Mr. Smith to ring you up _____ he comes back to the office.
   A. when   B. where   C. because   D. although
3. Young _____ he is, he has proved to be an able salesman.
   A. that   B. who   C. as   D. which
4. She didn't go to the party last night, _____ she had to finish her term paper.
   A. if   B. though   C. till   D. because
5. The policeman saw the thief _____ he appeared on the street corner.
   A. not until   B. as long as   C. the moment   D. only if
6. You can't get a driver's license _____ you are at least sixteen years old.
   A. if   B. unless   C. when   D. though
7. _____ you have any questions or needs, please contact the manager after 5:00 p.m.
   A. Because   B. Where   C. If   D. Though
8. _____ Susan gets onto the top of a tall building, she will feel very much frightened.
   A. Now that   B. Even though   C. Every time   D. Since
9. When he went out, he would wear sunglasses _____ nobody would recognize him.
   A. so that   B. now that   C. as though   D. in case
10. _____ he is still working on the project, I don't mind when he will finish it.
    A. In case   B. As long as   C. Even if   D. As far as
11. Li Lei didn't meet the famous American professor _____ he was on holiday in America last year.
    A. unless   B. until   C. if   D. whether
12. Few companies are interested in providing the software we need, _____ the market is small.
    A. although   B. since   C. so that   D. as if
13. The decision about such a big project cannot be made, _____ each member of the board agrees.
    A. if   B. unless   C. though   D. as
14. There was no proof to show that Charles had committed the crime, _____ he was set free.
    A. but   B. for   C. or   D. so

15. _____ we receive your application, we'll send you an email to confirm it.
    A. Once   B. Whatever   C. Whether   D. However

7.11 专项练习

1. Please put the book back _____ it belonged.
   A. the place where   B. what   C. where   D. that
2. She will call you back _____ she finishes dinner.
   A. as soon as   B. lest   C. in case   D. since
3. The price was very reasonable; I would gladly have paid _____ he asked.
   A. three times as much as   B. as much three times
   C. three times as much than   D. three times as many as
4. _____ you study during the semester, _____ you have to study the week before exams.
   A. The less, the less   B. The more, the less
   C. The better, the less   D. The more, the better
5. _____, the worse I seem to feel.
   A. When I take more medicine   B. Taking more of the medicine
   C. More medicine taken   D. The more medicine I take
6. Larry took a bus from New York to California _____ he could see the country.
   A. so that   B. in case   C. lest   D. now that
7. He had to borrow a little money from his brother _____ he could finish his education without working.
   A. in order to   B. so as to   C. so that   D. so
8. The robber ran away _____ the police appeared.
   A. at the moment   B. so that   C. as if   D. the moment
9. We missed the train _____ the bus to the railway station was late.
   A. because of   B. due to   C. caused of   D. because
10. Man can never send a rocket to the Mars _____ he knows the exact distance to the planet.
    A. when   B. since   C. if   D. unless
11. _____ everybody knows about it, I don't want to talk any more.
    A. For   B. Even   C. Since   D. However
12. Christopher Columbus was on his way to the Orient for silk _____ he discovered America.
    A. while   B. when   C. yet   D. but
13. _____ you talk to someone or write a message, you show your skills to others.
    A. By the time   B. Every time   C. Some time   D. At time
14. I recognized Tracy _____ she entered the room, even though we hadn't seen each other for years.
    A. whenever   B. the moment   C. once   D. by the time

15. _____, you can't go in without permission.
    A. No matter whoever you are   B. Whomever you are
    C. Whoever you are   D. No matter who are you

16. _____ you go, you can find new factories and shops, new schools and hospitals.
    A. Wherever   B. Where   C. When   D. Why

17. _____ we have begun talking about the matter, I had better tell you the truth.
    A. For now   B. Now that   C. Since that   D. Since

18. A rocket carries its own supply of oxygen, therefore, it can travel _____ there is no air.
    A. when   B. while   C. why   D. where

19. The thief ran away _____ he should be caught by the police.
    A. instead   B. until   C. unless   D. lest

20. Helen's anger was so great _____ she could not find the proper words for it.
    A. as that   B. as to   C. that   D. but that

21. _____ you return those books to the library immediately you will have to pay a fine.
    A. Until   B. Unless   C. Supposing   D. If

22. Although he is weak, _____ he is strong-minded.
    A. and   B. but   C. however   D. yet

23. A substance, _____ a solid, a liquid or a gas, may be a conductor or an insulator.
    A. if   B. whether   C. whatever   D. no matter

24. You will never be able to enter that university _____ you get very high scores on the college entrance examinations.
    A. if   B. as   C. although   D. unless

25. It has been only 30 years _____ television came to control American free time.
    A. after   B. ago   C. before   D. since

26. His salary as a taxi driver is much higher _____.
    A. in comparison with a teacher's   B. than that of a teacher
    C. than a teacher   D. than that of a teacher's

27. He took his raincoat with him _____ it should rain.
    A. else   B. if   C. lest   D. for

28. Our production will not increase _____ we introduce more efficient technique.
    A. except   B. if   C. as   D. unless

29. _____, it is quite easy to drill a hole on it with laser.
    A. Hard although the diamond is   B. Hard as the diamond is
    C. As the diamond is hard   D. How hard is the diamond

30. He has lived in this small town ever _____ he was a little boy.
    A. after   B. when   C. while   D. since

31. _____, she often behaves like a child.
    A. As old is she   B. As old she is   C. Old as is she   D. Old as she is

32. He made such a generous contribution to the university _____ they named one of the new buildings after him.

    A. as   B. that   C. which   D. when

33. She doesn't let him get off the train _____ he gets lost.

    A. if   B. because   C. in case   D. as

34. I will stay with you _____ there is a room free.

    A. even if   B. as though   C. as long as   D. in order to

35. Mr. Manson, who holds the office of Chairman, has _____ heavy a load that it is difficult for him to travel.

    A. such   B. so   C. quite   D. much

36. _____, he always treats others kindly and politely.

    A. World-famous professor as he is   B. A world-famous professor as he is
    C. As he is world-famous professor   D. Though he is world-famous professor

37. _____, the more money you will get.

    A. The more you sell tickets   B. The more you will sell tickets
    C. The more tickets you will sell   D. The more tickets you sell

38. While crossing the mountains, all the men had guns for protection _____ they should be attacked by the local people.

    A. for fear that   B. so that   C. in order that   D. such that

39. The doctor looks tired and sleepy simply _____ he has sat up all night with the patient.

    A. for   B. as   C. since   D. because

40. _____ it is a long, narrow country, the temperature varies considerably form north to south.

    A. Since   B. As   C. For   D. Although

第 8 章 一致关系

所谓一致（Concord 或 Agreement）是指句子中各句子成分之间或词语之间在语法形式上的协调关系。在英语中，一致关系主要是指两种类型的一致关系：一种是指主语和谓语动词之间在"人称"和"数"等方面的一致关系；另一种是指代词与其所指代的名词之间要保持一致关系。

8.1 主谓一致

8.1.1 三个原则

主谓一致通常遵循三个原则，即语法一致原则（Grammatical Concord）、意义一致原则（Notional Concord）和就近原则（Principle of Proximity）。

1）语法一致

这一原则主要是指主语和谓语动词从语法形式上取得的一致，主要表现在"数"的形式上保持一致：主语是单数形式，谓语也使用单数形式；主语是复数形式，谓语同时也使用复数形式。

Few students are waiting for you.

少数几个学生在等你。

Every boy comes on time.

每个男孩都是准时到。

A little bread is left in the basket.

篮子里剩了一点面包。

2）意义一致

这一原则主要是指有时主语和谓语的一致关系并非取决于其语法上的单、复数形式，而是取决于主语的单、复数意义：当主语在语法形式上虽为单数，但其意义上却是复数时，其谓语使用复数形式；当主语在语法形式上为复数，但其意义上却是单数时，谓语用单数形式。

The government have asked the country to decide by a vote.

政府要求全国投票表决。

Ten dollars is too cheap for this coat.

这件衣服只要十美元太便宜了。

3）就近原则

这一原则主要是指谓语动词的人称和单复数取决于最靠近谓语动词的主语中的中心

词的人称和单复数。

Only one out of five are going to pass the exam.

仅有五分之一的人将通过这个考试。

Either my brother or I am coming this night.

要么我要么我兄弟今晚去。

当 there be 句型的主语是一系列事物时，谓语应与最邻近的主语保持一致。

There is a pen, a knife and several books on the desk.

桌上有一支笔、一把刀和几本书。

8.1.2 基本规律

主谓一致所遵循的三个原则在实际使用中往往受到习惯用法和不同具体情况的制约，其中也有一些基本规律可以依循，分别以以下几个规律为主。

①以 -s 结尾的名词作主语时。

英语中的可数名词的语法表现形式通常是以 -s 或 -es 作为词的结尾，但以 -s 或 -es 结尾的名词并非全是可数名词的复数形式，它们通常表现为以下几种形式。

a. "形复义单"的名词作主语，如：news, measles（麻疹）, mathematics, physics, politics, works（工厂）, brains（智慧）, economics 等，其谓语动词用单数形式。

Generally measles occurs in children.

一般来说，麻疹出现在孩子们身上。

Physics is an important subject in middle schools.

在中学，物理是一门重要的课程。

b. 有些名词总是以复数形式出现，使用复数形式的谓语动词，如 glasses, clothes, trousers, shoes, compasses, chopsticks, scissors 等；但如果主语用 a kind of, a pair of, a series of 等加名词构成时，谓语动词一般用单数。

②以并列结构作主语时。

a. 由 and 连接的两个并列主语一般谓语动词用复数。

Plastics and rubber never rot.

塑料和橡胶永远不会腐烂。

b. 并列主语如果指的是同一个人、同一事物或同一概念时，谓语动词用单数形式。这时 and 后面的名词没有冠词。

The educator and writer is very popular among the youth.

既是教育家又是作家的他在年轻人中很受欢迎。

c. 当一个句子有两个主语，这两主语又是由 not only... but also, either... or..., neither... nor... 连接起来时，谓语动词和离它最近的主语保持一致。

Either they or she is to come.

不是他们就是她会去的。

d. 如果主语是单数，后面跟有 with, together, as well as, as much as, no less than, along with, with, like, rather than, together with, but, except, besides, including, in addition to 等词时，谓语动词通常用单数形式。

The manager with some workers was working during the holidays.

假日期间，这位经理和一些工人们一直在一起工作。

③以集体名词作主语时。

集体名词（Collective Noun）通常在语法形式上是单数形式，但在意义上却不一定都是单数。

a. 通常作复数的集体名词，如 government, committee, team, group, police, people, cattle, militia, poultry（家禽）等，作为主语时，其谓语动词使用复数形式。

The government have discussed the matter for a long time.

政府官员们已经讨论这个问题很长时间了。

The people are listening to a Beethoven symphony.

人们正在听贝多芬的交响乐。

b. 通常作不可数名词的集体名词，如 machinery, equipment, furniture, merchandise 等，作为主语时，其谓语动词使用单数形式。

A lot of machinery was imported from abroad.

很多机器是从外国进口的。

The suite of furniture he bought was quite expensive.

他买的那套家具太贵了。

c. 有一些集体名词既可以作单数，也可以作复数，如 audience, committee, class（班级），crew（全体船员或机组人员），family, government, public（公众）等。如果将该名词所表示的集体视为一个整体，则其谓语动词用单数。

That family is a very happy one.

这个家庭是一个非常幸福的家庭。

如果该名词强调的是组成集体的成员，则其谓语动词使用复数。

The class are taking notes carefully in class.

整个班上的同学在课堂上认真地做着笔记。

④当 some of..., most of..., half of..., all of..., the rest of... 等表达形式出现在主语中时，谓语的单复数由 of 后面的名词来决定。

The rest of the problem is very difficult.

剩下的问题很困难。

The rest of people are in the hall.

剩下的人在大厅里。

⑤如果主语由 more than one... 或 many a... 构成，尽管意义上是表示复数内容，但谓语动词仍用单数形式。

Many a student likes to read this book.

很多同学喜欢读这本书。

⑥表示度量、距离、金额、时间的复数名词或短语作主语，谓语常用单数。

Three miles is a long distance for Li Ming to run.

对李明而言，跑三英里这个距离太长了。

⑦动词不定式、动名词，或者主语从句作主语时，谓语动词一般用单数形式。

To say something is usually easier than to do something.

通常说比做容易。

8.2 代词一致

代词（Pronoun）包括人称代词（Personal Pronoun）、物主代词（Possessive Pronoun）、反身代词（Reflexive Pronoun）、指示代词（Demonstrative Pronoun）和疑问代词（Interrogative Pronoun）等。在英语中，代词（主要是人称代词、物主代词、反身代词以及相应的限定词）与其先行项在"数"（Number）、"性"（Gender）、"人称"（Person）方面要保持一致关系。

代词及其先行项要保持一致，代词的单复数形式、性、人称表现形式通常取决于其所指代对象的单复数形式、性和人称表现形式。

Miss White and I will go to Guangzhou. We will stay there for a month.

我和怀特小姐将去广州。我们将在那待一个月。

8.2.1 代词及其先行项的"数"的一致

①当先行项为 everyone, everybody, no one, nobody, anyone, anybody, someone, somebody 等复合词时，代词及其相应限定词通常按照语法一致原则使用单数形式。

If anyone calls, tell him I'll be back later.

如果有人打电话，告诉他我一会回来。

当先行项为 everything, anything, something, nothing 时，代词及其相应限定词通常按照语法一致原则使用单数形式。

Everything is ready, isn't it?

一切都准备好了，是吗？

②当先行词为某些集体名词时，随后的代词以及相应的限定词应该根据该集体名词所强调的意义而定。如果将该名词所表示的集体视为一个整体，代词及其相应限定词用单数；如果该名词强调的是组成集体的成员，则代词及其相应限定词使用复数。

The football team has won its third game.

这支足球队赢得了它的第三次胜利。

After having baths, the football team will come back to have a rest and then they will be out for tea.

洗完澡以后，足球队员们将回去休息一会儿，然后到外面去喝点茶。

8.2.2 代词及其先行项的"性"的一致

①代词的阴阳性取决于先行项的阴阳性。

The boy is always working hard. All the teachers like him very much.

这个男孩学习总是很努力。所有的老师都很喜欢他。

②英语中有些名词，如 baby, child, doctor, patient, lawyer, engineer, professor, student, teacher, scientist, customer, parent 等，既可以指男性，也可以指女性。当这类

词作为先行项时，代词及其相应限定词通常使用阳性。

③当先行项是无生命的名词时，代词以及相应的限定词通常使用中性代词，如 it, its, itself。但是如果说话人带有感情色彩也可以用阴性或阳性词来指代。例如人们常常用 she 来称呼自己的祖国、自己的爱车，船员用 she 来称呼 ship，等等。

8.2.3 代词及其先行项的"人称"的一致

"人称"也是语法范畴之一，是表示所指意义的语法形式。英语中，人称代词、物主代词、反身代词以及相应的限定词分为三种人称，即第一人称、第二人称和第三人称。第一人称是指说话人自己；第二人称是指说话的对象，即听话人；第三人称是指所谈论的对象。代词的三种人称又有单复数形式之分，还有主格（Subjective Case）和宾格之分（Objective Case）。

人称一致是指代词的人称形式必须和它的先行项保持一致，也就是说，在一句话中，代词和它的先行项必须保持人称上的一致。另外，在语篇中，说话人或者写文章的人必须保持人称一致，是以第一人称还是第三人称的口气说话，必须首尾一致。

Tom will visit his uncle this weekend.

汤姆这个周末要去他叔叔家。

8.3 实战演练

1. Doctor Richard, together with his wife and three children, (be) _____ to arrive in Beijing this afternoon.
2. Neither the clerks nor the manager (know) _____ anything about the accident now.
3. The manager, as well as his advisers, _____ to attend the world fair.
   A. are agreed　　　B. were agreed　　　C. have agreed　　　D. has agreed
4. Business and professional services _____ in the Yellow Pages.
   A. list　　　　　　B. is listed　　　　　C. are listed　　　　D. listed
5. While _____ at college, he got to know the professor and learned a lot from him.
   A. study　　　　　B. studying　　　　　C. studied　　　　　D. studies

8.4 专项练习

Fill in the following blanks with the proper forms of the words given in the brackets and fill in the proper pronouns in some sentences.

1. The writer and teacher (be) _____ quite popular among the students.
2. The teacher as well as the students (be) _____ looking forward to the summer holiday.
3. Five years (be) _____ a long time to wait for an answer.
4. What we want (be) _____ some water.
5. To say something (be) _____ usually easier than to do something.
6. There (be) _____ a pen, a knife and several books on the desk.

7. Statistics (show) _____ that most of the published and quoted scientific articles are related to medical science.
8. Nobody but Jack and Jane (have) _____ made great progress in the class recently.
9. Bread and butter (be) _____ what Americans usually have for breakfast.
10. Going to bed early and getting up early (be) _____ a good habit.
11. Plastics and rubber never (rot) _____ .
12. Every means (have) _____ been tried but with no end.
13. Not only he but also I (be) _____ good at English.
14. Each boy and girl (be) _____ given a gift on Christmas Day.
15. Everyone who read *Women in Love* said it (be) _____ one of the best books by Lawrence.
16. Many a writer of newspaper articles (have) _____ turned to writing novels.
17. Either they or he (be) _____ to come.
18. In our country, every boy and every girl (have) _____ the right to receive education.
19. Statistics (be) _____ his most difficult subject and they are all worried that he won't pass the test.
20. The police (have) _____ asked that anyone who saw the accident should get in touch with them.
21. A series of debates between the major candidates (be) _____ scheduled for the Labor Day weekend last week.
22. Neither of your suggestions (make) _____ sense.
23. Not only he but also I (want) _____ to work hard and pass the exam.
24. Either the teachers or the president (attend) _____ the meeting.
25. None of your projects (work) _____ out.
26. The teacher told us that to remember details, it (be) _____ important to take notes while listening to the lecture.
27. Many a child (learn) _____ to walk before he can speak.
28. My friend and classmate Paul (race) _____ motorcycles in his spare time.
29. Two hundred and fifty pounds (be) _____ too unreasonable a price for a second-hand car.
30. Politics (do not) _____ interest me.
31. The salesman told me that a good set of tires (be) _____ guaranteed to run at least fifty thousand miles.
32. Twenty minutes (seem) _____ a long time for one who waits.
33. David is one of the boys who (have) _____ a driving license.
34. Five multiplied by two (equal) _____ ten.
35. The audience (be) _____ taking their seats in the music hall.

36. Up to now, the majority of the undergraduates (have) _____ been enrolled for this selected course.
37. The mother along with her two children (go) _____ to the park.
38. I don't think one hundred dollars (be) _____ a big sum of money to him.
39. Jim is the only one of the staff members who (be) _____ to be promoted.
40. The government (have) _____ asked the country to decide by a vote.

第 9 章 倒 装

在英语中，如果谓语在前、主语在后就构成了倒装语序。倒装（Inversion）是一种语法手段，用于表示一定的句子结构或强调某一句子成分。倒装可以分为全部倒装和部分倒装两种形式。把整个谓语移到主语前面所形成的倒装称为全部倒装（Full Inversion）；把谓语动词的一部分移到主语前面所形成的倒装称为部分倒装（Partial Inversion）。

9.1 全部倒装

9.1.1 三种常见情况下的倒装

这三种情况分别是：①句子的开头是表示方位的副词 up, down, out, in, off, on, away, there, here 等，表时间或顺序的副词 then, now, first 等或表示地点的介词短语等；②句子的谓语动词是 be, lie, stand 等表示位置的静态动词或为 go, fall 等表示位置转移的动作词等；③句子真正的主语是名词。

Here comes the bus.
车来了。
There goes the bell.
铃声响起。
The door opened and in rushed a group of children, crying and laughing.
门开了，一群孩子叫着笑着冲了进来。
Then came the hour we had been looking forward to.
我们所期盼已久的时刻终于来到了。
In front of the house stood the children.
屋前站着一群孩子。
但如果主语是代词时，句子的主谓语序不变。
Here comes the bus.
Here it comes.
There goes the bell.
There it goes.

9.1.2 系表结构中的倒装

在系表结构中，如果主语长于句子的其他部分，通常将作为表语的部分置于句首，句子的主谓语须倒装，即倒装结构为"表语＋连系动词＋主语"。
①作表语的形容词提前至句首。

More important is the question how we should face challenges.

更重要的问题是我们如何面对挑战。

②作表语的非谓语动词词组提前至句首。

Sitting around the old man are boys and girls.

围着这位老人坐着的是一群孩子。

Gone are the days when they could do what they liked.

他们为所欲为的日子一去不复返了。

③作表语的介词短语提前至句首。

Among the visitors were a group of tourists from abroad.

在参观者当中有一群来自国外的游客。

9.1.3 以 so/neither/nor 开头的句子的倒装

其中，so 用于肯定句，neither 和 nor 用于否定句。

She is glad to hear that, so am I.

她很高兴听到那件事，我也是。

Tom will go to the zoo tomorrow, so will Mary.

汤姆明天要去动物园，玛丽也是。

Lucy can't do that by herself, neither can I.

露西不能独自完成那个任务，我也不能。

He didn't laugh at you, nor did he say anything.

他没有取笑你，也没有说任何关于这方面的事。

如果以 so 开头的句子表示的是对于前面别人所说内容和情况加以肯定，而不是对于前面内容的一部分进行重复，则无须倒装。

—Xiao Ming is good at English.

小明英语很好。

—So he is, and so are you.

是的，他的英语很好，你的英语也很好呀。

9.1.4 其他情况下的倒装

①有时将直接宾语置于句首，句子主谓也须倒装。这类倒装（强调表语）常含有如 say, ask, request 等表示说话的谓语动词。

"I do think", said Tom, "she is right!"

"我真的这么认为，"汤姆说道，"她是对的！"

②there be 句型中，通常要用完全倒装，即 there + be + 主语。

There are several boys and girls in the classroom.

教室里有一些男孩和女孩。

There are 30 days in June.

六月份有 30 天。

除了最常见的 there be 句型以外，there 还可以接 appear, exist, lie, remain, seem to be, stand 等，一般都译成"有"的含义，构成完全倒装句。

There stands a tower at the top of the hill.

山顶上有座塔。

There appeared to be a man in red in the distance.

远处有个穿红色衣服的人。

③如果主语过长，通常也使用倒装以保持句子的平衡。

Inside the pyramids are the burial（埋葬的） rooms for the kings and queens and long passages to the rooms.

在金字塔里面是埋葬国王和王后的墓室以及通往墓室的长长的通道。

④在某些表示祝愿的句型中须倒装。

May you Merry Christmas and Happy New Year!

祝愿你圣诞快乐、新年快乐！

9.2　部分倒装

部分倒装句的语序通常是将强调部分置于句首，后面接助动词，然后再接主谓结构；或者是把其他句子成分提前，起到强调作用。

9.2.1　疑问句中的部分倒装

疑问句分为两种类型，即一般疑问句和特殊疑问句。在一般疑问句中，通常将助动词放于句首，再接主谓结构；在特殊疑问句中，通常将特殊疑问词放于句首，后面接助动词，然后接主谓结构。

Has he seen the film?

他看过这部电影没有？

Why did you think so?

你为什么这么想？

Where did you go yesterday?

昨天你去了哪？

9.2.2　以否定词开头的句子的部分倒装

hardly, never, not, little, neither, nor, rarely, seldom, by no means, in no time, in no way, no more, no longer, not only, no sooner, on no occasion, under no circumstances 等具有否定意义的词或词组位于句首时，句子须用部分倒装。

Never have I received such a beautiful present.

我从未接受过这么漂亮的礼物。

Not only is he a writer, but also he is an educator.

他不仅是一位作家，还是一位教育家。

Not until one week later did she give me a reply.

直到一个星期以后，她才给我答复。

还有一些表示否定意义的词组所引导的句子，常常使用部分否定的形式，常见的搭配形式有：hardly/scarcely…when…, no sooner…than…, not until…, not only…

but also... 等。这些词组所引导的两个分句，将前一个分句中的主谓做部分倒装，后一个分句中的主谓语序不变。

  Not only was Churchill a statesman, but also a poet.
  丘吉尔不仅仅是一位政治家，还是一位诗人。
  Hardly had he begun to speak when his father stopped him.
  他刚开口发言就被父亲制止了。

但是 neither/not... nor 引导两个分句时，这两个分句中的主谓均要倒装。

  Not could the patient eat, nor could he drink.
  那个病人既不能吃，也不能喝。

9.2.3 以 only 开头的句子的部分倒装

由"only + 副词""only + 介词短语""only + 状语从句"等所构成的状语部分放于句首表示强调时，句子须采用部分倒装。

  Only then did I realize that I was wrong.
  只有在那时我才意识到错了。
  Only at home does he feel happy.
  只有在家里他才感到快乐。
  Only when we complete the task can I stop worrying.
  只有当我们完成任务时，我才能够放心。

9.2.4 so/such 用于句首时的部分倒装

  So quickly did they finish their work that they could go back home early.
  他们如此迅速地完成了工作，可以尽早回家。
  Such a good place is Sichuan that many people home and abroad visit here each year.
  四川是这样的一个好地方，每年都有好多国内外的游客来此游览。

9.2.5 省略了从属连接词 if 的虚拟条件从句的部分倒装

在虚拟条件从句中，可以省略从属连接词 if，即将谓语中的 be 动词的过去式 were 或助动词 had, should 等移到主语之前。

  Had I known it earlier, I wouldn't let he go.
  如果早知道这样，我是不会让他去的。
  Were I you, I would work hard.
  如果我是你，我一定会好好学习。

9.2.6 由 as 引导的部分倒装

as 引导的状语从句，也可以将被强调句子成分置于句首形成部分倒装，一般分为以下四种情况。

  ①当 as 引导比较状语从句时，即用于 as + *adj.*/*adv.* + as 结构中，可以强调的 *adj.*/*adv.* 这一部分置于句首，此时须省略掉第一个 as，就形成部分倒装句。

  Cautious as her sister (was), she didn't seem willing to give a reply immediately.
  正如她姐姐一样谨小慎微，她似乎不愿意立即给一个答复。
  She does everything with a smile on her face, happy as a lark (is).

她做任何事情都总是面带笑容，快乐得像一只百灵鸟。

②当 as 引导让步状语从句时，其意义和 although，though 一样，即表示"尽管"之意，可以用于部分倒装句。

Smart as she is, she knows how to deal with the problem.

聪明如她，一定知道怎样处理这个问题。

Young as he was, he knew what he wanted to be.

他虽年轻，但很清楚自己要做一个怎样的人。

③当 as 引导原因状语从句时，可以将被强调部分置于句首，形成部分倒装句。

Tired as he was, we decided not to disturb him.

因为他太累了，我们决定不打扰他。

④在某些时候 as 在意义上与 so 是相同的，此时与 so 的用法一样是重复前面的内容，意义是"也、也是"，此时使用完全倒装。

She is good at English, so/as is he.

她的英语很好，他也一样。

9.3 实战演练

1. Only when we had finished all the work _____ that it was too late to take a bus home.
   A. did we realize　　B. will we realize　　C. we did realize　　D. we will realize

2. Not until the day before yesterday _____ to give a speech at the meeting.
   A. he agreed　　B. does he agree　　C. he agrees　　D. did he agree

3. Not until yesterday _____ anything about the project that will be completed soon.
   A. did I learn　　B. have I learnt　　C. I learnt　　D. that I learnt

4. He is used to flying by air and on no occasion _____ frightened.
   A. he has ever felt　　　　　　B. he ever feels
   C. ever does he feel　　　　　D. has he ever felt

5. So _____ after she learned the good news that she could hardly fall asleep that night.
   A. excited the mother was　　　　B. was the mother excited
   C. the mother was excited　　　　D. excited was the mother

6. So loudly _____ that people could hear it out in the street.
   A. did the students play the music　　B. the students playing the music
   C. the students played the music　　 D. have the students played the music

7. _____ last Friday, he would have got to Paris.
   A. Would he leave　　　　　B. Had he left
   C. If he is to leave　　　　　D. If he was leaving

8. Since Dick was busy, he rarely had time to go to the cinema; _____ .
   A. Jane did too　　　　　B. Jane didn't as well
   C. so did Jane　　　　　　D. nor did Jane

9. _____ got in the wheat than it began to rain heavily.
   A. No sooner have they   B. No sooner had they
   C. No sooner they have   D. No sooner they had

10. Not until all fish died in the river _____ how serious the pollution was.
    A. did the government realize   B. the government did realize
    C. the government realized   D. had the government realized

11. Only when we hurried to the airport _____ the flight was cancelled.
    A. we found   B. did we find   C. have we found   D. we have found

12. Not until yesterday _____ anything about the new advertising campaign.
    A. I learned   B. have I learned   C. did I learn   D. that I learned

13. Hardly _____ his speech when a young woman in the audience rose to make a protest.
    A. George finished   B. does George finish
    C. George had finished   D. had George finished

14. No sooner _____ than I realized I'd left the document at home.
    A. have we sat down   B. had we sat down
    C. we had sat down   D. we sat down

15. Only after we really understand your business _____ a suitable insurance programme for you.
    A. can we recommend   B. we can recommend
    C. recommend we can   D. recommend can we

16. No sooner _____ his job in a small company than he received an offer from a big international firm.
    A. he quit   B. he had quit   C. had he quit   D. does he quit

9.4 专项练习

1. _____ for your help, I'd never have been able to achieve such a success.
   A. Had it not   B. Had it not been   C. If it were not   D. If I had not been

2. _____ have I seen a better performance.
   A. Everywhere else   B. Everywhere   C. Nowhere else   D. Nowhere

3. Not until all the fish died in the river, _____ how serious the pollution was.
   A. did the villagers realize   B. the villagers did realize
   C. the villagers realized   D. didn't the villagers realize

4. _____ can you expect to get a pay rise.
   A. Only with hard work   B. Although work hard
   C. With hard work   D. Now that he works hard

5. Listen, there _____ .
   A. the bell goes   B. the bell going   C. going the bell   D. goes the bell

· 122 ·

6. They didn't manage to do so. _____ .
   A. Neither did we B. Neither we did C. Neither we do D. Neither do we
7. Many a time _____ not to play with fire but he turns a deaf ear to the warnings.
   A. the child being told   B. has the child been told
   C. has been told the child   D. the child has been told
8. _____ , mother will wait for him to have dinner together.
   A. However late is he   B. However he is late
   C. However late he is   D. However is he late
9. They had just taken their seats, then _____ .
   A. came the chairman   B. the chairman comes
   C. the chairman came   D. comes the chairman
10. Only in this way _____ do it well.
    A. we can   B. we could   C. can we   D. must we
11. Hardly _____ when it began to rain.
    A. did he arrive   B. arrived he
    C. he had arrived   D. had he arrived
12. Jack is a student and studies at the No. 2 Middle School. _____ .
    A. It was the same with Mike   B. So is Mike
    C. So it is with Mike   D. So does Mike
13. _____ tell me _____ to go there with me?
    A. They won't; why don't they want   B. Could you; why they don't want
    C. They won't; why they don't want   D. Could you; why won't they want
14. In the cottage _____ Uncle Tom many years ago.
    A. lived there   B. there lived   C. lives there   D. there lives
15. _____ that I couldn't be absorbed in the work.
    A. They made such talked   B. It was noise outside
    C. So loudly they talked   D. Such a loud noise did they make
16. Many a time _____ me good advice.
    A. he has given   B. has he given   C. he gave   D. does he give
17. Not until noon _____ snowing.
    A. had it stopped B. it stopped   C. in the stopped   D. did it stop
18. Only by this means _____ .
    A. can we hope to succeed   B. we can hope to success
    C. can we hope to success   D. we can hope to succeed
19. Tom doesn't want to take part in any school activities, _____ .
    A. and David doesn't too   B. and so doesn't David
    C. and David doesn't either   D. and either does David

20. _____, it is quite easy to drill a hole in it with a eraser.
    A. Hard as a diamond is   B. Hard a diamond is
    C. As a diamond is hard   D. How hard is a diamond
21. He listened so carefully that not a single word _____.
    A. did he miss   B. did he never miss
    C. he missed   D. he never missed
22. Hardly _____ when it started raining.
    A. had the game begun   B. the game had began
    C. the game began   D. did the game begin
23. Only after I read the text over again _____ its main idea.
    A. I did know   B. did I know   C. I could know   D. that I knew
24. _____ been asked to sing an English song.
    A. Before have I never   B. Never before have I
    C. Have never I   D. I never have
25. By no means _____ look down upon the disabled.
    A. should we   B. we shall   C. we ought   D. we should
26. Seldom _____ any mistakes during my past few years of working here.
    A. did I make   B. shall I make   C. I did make   D. would I make
27. _____ who had been in prison for seven years.
    A. In the robbery a man involved   B. Involved a man in the robbery
    C. Involved a man in the robbery   D. Was a man involved in the robbery
28. Only when I finish my homework _____ watch TV.
    A. can I be allowed to   B. can I be allowed
    C. I can be allowed   D. I can be allowed to
29. On a hill in front of them _____.
    A. stands a great castle   B. a great castle stands
    C. stand a great castle   D. a great castle stand
30. Not a single song _____ at yesterday's party.
    A. she sang   B. sang she   C. did she sing   D. she did sing
31. No sooner _____ the telephone rang.
    A. he had got home than   B. had he got home than
    C. had he got home then   D. he had got home then
32. Only when class began _____ that he had left his book at home.
    A. should he realize   B. will he realize
    C. did he realize   D. he did realize
33. The old couple have been married for 40 years and never once _____ with each other.
    A. had they quarreled   B. they have quarreled
    C. they had quarreled   D. have they quarreled

34. So excited _____ that he couldn't say a word.
    A. was he seeming	B. did he seem
    C. he seemed	D. he did look
35. Only when you have finished your homework _____ go home.
    A. you will	B. you can	C. can you	D. would you
36. David's mother seldom does her homework on Sunday. _____
    A. So does my mother.	B. My mother doesn't, too.
    C. My mother isn't, either.	D. Nor does my mother.
37. _____ at the railway station when it began to rain.
    A. Hardly had he arrived	B. No sooner arrived he
    C. Hardly he had arrived	D. No sooner did he arrive
38. Not only _____ those who lay behind, but we should try to help them.
    A. we should look down upon	B. should we look down upon
    C. shouldn't we look down upon	D. we shouldn't look down upon
39. _____ it rain tomorrow, we would have to put off the sports meeting.
    A. Were	B. Would	C. Will	D. Should
40. Only by reading extensively _____ your horizons.
    A. can you widen	B. you will widen
    C. therefore you widen	D. you may widen
41. —Do you know Jim quarrelled with his brother yesterday?
    —I don't know, _____.
    A. nor don't I care	B. I don't care neither
    C. nor do I care	D. I don't care also
42. _____ today, he would get there by Friday.
    A. Were he to leave	B. Were he leaving
    C. Would he leave	D. Had he left
43. Not until I began to work _____ how much time I had wasted.
    A. didn't realize	B. I realized
    C. I didn't realize	D. did I realize
44. _____ that it was made into a film.
    A. So the book was successful	B. So great the success of the book was
    C. So great was the success of the book	D. So successful the book was
45. Only by practicing a few hours every day _____ be able to pass the exam.
    A. will you	B. can you	C. you will	D. you can
46. Not until the early years of the 19th century _____ what heat is.
    A. man did know	B. did man know
    C. didn't man know	D. man knew

47. Autumn coming, down _____ .
    A. fall the leaves   B. falling the leaves
    C. the leaves fall   D. do the leaves fall
48. _____ so busy, I should come to help you.
    A. If I am not   B. Were I not   C. Was I not   D. If I were not
49. _____ got into the room _____ the telephone rang.
    A. He hardly; then   B. He had not; than
    C. Hardly had he; when   D. Not had he; when
50. _____ snacks and drinks, but they also brought cards for entertainment when they had a picnic in the forest.
    A. Not only did they bring   B. Not only they brought
    C. Not only brought they   D. Not only they did bring
51. _____ I would see you here.
    A. Little did I dream   B. Little do I dream
    C. I dreamed little   D. Little I dreamed
52. There _____ .
    A. come they   B. they are come   C. they come   D. they will come
53. _____ that he could not speak for a long time.
    A. So frightened he was   B. So frightened was he
    C. Was he so frightened   D. Frightened was he
54. —Why didn't you buy it?
    —_____, nor did the color agree with me.
    A. Neither was the price satisfactory   B. Because the price was high
    C. For I disliked its material   D. Not only didn't it fit me
55. Not only _____ polluted but _____ crowded.
    A. was the city; were the streets   B. was the city; the streets were
    C. the city was; the streets were   D. the city was; were the streets
56. —Did she write anything after that?
    —No, _____ anything.
    A. but she didn't read   B. and she also didn't read
    C. nor did she read   D. neither she read
57. Not a single word _____ at the beginning.
    A. has he said   B. he said   C. he has said   D. did he say
58. Only in an hour ago _____ out why he was absent.
    A. did the teacher find   B. the teacher found
    C. did the teacher found   D. had the teacher found
59. Hardly _____ when the bus suddenly pulled away.
    A. did they get to the bus stop   B. they had got to the bus stop

C. they got to the bus stop   D. had they got to the bus stop
60. _____ I had time, I would have run round that lake again.
    A. If   B. Unless   C. When   D. Had
61. —I went to visit the Great Wall yesterday afternoon.
    —Oh, did you? _____.
    A. So did I   B. So I did   C. Neither I did   D. Nor did I
62. —I don't think I can walk any further.
    —_____. Let's stop here for a rest.
    A. I didn't think so B. Neither do I   C. Neither can I   D. I think so
63. _____, I would have given you his address.
    A. Had you asked me   B. You had asked me
    C. Should you have asked me   D. If you asked me
64. Little _____ that she was seriously ill herself.
    A. was Susan known   B. knew Susan
    C. Susan knew   D. did Susan know
65. _____ that they had made an important discovery in science.
    A. Little did they realize   B. They had realized little
    C. Little they realized   D. Little had they realized
66. _____ the plane.
    A. Down fly   B. Down was flying   C. Down flew   D. Flew down
67. _____ his appearance that no one could recognize him.
    A. Strange so was   B. So strange was
    C. Was so strange   D. So was strange
68. Not only _____ a promise, but he also kept it.
    A. had he made   B. did he make   C. he had made   D. he makes
69. _____ absurd was his manner that everyone stared at him.
    A. Such   B. Much   C. So   D. Too
70. "I thought he was present at the meeting." "_____."
    A. So did he   B. So do I   C. So was he   D. So he was

第10章 强 调

　　强调是英语中常见的修辞现象之一,其目的是突出句子中的某一部分。英语中,表示强调的方法一般分为三种:位置强调、词或词组强调、句型强调。

10.1　位置强调

　　在英语中,句子一般的语序是主语、谓语、宾语、状语或者主语、谓语、表语等顺序,但是有时将句子的某个非主语成分置于句首,从而形成完全或部分倒装的形式,以此来强调句子的这个成分。(参见第九章:倒装)

10.2　词或词组强调

　　在英语中,人们往往用一些特殊的词或词组对句子中被强调的部分进行夸张,从而达到强调的目的。这类词分别表现为以下几种形式。
　　①将助动词do及其各种时态表现形式放于句子的谓语前,形成对句子谓语的强调。
　　I do hope you could recover as soon as possible!
　　我诚心祝愿你早日康复!
　　She did go to Beijing yesterday.
　　她昨天的确去了北京。
　　Do do your homework now!
　　你现在必须做家庭作业。
　　②用某些副词或副词词组以加强语气,达到强调的目的。
　　a. 用very, so, only, just, single, pretty, such 等副词修饰名词或形容词,达到强调的目的。
　　Only Susan passed the exam.
　　只有苏珊通过了考试。(强调主语Susan)
　　Tom is the very man he is looking for.
　　汤姆正是他在寻找的人。(强调表语man)
　　There is not a single customer in the market this afternoon.
　　今天下午超市里连一个人都没有。(强调主语customer)
　　The roses smell pretty sweet.
　　玫瑰闻起来是如此的香甜。(强调表语sweet)

b. 用 very much, very, never 副词或副词词组和 particularly, extremely, terribly, pretty, really, awfully, badly, deeply, strongly 等以 -ly 结尾的副词来加强语气进行强调。

She likes to read this book very much.

她非常喜欢读这本书。（强调谓语 like）

He loves Mary deeply.

他深深地爱着玛丽。（强调动词 love）

Jim was terribly wounded.

吉姆伤得很重。（强调表语 wounded）

c. 用 even, much, a few, a great deal, rather, still, by far, a little 等程度副词或副词词组用来强调形容词和副词的比较级。

He works even harder than John.

他比约翰工作努力得多。

This watch is much expensive than that one.

这块表比那块要贵得多。

d. 将 quite, great 等副词放于数量词前进行强调。

There are quite a lot of people who are waiting for the bus.

有好多好多的人正在等车。

③当反身代词在句中充当次要成分时，即如果被省略，不会影响句子的结构和句意的表达时，可以起到强调的作用。

I myself will solve this problem this night.

今晚，我将亲自来解决这个问题。

（这句话如果去掉 myself，则不会影响句子的结构和句意的表达，在此起到强调作用，强调主语 I。）

Are you sure that she could do it by herself?

你确信她可以独自完成这个任务吗？

（在此句中 by herself 作为状语使用，herself 不能去掉，否则就会影响句意的表达，是一个主要语法成分，不起强调作用。）

④用短语 in no way, in no case, in every way, by all means, not... at all, on earth, under the sun, in the world 表示强调，其意义通常是"决不、完全、一定、根本不、究竟、确实"等。

He doesn't smoke at all.

他根本不抽烟。

Who on earth helped you?

究竟是谁帮助的你？

⑤重复某一词或短语来进行强调。

He thought and thought, and suddenly he got a good idea.

他想啊想啊，突然想到了一个好主意。

10.3 句型强调

① "It is + 被强调部分 + that" 是英语中最常用的强调句型。

a. "It is + 被强调部分 + that" 中的 "It is" 部分的时态应根据具体情况而变：如果原句是现在时或将来时，则用 "It is"；如果原句是过去时，则应该用 "It was"。

I met Li Ming at airport yesterday.

我昨天在机场遇见了李明。

— It was Li Ming that I met at airport yesterday.

我昨天在机场遇见的正是李明。

Xiao Hu is waiting for you.

小胡在等你。

— It is you that Xiao Hu is waiting for.

小胡在等的正是你。

b. 如果"被强调部分"强调的是人，则可以用 who 代替 that；但是如果"被强调部分"是时间、地点、原因、方式等时，只能用连词 that，不能使用 when, where, why, how 等代替。

It is Lucy that/who will have an interview this Friday.

露西正是星期五要进行面试的人。

It is because Rose is ill that they couldn't go to the Great Wall today.

正是因为罗斯病了，他们今天不能去长城了。

c. 在 "It is + 被强调部分 + that" 这一强调句型中，即使"被强调部分"是复数，It 后面也始终用单数形式。

It was Mr. and Mrs. White who ordered the room.

订房间的人正是怀特先生和他太太。

d. 强调主语时，that 或 who 后面的谓语要与被强调的主语的单复数保持一致。

It is Susan who is talking with a boy in the classroom.

在教室里跟一个男孩说话的正是苏珊。

It is Lisa and Nancy that are singing.

正在唱歌的正是丽萨和南希。

e. 有时这一强调句型会用到 not until 来强调某一个时间点，此时，not until 放在 It is 和 that 之间，其句型变成 "It is not until + 被强调时间点 + that"。

It was not until 30 years old that he got married.

直到 30 岁他才结婚。

f. 强调句中的 be 前可用表推测的情态动词：must, can, may 等。

It must be David who gave a call to Jane.

一定是大伟给简打的电话。

g. 强调句型不用于强调谓语、表语及 since, as 等引导的原因状语从句。

As it rained, we all stayed at home.

由于下雨我们都待在家里。

It was as it rained that we all stayed at home. （错）

②在特殊疑问句中，只有疑问词可以被强调，其他部分不能被强调，其强调句型是"特殊疑问词 + be + it that"。

Why is Jimmy late for class?

为什么吉米上课迟到？

— Why is it that Jimmy is late for class?

What made her so happy?

是什么使得她如此高兴？

— What was it that made her so happy?

③通过感叹句来表达强烈的感情，突出说话人的情感。

What a fine day it is!

多好的天气啊！

How beautiful are the flowers!

多美的花啊！

How could you ask such a silly question!

你怎么会问这么愚蠢的问题！

10.4 实战演练

1. It was because I wanted to buy a dictionary _____ I went downtown yesterday.
   A. but   B. and   C. why   D. that

2. It was not until the accident happened _____.
   A. when I realized my carelessness   B. that I realized my carelessness
   C. as I realized my carelessness   D. when my carelessness has been realized

3. It was because of his good performance at the interview _____ he got the job with the big company.
   A. so   B. what   C. that   D. while

4. It was in their London branch _____ we met and discussed the Issue.
   A. that   B. which   C. how   D. what

5. It was soon after the economic crisis _____ sales of e-business started to grow.
   A. why   B. how   C. where   D. that

6. It was not until yesterday _____ the business negotiation finally came to a successful end.
   A. when   B. that   C. since   D. after

10.5　专项练习

1. It was at the school gate _____ I met an old friend of mine after class.
   A. where　　　B. why　　　C. which　　　D. that
2. Mary speaks in a low voice: _____ is difficult to know what she is saying.
   A. that　　　B. it　　　C. so　　　D. she
3. It was _____ I met Mr. Green in Shanghai.
   A. many years ago that　　　B. many years that
   C. many years before　　　D. many years when
4. Was it at the school gate _____ the girl picked up the purse?
   A. when　　　B. at which　　　C. that　　　D. which
5. _____ to travel by boat on a hot summer night!
   A. How pleasant it is　　　B. So pleasant
   C. Such a pleasant　　　D. How pleasant is it
6. It was not until 1920 _____ regular radio broadcasts began.
   A. that　　　B. when　　　C. which　　　D. since
7. It was not _____ she took off her dark glasses _____ I realized she was a famous film star.
   A. when; that　　　B. until; when　　　C. until; that　　　D. when; then
8. It wasn't _____ him in.
   A. I who let　　　B. I what let　　　C. me whom let　　　D. I which let
9. It was during the Second World War _____ he died.
   A. when　　　B. before　　　C. that　　　D. after
10. _____ the Christmas shopping season begins.
    A. It is after Thanksgiving that　　　B. After Thanksgiving it is
    C. It is Thanksgiving that　　　D. That is after Thanksgiving
11. It was on October 1st 1949 _____ new China was founded.
    A. which　　　B. that　　　C. as　　　D. when
12. Was it in this palace _____ the last emperor died.
    A. in where　　　B. in which　　　C. that　　　D. which
13. It was not until she had arrived home _____ she remembered her appointment with the doctor.
    A. when　　　B. while　　　C. and　　　D. that
14. It was about 600 years ago _____ the first clock with a face and an hour hand was made.
    A. that　　　B. before　　　C. until　　　D. when
15. It was not until eleven o'clock _____ he went to bed.
    A. in which　　　B. when　　　C. at which　　　D. that

16. _____ is not everybody _____ can draw so well.
    A. It; all   B. There; who   C. It; that   D. There; that
17. So _____ that no fish can live in it.
    A. shallow the lake is   B. the lake is shallow
    C. shallow is the lake   D. is the lake shallow
18. My bike is missing. I can't find _____ anywhere.
    A. it   B. that   C. ones   D. one
19. —Who's that?
    —_____ Professor Li.
    A. That's   B. He's   C. It's   D. This's
20. _____ was Jane that I saw in the library this morning.
    A. That   B. He   C. She   D. It
21. _____ you met the foreigner from Canada.
    A. Where was it that   B. Who it was that
    C. Where was that   D. Where it was that
22. It was not until late in the evening _____ her husband arrived home.
    A. which   B. how   C. that   D. when
23. —Have you ever seen a whale alive?
    —Yes, I've seen _____.
    A. such   B. that   C. it   D. one
24. The color of my coat is different from _____ of yours.
    A. that   B. this   C. it   D. one
25. _____ four years since I joined the Army.
    A. There was   B. It is   C. It was   D. There is
26. How long _____ to finish the work?
    A. will it take you B. will take you   C. you'll take   D. you'll take it
27. It _____ Mike and Mary who helped the old man several days ago.
    A. was   B. were   C. are   D. had been
28. _____ electricity plays an important part in our daily life?
    A. Why was it that   B. Why is it
    C. Why is it that   D. Why it is that
29. It was _____ who respected all their teachers.
    A. them   B. they   C. themselves   D. their
30. Who was it _____ wanted to see me just now.
    A. when   B. who   C. when   D. that
31. Was it _____ he was seriously ill that he didn't come to school yesterday.
    A. although   B. that   C. since   D. because
32. Who is it _____ is waiting outside the room?
    A. who   B. which   C. whom   D. that

33. _____ good time they are having at the party now!
    A. What   B. How a   C. What a   D. How
34. It was after he had made an investigation _____ he came to know the truth.
    A. where   B. when   C. and   D. that
35. It was in the rice fields _____ we had our league meeting.
    A. that   B. where   C. in which   D. on which
36. It was in the park _____ I met his uncle the day before yesterday.
    A. in which   B. where   C. when   D. that
37. It's her very cleverness _____ makes it difficult for her to work with others.
    A. what   B. that   C. which   D. for that
38. _____ will do you good to do some exercise every morning.
    A. Those   B. It   C. There   D. You
39. We think _____ our duty to pay taxes to our government.
    A. that   B. it   C. its   D. this
40. _____ progress you have made!
    A. What great   B. How great a   C. What a great   D. How great
41. _____ terrible weather we've been having these days!
    A. What   B. How   C. How a   D. What a
42. It was the training that he had as a young man _____ made him such a good engineer.
    A. that   B. has   C. who   D. what
43. Was it because he was ill _____ he asked for leave?
    A. and   B. that's   C. that   D. so
44. Is it _____ who wants to see you.
    A. him   B. himself   C. his   D. he
45. It was only when I reread his poems recently _____ I began to appreciate their beauty.
    A. so   B. then   C. that   D. until
46. It was _____ he said _____ disappointed me at that time.
    A. what; that   B. what; what   C. that; what   D. that; that
47. _____ from Beijing to London!
    A. How long away it is   B. What a long way it is
    C. How long way is it   D. What a long way is it
48. The climate of Shanghai is better than _____ of Nanjing.
    A. it   B. that   C. which   D. what
49. It was not until he entered the classroom _____ he realized that he had forgotten to do the homework.
    A. that   B. when   C. where   D. before
50. It was between 1830 and 1835 _____ the modern newspaper was born.
    A. how   B. which   C. that   D. when

第 11 章 构 词 法

对于多数中国英语学习者来说,如何扩大词汇量一直是个难题。实际上,英语单词的构成有一定的规律和方法,掌握构词法对于扩大词汇量有很大帮助。英语构词法主要有派生法、转化法、合成法、截短法、首字母缩略法、混合法。

11.1 派生法

在一个词的词根前面或后面加上某个词缀构成新词的方法叫派生法。分为前缀和后缀。

11.1.1 前缀

在多数情况下,前缀会改变词的意义。

1) 表否定的前缀

①dis- 用于名词、动词前表否定。(不、反向)

disconnect, disarm, disagree, disadvantage, disable, discourage, discover, dishonesty, disillusion, disinterest, dislodge, disorder, disqualify, dissatisfy, distrust, disuse

②in- 通常用于形容词前表否定。(变体:il-, im-, ir-)

incomplete, inaccurate, inappropriate, incapable, incorrect, indifferent, indivisible, infinite, inflexible, inimitable, inoperative, insensitive, insignificant

il- 用于以字母 l 开头的形容词前表相反。

illegal, illegible, illiberal, illimitable, illiterate, illogic

im- 用于以字母 m 开头的形容词前表相反。

immaterial, immature, immemorial, immobile, immoderate, immodest, immortal, immovable

ir- 用于以字母 r 开头的形容词前表相反。

irrational, irrealizable, irregular, irrelevant, irreligious, irremovable, irresponsible

③non- 用于名词、形容词和副词前。(不、不重要、缺少传统特征的)

nonhero, nonbook, nonconductor, non-confidence, non-dollar, non-effective, non-metal, non-natural

④un- 用于形容词、分词前。(不、非)

unable, unacceptable, unanswered, unattractive, unbroken, unconnected, uncontrolled, undecided, undeveloped, unemotional, unemployed, unforgettable, unfriendly, unimportant, unimproved, unnecessary, unpunished, untitled, untouchable, unusual

2) 表其他意义的前缀

①mis- 用于动词、名词前。（坏、错、误）

misdirect, misunderstand, misbelief, mislead, mistreat, misuse

②co- 用于名词、动词前。（共同、一起、相互）

coact, coexist, cooperate, co-owner

③over- 用于动词、名词、形容词前。（过）

overwork, overeat, overconfident, overestimate, overpressure, overprotect, oversleep

④under- 用于动词前。（低于、少于、不足）

underdevelop, underestimate, undervalue, underwrite

⑤bi- 用于形容词、名词前。（双、两个）

bi-lingual, bicycle, bilateral

⑥micro- 用于名词前。（微型的、小的）

microphone, microphotograph, microprint, microsecond, micromotor

⑦anti-用于名词、动词、形容词前。（反、抵消）

anti-tank, anti-war, anti-society

⑧pre-/post 用于名词、动词前。（前/后）

preface, postwar

⑨re-用于名词、动词前。（再、重新）

rearrange, restore

⑩ex-用于动词前。（使、做）

exchange

11.1.2 后缀

1) 名词后缀

①-er/-or/-ee, -eer, -ist, -ese, -ess, -ant（用于动词后）构成表示人或物的名词。

manager, teacher, singer, author, calculator, employer, operator, employee, interviewee, engineer, volunteer, artist, dentist, pianist, scientist, Japanese, actress, waitress, hostess, assistant, applicant

②-ment, -ance/ence, -ure, -ation/sion, -al（用于动词后）, -ity, -th, -ty, -ness（用于形容词后）, -ship（用于名词后）构成表示行为、性质、状态的抽象名词。

development, equipment, judgment, acceptance, confidence, difference, independence, failure, pressure, decision, preparation, translation, information, abbreviation, regulation, recommendation, organization, operation, participation, conversation, globalization, innovation, expectation, refusal, arrival, survival, proposal, ability, reality, unity, length, truth, wealth, width, warmth, safety, darkness, kindness, friendship, scholarship, leadership, membership, hardship

③其他名词后缀。

-age, -ing（用于动词后）

courage, storage, marriage, building, learning, writing

-dom（用于形容词或名词后）
freedom，kingdom，wisdom
-hood（用于名词后）
childhood，fatherhood，manhood，neighborhood

2）形容词后缀

①-able，-tive，-ent（用于动词后）。
acceptable，available，suitable，drinkable，movable，reasonable，collective，decisive，dependent，consistent

②-al，-ful，-less，-ish，-ly，-y，-ary（用于名词后）。
natural，national，additional，powerful，faithful，careful，careless，hopeless，helpless，childish，selfish，friendly，motherly，thirsty，noisy，secondary，imaginary，revolutionary

3）动词后缀

-ise/ize，-en，-ify（用于形容词后）
realize，modernize，deepen，fasten，sharpen，shorten，widen，beautify，purify，verify，modify

（例外：strengthen，lengthen，organize 是由名词加后缀构成的）

4）副词后缀

①-ly（用于形容词后）。
carefully，regularly，terribly

②-ward（用于名词后）。
backward，forward，homeward

③-wise（用于形容词、名词后）。
otherwise，likewise，clockwise

11.2 转化法

在词形不变的情况下，一个单词由一种词性转换成另一种词性。

11.2.1 动词转化为名词

Let's have a look at the pictures.
我们来看一下这些图片。
He usually goes out for a walk after supper.
他通常晚餐后出去散步。
We have made a big step out to the space.
我们已经朝太空迈出了一大步。

11.2.2 名词转化为动词

Did you book a seat on the plane?
您在飞机上订座位了吗?
Please hand me the book.

请把那本书递给我。
You should <u>shoulder</u> responsibilities in this matter.
这件事你应该承担责任。
May I ask who <u>chairs</u> the meeting?
我可以问一下谁主持会议吗?
She <u>nursed</u> her husband back to health.
她精心照顾她丈夫使他恢复健康。

11.2.3 形容词转化为名词

形容词转化为名词一般情况下前面要加 the。
<u>The old</u> in the village are living a happy life.
村里的老人过着幸福的生活。
<u>The injured</u> were sent to hospital immediately.
伤员立即被送到了医院。
<u>The rich</u> are not necessarily happier than the poor.
富人不一定比穷人幸福。

11.3 合成法

由两个或两个以上的词合成一个新词的构词法称为合成法。合成词之间有的要用连字符连接，有的直接连接在一起。

11.3.1 合成名词

名词 + 名词	weekend, headache
名词 + 动词	daybreak, haircut
名词 + 动名词	handwriting, oil-painting
名词 + 及物动词 + er/or	pain-killer
代词 + 名词	she-wolf
动词 + 名词	typewriter, bottle-opener, postman
动名词 + 名词	reading-room, sleeping-pill
形容词 + 名词	gentleman, blackboard
副词 + 动词	outbreak

11.3.2 合成形容词

名词 + 形容词	snow-white, duty-free
名词 + 现在分词	English-speaking, breathtaking
名词 + 过去分词	man-made, heartfelt
数词 + 名词 + ed	five-storeyed
形容词 + 名词 + ed	noble-minded, white-haired, warm-hearted
形容词 + 现在分词	good-looking
副词 + 现在分词	hard-working

副词 + 过去分词　　　　　well-known

11.3.3　合成动词
名词 + 动词　　　　　　　sleep-walk, air-condition, baby-sit
形容词 + 动词　　　　　　white-wash
副词 + 动词　　　　　　　overthrow, mass-produce

11.4　截短法

把词缩短的方法就叫截短法。

11.4.1　略去后部
examination—exam, mathematics—maths, memorandum—memo, kilogram—kilo, laboratory—lab, advertisement—ad, taxicab—taxi

11.4.2　略去前部
aeroplane—plane, telephone—phone

11.4.3　略去两头
influenza—flu, refrigerator—fridge, prescription—script

11.5　首字母缩略法

11.5.1　按字母读
IOC（International Olympic Committee，国际奥林匹克委员会）
IMF（International Monetary Fund，国际货币基金组织）
CCTV（China Central Television，中国中央电视台）
UN（United Nations，联合国）

11.5.2　作为一个词读
NATO（North Atlantic Treaty Organization，北大西洋公约组织）
SALT（Strategic Arms Limitation Talks，战略武器限制谈判）
OPEC（Organization of Petroleum Exporting Countries，石油输出国组织）

11.6　混合法

将两个词混合或各取一部分合在一起构成新词的方法叫混合法。

11.6.1　首 + 尾
motel［mo（tor）+（ho）tel］　汽车旅馆
smog［sm（oke）+（f）og］　烟雾
brunch［br（eakfast）+（l）unch］　早午餐
telecast［tele（vision）+（broad）cast］　电视广播

11.6.2 原形+尾

carbecue〔car + (bar) becue〕 热压熔化废旧汽车的装置
lunarnaut〔lunar + (astro) naut〕 登月宇航员
workfare〔work + (wel) fare〕 工作福利制（指政府规定失业者必须参与社区工作或接受职业培训才能领取社会保障金的制度）
newscast〔news + (broad) cast〕 （收音机或电视的）新闻广播

11.6.3 首+原形

helipad〔heli (copter) + pad〕 直升机停机坪
medicare〔medi (cal) + care〕 医疗保健制度
telediagnosis〔tele (vision) + diagnosis〕 （医生与病人通过双向电视进行的）远距离诊断

11.6.4 首+首

psywar〔psy (chological) + war (fare)〕 心理战
Amerind〔Amer (ican) + Ind (ian)〕 美洲印第安人
sitcom〔sit (uation) + com (edy)〕 情景喜剧

11.7 实战演练

1. Obviously, nuclear power can never be the only (solve) _____ to energy crisis.
2. Nobody at the meeting would (belief) _____ that the new proposal could be carried out smoothly.
3. The lecture was so (bore) _____ that many of the students in the classroom fell asleep.
4. The government is trying to find a way to deal with the problem of pollution (effective) _____.
5. Sandy made quite a number of (apply) _____ for a management position but failed every time.
6. The graduates had a (cheer) _____ farewell party before leaving the college.
7. Although he was (deep) _____ hurt by what she said to him, he made no reply.
8. I'm not sure whether we can gain any profit from the (invest) _____.
9. The organization started a (nation) _____ campaign against cigarette smoking in public places.
10. Application for this training course should be sent (direct) _____ to the admission office.
11. The manager was (entire) _____ unaware of the trouble with the heating system in the hotel until this week.
12. I'm afraid there is not much (differ) _____ in their points of view.
13. I am sure the secretary who has just been hired will proved an efficient (employ) _____.

14. I've heard that the musical group will set off for Hong Kong to give a three-day (perform) _____.
15. After the flood, life was (extreme) _____ difficult for the farmers in this area.
16. Before the flight takes off, all the passengers are asked to (fast) _____ their seat belts.
17. I cannot go shopping with you because I have an (appoint) _____ with my dentist this afternoon.
18. The father wants to know why his son (question) _____ by the police last week.
19. Following the (settle) _____ of the strike, the train service is now back to normal.
20. We should read more and see more in order to (wide) _____ our horizons.
21. Some experts suggest that we slow down the (economy) _____ growth in the country.
22. Doing a second job to earn more money also means you have to pay (addition) _____ income tax.
23. We are not short of raw materials at the moment, but we need reliable (equip) _____.
24. Following the (success) _____ settlement of the strike, the train service is now back to normal.
25. If a business wants to sell its products (international) _____, it should do some world market research first.
26. It is (reason) _____ for parents to pay for their children's education.
27. At the meeting a (propose) _____ was put forward by John Smith.
28. It has been a long winter, and we're (eager) _____ waiting for the coming of spring.
29. They fully recognized the enormous (strong) _____ and influence of the union.
30. My sister has recently got a job as a (reception) _____ in a hotel.
31. Provided that there is no (object) _____, we will begin with the next item.
32. There has not been a favorable (respond) _____ to your plan so far.
33. Buying a house in such a neighborhood can be a (cost) _____ business.
34. The businessman lost a (gold) _____ chance to make a big fortune.
35. You should be aware that this rare bird was on the list of human (protect) _____.
36. Did you get the (permit) _____ from the authorities to run the business?
37. Nowadays, electronic (pay) _____ is a more convenient way to pay for purchases than cash and check.
38. The (grow) _____ of online shopping is producing a fundamental change in consumer behavior.
39. It is the (responsible) _____ of the Human Resources Department to employ new staff members.
40. I have worked part-time to earn some money to continue my (educate) _____.
41. More than half of the staff say they won't feel (comfort) _____ when talking to their boss.
42. All types of water pollution are (harm) _____ to the health of humans and animals.

43. If you give us any opportunity to deal in your products, the result will be (entire) _____ satisfactory.
44. The manager stressed the (important) _____ of developing a long-term strategy for the company.
45. Working from home is flexible and beneficial not only to the employees but also to the (employ) _____.
46. The local government has decided to spend more money on the (equip) _____ of the hospitals in the rural area.
47. I tried to fix the computer myself, but that just made it (bad) _____ than I had expected.
48. Winning three gold medals is the most remarkable (achieve) _____ he has made so far.
49. In order to deal (effective) _____ with the frequent railroad accidents, a special committee has been set up.
50. In addition to the (require) _____ courses, there are still some other courses to be individually chosen.
51. If you want to be (success) _____ in life, you should be honest and self-confident.
52. The engineer put forward a (suggest) _____ at the meeting to improve the public traffic system.
53. I am (please) _____ to inform you that you have won the first prize.
54. The expert made a very (help) _____ suggestion for the project.
55. According to the report (publish) _____ yesterday, an increasing number of young people are involved in community activities.
56. In his speech, the manager expressed his thanks to those who have made their (contribute) _____ to the company.
57. To her (disappoint) _____, the girl was denied the job she had applied for.
58. Communication via eye contact seems to be (particular) _____ important in some cases.
59. As more customers will attend the meeting, we need to prepare some (addition) _____ chairs.
60. These apartments allow older people to keep their (independent) _____, while having medical care available.
61. We hope to bring together all the parties (direct) _____ involved in the conflict.
62. We should continue to give full and (act) _____ support to the United Nations.
63. Budgeting is an important part of the (manage) _____ control process in any organization.
64. We're pleased to announce that your (apply) _____ for the membership has been accepted.
65. The company offers a variety of roles (suit) _____ for the goals, backgrounds and talents of its employees.

66. We make every effort to ensure that our transaction process is safe and that your (person) _____ information is secure.

11.8 专项练习

Ⅰ. **Choose the best answer to complete each sentences.**

1. He was _____ enough not to tell me that he had been promoted.
   A. care　　　　B. careful　　　　C. careless　　　　D. cared
2. The college student died for saving the child, so his _____ is heavier than Mount Tai.
   A. die　　　　B. dead　　　　C. died　　　　D. death
3. The girl looked _____ at her brother who was badly wounded.
   A. sadly　　　　B. sadness　　　　C. sadless　　　　D. sad
4. Tom is an expert at chemistry. We all call him a _____.
   A. chemistry　　　　B. chemical　　　　C. chemist　　　　D. physician
5. The three-_____ chair isn't suitable for an old man. He may fall off.
   A. legging　　　　B. legged　　　　C. legs　　　　D. leg
6. He became the _____ engineer in the country.
   A. lead　　　　B. leader　　　　C. leading　　　　D. leadership
7. When the teacher praised him for working out the maths problem, Jack looked _____ about at his classmates.
   A. proud　　　　B. proudly　　　　C. pride　　　　D. pridely
8. To everyone's _____, he finished the job quite well.
   A. satisfied　　　　B. satisfactory　　　　C. satisfying　　　　D. satisfaction
9. He tries to write _____ in English. I believe he can write _____ passage in English.
   A. 600 words, a 600-words　　　　B. 600-word, a 600-words
   C. 600 words, a 600-word　　　　D. 600 words, a 600-words
10. You should not enter the spot without the _____ of the police.
    A. permit　　　　B. permission　　　　C. permitting　　　　D. permittance
11. They took him to the police _____.
    A. headquarters　　　　B. headline　　　　C. headmaster　　　　D. headache
12. If animal escape was no accident, he did it _____.
    A. intend　　　　B. intention　　　　C. intentionally　　　　D. intentional
13. The receptionist welcomed all the guests with a _____ smile.
    A. practice　　　　B. practise　　　　C. practical　　　　D. practiced
14. The _____ ordered him to pay a $1,000 fine.
    A. judger　　　　B. judgement　　　　C. judge　　　　D. judgment

15. My TV is out of order. Can you tell me what the _____ news about financial crisis in Wall Street is?
    A. lately   B. latest   C. later   D. latter
16. The Great Wall is more than 3,000 kilos in _____.
    A. longer   B. length   C. long   D. longing
17. To his _____, he passed the exam easily.
    A. joy   B. joyful   C. joyless   D. joyness
18. Australia is an _____ country.
    A. English-speaking   B. speak-English
    C. spoken-English   D. English-spoken
19. How _____ he is! He is always acting _____. He is really a _____.
    A. foolish; foolishly; fool   B. fool; foolish; fool
    C. foolish; fool; fool   D. foolishly; foolish; fool
20. The necklace is of great _____.
    A. valuable   B. value   C. valueless   D. unvaluable
21. There were _____ fish in the river in Amazon.
    A. in danger   B. danger   C. dangerous   D. dangerless
22. The letter "b" in the word "debt" is _____.
    A. sound   B. silent   C. silence   D. sounded
23. The baby looked at me _____.
    A. stranger   B. strangely   C. strange   D. strangeless
24. The black people fought for their _____ bravely to get rid of slavery.
    A. free   B. freely   C. freedom   D. frees
25. What you said sounded _____ but I believe it was not true.
    A. reasonable   B. reasonful   C. reasonless   D. unreason
26. We have to learn _____ technology from other countries.
    A. advance   B. advancing   C. advantage   D. advanced
27. The old men live in a village _____. They come here almost every day to chat.
    A. nearby   B. near   C. nearly   D. near by
28. He is an _____ in the army, not an _____ in the government. You can not easily find him in his _____.
    A. official; officer; office   B. officer; office; official
    C. official; official; official D. officer; official; office
29. You should give up smoking if you want to keep _____.
    A. health   B. healthy   C. healthily   D. healthier
30. _____ speaking, I didn't do it on purpose.
    A. Honestly   B. Honest   C. Honesty   D. Dishonest

31. If there are more than 4 people, it's more _____ to travel by car than by coach.
    A. economics   B. economy   C. economic   D. economical
32. _____ his brother, Tom is lively and makes friends easily with others.
    A. Unlike   B. Liking   C. Alike   D. Dislike
33. That was a _____ trade fair; we made many contracts with companies from all over the country.
    A. fruit   B. fruitless   C. fruitful   D. fruits
34. I hope you can take it into _____.
    A. consider   B. considered   C. consideration   D. considering
35. She gave me a very good _____ with her fluent English.
    A. impress   B. impression   C. impressive   D. impressed

Ⅱ. **Complete the following sentences with the proper forms of the words given in the brackets.**

1. There they found _____ (accommodate) at reasonable price.
2. She won _____ (accept) by the family only through extraordinary diligence.
3. Our baby sister is an _____ (add) to our family.
4. Most people are against the _____ (add) tax.
5. _____ (act) speaks louder than words.
6. The _____ (act) cost of building this apartment is much more than we expected.
7. The poor young man is eager to have a chance to receive _____ (advance) education.
8. If you travel on business, you can get a travel _____ (allow) that covers hotel and restaurant bills.
9. To my _____ (amaze), he has known the truth.
10. The _____ (analyze) of the blood on the murder spot showed some valuable clues to the police.
11. He was _____ (anxiety) for his mother's coming.
12. There are many _____ (appetite) foods in the supermarket.
13. Never judge a man by his _____ (appear).
14. He showed his _____ (approve) by nodding his head.
15. My early _____ (arrive) made him very surprised.
16. She is an _____ (art) in the kitchen.
17. Countries all over the world offered financial _____ (assist) to the quake-hit areas.
18. There is a high _____ (attend) at his lecture.
19. Without the _____ (aware) of the danger, the little boy went into the wild forest alone.
20. The neighbors speak highly of Tom's good _____ (behave).
21. Usually kids have _____ (bound) imagination.
22. _____ (care) people tend to make more mistakes.

23. The apartments in the _____ (center) position in the city are not available now.
24. He plans to take a _____ (challenge) course of the study this semester.
25. This photo reminds me of my _____ (child).
26. We usually _____ (class) books by subjects in a library.
27. I appreciate the _____ (color) leaves in the fall.
28. My English teacher has a large _____ (collect) of stamps.
29. The shop received a lot letters of _____ (complain).
30. _____ (confident) is important to your success.
31. He was often absent from my class, _____ (consequence) he failed the exam.
32. He made a _____ (consider) sum of money abroad.
33. It's _____ (consider) of you to send me so beautiful flowers on my birthday.
34. We should take the weather into _____ (consider) when thinking of traveling.
35. You'd better buy a glass _____ (contain) to put the fish in.
36. The man is full of _____ (curious) though he knows a lot.
37. The troops must have used _____ (dead) weapons.
38. In the past, young people could not make a _____ (decide) by themselves about the marriage.
39. The best _____ (defend) is offence.
40. A dictionary usually gives a _____ (define) to words.
41. There is no _____ (deliver) of goods if you live outside the city.
42. American teenagers like to be _____ (depend). They do many things on their own.
43. They didn't know the _____ (deep) of the well.
44. Our desks are covered with a lot of _____ (dirty).
45. The scientist made a new _____ (discover) in medical science.
46. I got a _____ (distance) telephone call from a Canadian friend.
47. It is a small village in the _____ (east) coastline of China.
48. Going by train is more _____ (economy) than going by bus.
49. The medicine is an _____ (effect) cure for a headache.
50. The Bird Nest is being built with great _____ (efficient) and speed.
51. He always appears to be _____ (energy) in front of his colleagues.
52. People's senses of _____ (environment) protection are becoming stronger.
53. It's _____ (evidence) that you are cheated.
54. There is no _____ (except) to this rule.
55. Her eyes shine with _____ (expect).
56. The only _____ (explain) for his behavior is that he's crazy.
57. As the saying says, "_____ (fail) is the mother of success".
58. Every boss wants to have _____ (faith) employees.
59. She chooses to be a teacher because she likes the _____ (flexible) of teachers' working

hours.
60. The next _____ (fly) will take off at 10 a.m.
61. Environment pollution is a _____ (globe) problem.
62. The whole world are amazed at the rapid _____ (grow) of China.
63. I did the work with my supervisor's _____ (guide).
64. The girl looked at him with an expression of _____ (hate).
65. The man is 5 feet in _____ (high).
66. _____ (Honest) is the best policy.
67. You should know it is _____ (legal) to steal things from supermarket.
68. There is steady _____ (increase) in population.
69. I have got three _____ (invite) to parties.
70. We should not _____ (judgment) a person by his appearance.
71. I have a good _____ (know) of Paris.
72. Your dress is not the right _____ (long); it is too short.
73. The little girl has been _____ (long) for this book for a long time.
74. He _____ (loose) his collar of his overcoat.
75. The _____ (lose) of my mobile phone meant that I had to buy a new one.
76. The make-up has a _____ (magic) effect on her skin.
77. The _____ (major) of the students in our class have brown eyes; only two have blue eyes.
78. A _____ (month) paper is printed every month.
79. She gives me _____ (mother) love.
80. The people in the city are annoyed at the _____ (noise) traffic.
81. She likes to live in the _____ (north) part of the country.
82. We go for walks in the park _____ (occasion).
83. That man was the _____ (origin) owner of this house.
84. I am sure what he said is _____ (part) true.
85. Have _____ (patient); you can work out the mathematics problem.
86. He likes the _____ (poet) written by Li Bai.
87. There is no _____ (possible) of his coming.
88. The girl's _____ (present) was hardly noticed.
89. The highest _____ (prior) of governments has been given to the development of the quake-hit areas.
90. We must respect other's _____ (private).
91. Our company sells plastic _____ (produce).
92. There is no _____ (prove) that he was not there then.
93. I can't agree to your _____ (propose).
94. You have to get the _____ (qualify) for this job first.

95. What you said sounds _____ (reason).
96. I want to keep this book for _____ (refer).
97. Your _____ (refuse) of my help hurt me.
98. It's not _____ (rely) to judge a man by his appearance.
99. If you want to see a movie there, you'll have to make a _____ (reserve), or there will be no tickets.
100. I find it rather _____ (risk) to invest in this company.
101. The mother is concerned about her son's _____ (safe).
102. For a few students from remote areas, _____ (scholar) were sources of financial support.
103. We should focus on the _____ (science) development of the country.
104. In the developed countries, there's a great _____ (short) of work force.
105. _____ (short) afterwards, the police stopped the car and both men were arrested.
106. Try to _____ (simple) your explanation for the elderly people.
107. He felt _____ (sleep) the whole day.
108. Every one should contribute to the _____ (social).
109. He said there was no simple _____ (solve) to the unemployment problem.
110. Her local doctor couldn't tell what was wrong, so he was sent to see a _____ (special).
111. The book was written _____ (specific) for women.
112. _____ (speak) is learnt in the first years of life.
113. Were you _____ (succeed) in inviting him to the party?
114. Her _____ (succeed) as a popular singer was short.
115. My grandpa is very _____ (talk).
116. A few of them are trained to be _____ (technical).
117. His father _____ (threat) to beat the boy if he left the room again.
118. The shopping mall sells a _____ (vary) of goods.
119. There are _____ (vary) colors to choose from.
120. The baby's _____ (weigh) was 3 kilos.

附录 A 单词及专业词汇表（A 级）

单　词　表

（说明：[C] 可数名词；[U] 不可数名词；[P] 复数）

单词	释义
A	
abandon	*v.* 放弃
ability	*n.* 1. 能力　　2. 能耐，本领
aboard	*adv. & prep.* 1. 在船（或飞机、车）上　　2. 上船（或飞机、车）
abroad	*adj.* 到国外，在国外
absent	*adj.* 缺席，不在
absolute	*adj.* 绝对的，完全的
absorb	*v.* 1. 吸收　　2. 吸引……的注意，使全神贯注
abstract	*adj.* 抽象的　　*n.* [C] 摘要，梗概
abundant	*adj.* 丰富的，充裕的
accent	*n.* 口音，腔调
accept	*v.* 1. 接受，领受　　2. 同意，认可
access	*n.* [U] 1. 接近，进入　　2. 通道
accident	*n.* [C] 1. 意外的事，偶然的事　　2. 事故
accommodations	*n.* [P] 膳宿，住宿
accompany	*v.* 1. 陪伴，陪同　　2. 伴随，和……一起发生　　3. 为……伴奏
accomplish	*v.* 完成，实现
according	*adj.* 按照，根据
account	*n.* [C] 叙述，说明
accumulate	*v.* 积累，积聚
accurate	*adj.* 准确的，精确的
accuse	*v.* 1. 指责　　2. 指控
accustomed	*adj.* 习惯的，惯常的
achieve	*v.* 1. 完成，实现　　2. 达到，得到
achievement	*n.* 成就，成绩
acknowledge	*v.* 1. 承认　　2. 致谢
acquire	*v.* 取得，获得，学到
action	*n.* 1. 行动，行动过程　　2. 作用
active	*adj.* 1. 活跃的，敏捷的，积极的　　2. 在活动中的

activity	*n.* 活动，活跃
actual	*adj.* 实际的，事实上的，真实的
actually	*adv.* 实际上，真实地，竟然
adapt	*v.* 使适应，使适合
addition	*n.* 1. 加，加法　2. 附加物，新增产品
additional	*adj.* 附加的，另外的，补充的
adequate	*adj.* 1. 充足的，足够的　2. 适当的，胜任的
adjust	*v.* 1. 调节，改变……以适应　2. 校正，调整，校准
admire	*v.* 钦佩，赞赏，羡慕
admission	*n.* [U] 1. 准许进入　2. 入场费　[C] 承认，供认
admit	*v.* 1. 承认，供认　2. 准许……进入，准许……加入
adopt	*v.* 1. 收养　2. 采取，采纳，采用
advanced	*adj.* 1. 先进的，高级的　2. 预先的
advantage	*n.* 1. 优点，优势　2. 利益，好处
adventure	*n.* [U] 冒险　[C] 奇遇
advertise	*v.* 1. 登广告　2. 宣扬
advertisement/ad	*n.* 广告
advise	*v.* 劝告，建议
affair	*n.* 事情，事件
affect	*v.* 1. 影响　2.（在感情方面）打动
afford	*v.* 1. 买得起，负担得起　2. 提供，给予
agency	*n.* [C] 代理（处），代办（处）
agenda	*n.* [C] 1. 会议事项　2. 议事日程
agent	*n.* [C] 代理人，代理商
agreement	*n.* [U] 同意，一致　[C] 协定，协议
agriculture	*n.* [U] 农业
aid	*n.* 1. 帮助，援助　2. 助手，辅助手段　*v.* 帮助，援助
aim	*v.* 1. 把……瞄准，把……对准　2. 致力于，旨在
	n. 1. 瞄准，对准　2. 目标，目的
alarm	*n.* [U] 惊恐　[C] 报警器
	v. 1. 使惊恐　2. 向……报警
alcohol	*n.* 酒精，乙醇
alike	*adj.* 同样的，相像的
alive	*adj.* 1. 活着的　2. 有活力的，活跃的
allow	*v.* 1. 允许，准许　2. 给予（金钱、时间）
allowance	*n.* 津贴，补助
alone	*adj.* 单独的，孤独的　*adv.* 仅仅，只
alter	*v.* 改变，变更
alternative	*n.* 1. 可供选择的事物　2. 选择余地　*adj.* 二者选择其一的
amaze	*v.* 使大为惊奇，使惊愕
ambassador	*n.* 大使，使者
ambition	*n.* 雄心，野心，企图

ambitious	*adj.* 1. 有雄心的，野心勃勃的，志向远大的　　2. 豪迈的　　3. 热望的
amend	*v.* 修正，修订
amount	*n.* 数量　　*v.* 合计，共计
amuse	*v.* 1. 逗乐，逗笑　　2. 给……提供娱乐
analysis	*n.* 分解，分析
analyze	*v.* 分解，分析
ancestor	*n.* 1. 祖先　　2. 先驱
ancient	*adj.* 古代的，古老的
anger	*n.* 怒，愤怒　　*v.* 使发怒，激怒
angry	*adj.* 愤怒的，生气的
anniversary	*n.* [C] 1. 周年　　2. 周年纪念
announce	*v.* 宣布，宣告
annoy	*v.* 使恼怒，使烦恼
annual	*adj.* 每年的，年度的　　*n.* 年刊，年鉴
anticipate	*v.* 1. 预期　　2. 希望
anxiety	*n.* 1. 忧虑，焦虑　　2. 渴望，热望
anxious	*adj.* 1. 焦虑的，发愁的　　2. 渴望的，急切的
apartment	*n.* [美] 公寓
apologize/~se	*v.* 道歉，认错
apology	*n.* 道歉，认错
apparent	*adj.* 1. 表面上的　　2. 显然的，明显的
appeal	*n. & v.* 1. 恳请，呼吁　　2. 吸引　　3. 上诉
appear	*v.* 1. 出现，显露　　2. 看来好像，似乎
appearance	*n.* 1. 出现，露面　　2. 外观，外貌
appendix	*n.* 1. 附录　　2. 附属物
appetite	*n.* 1. 食欲，胃口　　2. 欲望，爱好
appetizing	*adj.* 1. 开胃的　　2. 刺激欲望的
applause	*n.* 1. 鼓掌　　2. 欢呼
appliance	*n.* 1. 电器用具　　2. 装备
applicant	*n.* 请求者，申请者
application	*n.* 1. 申请，申请表　　2. 应用，实施
apply	*v.* 1. 申请，请求　　2. 应用，运用　　3. 适合于
appoint	*v.* 1. 任命，委派　　2. 约定，指定（时间、地点）
appointment	*n.* 约定，指定（时间、地点）
appreciate	*v.* 1. 重视，欣赏　　2. 领会，充分意识到　　3. 为……表示感激
approach	*v.* 靠近　　*n.* 1. 接近　　2. 途径，入门　　3. 方式，方法
appropriate	*adj.* 适当的，恰当的　　*v.* 拨（尤指款项）
approval	*n.* 1. 赞成，同意　　2. 认可，批准
approve	*v.* 1. 赞成，同意　　2. 批准，核准
arbitration	*n.* 仲裁，公断
argument	*n.* 1. 争论，争辩　　2. 理由，论据
arise	*v.* 1. 出现，发生　　2. 由……引起，起源于

arouse	*v.* 1. 引起，激起，唤起　2. 唤醒
arrange	*v.* 1. 安排，筹划　2. 整理，排列，布置
arrest	*v. & n.* 逮捕，拘留
arrival	*n.* 到达，到来
arrive	*v.* 1. 到来，到达　2. 达到，得出
artificial	*a.* 1. 人工的，人造的，人为的　2. 假的，矫揉造作的
artist	*n.* 艺术家，美术家
aspect	*n.* 方面
assess	*v.* 对……进行评估，评价
assign	*v.* 1. 指派，选派　2. 分配，布置（作业）　3. 指定（时间、地点等）
assignment	*n.* 1. （分派的）任务　2. 分配，指派
assist	*v.* 帮助，协助
assistant	*n.* 1. 助手，助理　2. 助教　*adj.* 助理的，辅助的，副的
associate	*v.* 1. 把联系在一起，使结合在一起　2. 交往
	n. 伙伴，合伙人　*adj.* 副的
association	*n.* 1. 协会，社团　2. 联合，结合，交往　3. 联想
assume	*v.* 1. 假定，假设　2. 承担
assure	*v.* 1. 说服，使……相信　2. 向……保证
astonish	*v.* 使惊讶
athlete	*n.* 运动员
Atlantic	*adj.* 大西洋的　*n.* the Atlantic 大西洋
atmosphere	*n.* 1. 大气，大气层　2. 气氛
attach	*v.* 1. 系，贴，装，连接　2. 使……成为一部分，使附属　3. 使依恋
attack	*v.* 攻击，进攻　*n.* 1. 攻击，进攻　2. （疾病的）突然发作
attempt	*v. & n.* 企图，试图
attend	*v.* 1. 出席，参加　2. 照顾，照料　3. 专心于，致力于
attendant	*n.* 服务员　*adj.* 伴随的，陪同的
attention	*n.* 注意，留心
attitude	*n.* 1. 态度，看法　2. 姿势
attractive	*adj.* 有吸引力的，引起注意的
audience	*n.* 听众，观众，读者
authority	*n.* 1. [P] 官方，当局　2. 当权者　3. 权力，权威
authorize	*v.* 授权，委任
automatic	*adj.* 自动的
automobile/auto	*n.* 汽车
available	*adj.* 1. 可利用的，可获得的　2. 可取得联系的
avenue	*n.* 林荫道，大街
average	*n.* 平均数，平均　*adj.* 1. 平均的　2. 平常的，通常的　*v.* 平均
avoid	*v.* 避免，避开
await	*v.* （人）等候，期待；（事件等）等待（处理）
awake	*adj.* 醒着的　*v.* 唤醒，使觉醒
award	*n.* 奖，奖品　*v.* 授予，给予

aware	*adj.* 意识到的，知道的
awful	*adj.* 1. 令人敬畏的，可怕的　　2. 极度的，极坏的
awkward	*adj.* 1. 粗笨的，笨拙的，不灵活的　　2. 尴尬的，棘手的

B

bachelor	*n.* 1. 单身汉　　2. 学士
background	*n.* 背景，经历
baggage	*n.* [U] 行李
balance	*v.* 1. 使平衡　　2. 称（重量）
	n. 1. 天平，称　　2. 平衡，均衡　　3. 结存，结欠
banquet	*n.* 宴会，酒会　　*v.* 宴请
bare	*adj.* 1. 赤裸的，不穿衣服的，不戴帽子的　　2. 光秃秃的，无遮盖的
	3. 仅仅的，勉强的
	v. 露出，暴露
bargain	*n.* 1. 交易　　2. 特价商品　　*v.* 讨价，还价
barrier	*n.* 1. 栅栏，屏障　　2. 障碍，障碍物
base	*n.* 1. 基，底　　2. 基础　　*v.* 把……建在……基础上
basic	*adj.* 基本的，基础的
basis	*n.* 基础，根据
bath	*n.* 1. 浴，洗澡，洗澡水　　2. 浴缸　　*v.* 给……洗澡
bathe	*v.* 1. [美] 给……洗澡　　2. 游泳
bathroom	*n.* 1. 浴室　　2. 盥洗室
battery	*n.* 电池（组）
bear	*n.* 熊　　*v.* (bore, born/borne) 1. 忍受，容忍　　2. 负担，承担
	3. 结（果实），生（孩子）
beast	*n.* 兽，野兽，牲畜
beat	*v.* (beat, beaten) 1.（接连地）打，击　　2.（心脏等）跳动
	3. 打败，战胜
	n. 1.（心脏等的）跳（声）　　2. 有节奏的敲击（声）
beautiful	*adj.* 美的，美丽的
beauty	*n.* 1. 美，美丽　　2. 美人，美的东西
behave	*v.* 1. 举止　　2.（机器等）运转
behavio(u)r	*n.* 1. 行为，举止　　2.（机器等）运转情况
belief	*n.* 1. 相信　　2. 信念，信仰
believe	*v.* 1. 相信，笃信　　2. 认为
belong	*v.* 1.（在分类上）属，划归于　　2.（在所有权、关系等方面）属于
bend	*v.* (bent, bent) 使弯曲，使屈从　　*n.* 弯曲，弯道
benefit	*n.* 益处，好处　　*v.* 有益于，得益
bet	*v.* 打赌，以……打赌，与……打赌　　*n.* 1. 打赌　　2. 赌金，赌注
bid	*n. & v.* (bid, bade; bid, bidden) 出价，投标
bind	*v.* [bound, bound] 捆绑，捆扎
biology	*n.* 生物学

bite	*v.* (bit, bitten) & *n.* 咬，叮
bitter	*adj.* 1. 痛苦的　　2. 有苦味的
blame	*v.* 1. 指责，责备，责怪　　2. 归咎于，把……归咎于
	n. 1. （过错、事故等的）责任　　2. 指责，责备
blank	*adj.* 1. 空白的，空着的　　2. 茫然的，没有表情的
	n. 空白，空白处，空白表格
blend	*v.* 混合　　*n.* 混合物
block	*n.* 1. 街区，街段　　2. 大块（木料或石料，金属，冰）
	3. 障碍物，阻塞物　　*v.* 堵塞，阻塞
blouse	*n.* [C]（妇女穿的）短上衣，女衬衫
board	*n.* 1. 板，木板，纸板　　2. 委员会，董事会
	3. （指包饭的）伙食　　*v.* 上（船，车，飞机）
boil	*v.* 沸腾，煮沸
bold	*adj.* 1. 勇敢的，无畏的　　2. 冒失的　　3. 粗体的，黑体的
bomb	*n.* 炸弹　　*v.* 轰炸，投弹
bond	*n.* 1. 团结，联系　　2. 公债，债券
bonus	*n.* 奖金，额外酬金
border	*n.* 1. 边，边缘，界线　　2. 边界，边境
	v. 与……接壤，毗邻，接近
bore	*v.* 1. 使厌烦，使厌倦　　2. 钻（孔），凿（井），挖（通道）
	n. 令人厌烦的人（或事）
boring	*adj.* 枯燥的
born	*adj.* 1. 出生的，产生的　　2. 天生的
borrow	*v.* 借，借入
bother	*v.* 1. 打扰，麻烦　　2. 担心，烦恼　　*n.* 烦恼
bound	*adj.* 1. 一定的，必然的　　2. 受约束的，有义务的
	3. 开往（或驶往）……的
	v. 跳跃，弹回
boundary	*n.* 1. 分界线　　2. 边界
branch	*n.* 1. [C] 树枝，分枝　　2. （机构的）分部，分号
	3. （学科的）分科，分支
brand	*n.* [C] 商标，（商品的）牌子
	v. 1. 打烙印于，以烙铁打（标记）　　2. 把……铭刻，铭刻于
break	*v.* (broke, broken) 1. 打破，使破裂　　2. 损坏，弄坏
	3. 破坏，违反　　4. 中止，中断
	n. （课间、工间）休息时间
breath	*n.* [U] 气息，呼吸
breathe	*v.* 1. 呼吸　　2. 屏息
brief	*adj.* 简短的　　*v.* 向……作简要的介绍
brochure	*n.* 小册子
broker	*n.* 经纪人
budget	*n.* 预算（表）　　*v.* 编列预算

bulletin	*n.* 公告，告示
burden	*n. & v.* 负担
burn	*v.* 1. 燃烧　2. 烧毁　3. 灼烧　*n.* 烧伤，灼伤
burst	*v. & n.* 爆炸，爆裂
bury	*v.* 埋葬，掩埋
button	*n.* 纽扣，按钮　*v.* 扣上，扣紧

C

cable	*n.* 1. 索，缆　2. 电缆　3. 电报　*v.* 发电报
calculate	*v.* 1. 计算，核算　2. 计划，打算
calendar	*n.* 日历，月历
camp	*n.* 野营，营地，帐篷　*v.* 设营，宿营
campaign	*n.* 战役，运动
campus	*n.* 校园
canal	*n.* 运河，沟渠
cancel	*v.* (cancelled, cancelled) 1. 取消，撤销　2. 删去，划掉
cancer	*n.* 癌
candidate	*n.* 1. 候选人，候补者　2. 投考者，申请求职者
capable	*adj.* 有能力的，有才能的
capacity	*n.* 1. 容量，容积　2. 能力
capital	*n.* 1. 资本，资金　2. 大写字母　3. 首都　*adj.* 主要的，基本的
captain	*n.* 1. 上尉，队长　2. 船长，舰长
capture	*v. & n.* 捕获，俘获
career	*n.* 生涯，职业
cargo	*n.* 船货，货物
case	*n.* 1. 情况　2. 病例　3. 案件　4. 箱，盒
cash	*n.* 钱，现款
cashier	*n.* 出纳员，收银员
cassette	*n.* 盒式录音带
cast	*v.* 1. 投，扔，抛　2. 浇筑，铸造
casual	*adj.* 1. 随便的，非正式的　2. 偶然的，碰巧的
catalogue	*n.* 目录，目录簿（册）　*v.* 1. 将……编入目录　2. 将（书籍、资料等）编目分册
cause	*n.* 1. 原因，起因，理由　2. 事业，(奋斗的)目标　*v.* 使产生，引起
cease	*v. & n.* 停止，终止
ceiling	*n.* 1. 天花板　2. 上限
celebrate	*v.* 庆祝
cell	*n.* 1. 细胞　2. 小房间　3. 电池
central	*adj.* 1. 中央的，中心的　2. 主要的，起支配作用的
century	*n.* 世纪，百年

ceremony	*n.* 1. 典礼，仪式　　2. 礼节，礼仪
certificate	*n.* 证（明）书，执照
chain	*n.* 1. 链，链条　　2. 一连串，连锁　　*v.* 用链条拴住
challenge	*n.* 挑战，困难　　*v.* 向……挑战
champagne	*n.* 香槟酒
champion	*n.* 冠军
channel	*n.* 1. 海峡，水道，航道　　2. 渠道　　3. 频道
chapter	*n.* 章，回，篇
character	*n.* 1. 性格，品质　　2. 特性，特征　　3. 人物，角色　　4.（书写或印刷）符号，（汉）字符
characteristic	*adj.* 特有的，典型的　　*n.* 特性，特征
charge	*v.* 1. 索价，要……支付　　2. 控告，指控　　3. 充电　　*n.* 1. 价钱，收费　　2. 控告，指控　　3. 电荷，充电
chart	*n.* 图，图表
chase	*v. & n.* 追逐
chat	*v.* 1. 闲谈　　2. 畅谈
cheat	*v.* 欺骗，骗取，作弊　　*n.* 1. 欺骗，欺诈行为　　2. 骗子
check	*v.* 1. 检查，核对　　2. 制止　　*n.* 1. 检查，复核　　2. 支票
cheerful	*adj.* 愉快的，高兴的
chemical	*adj.* 化学的　　*n.* 化学制品
chemist	*n.* 药剂师，化学家
cheque	*n.* 支票
chief	*n.* 首领，领袖　　*adj.* 主要的，首要的
choice	*n.* 1. 选择，抉择　　2. 供选择的品种　　*adj.* 上等的，精选的
choose	*v.*（chose，chosen）选择，挑选
Christian	*n.* 基督教徒　　*adj.* 基督教的
Christmas	*n.* 圣诞节
cigaret(te)	*n.* 香烟
circle	*n.* 1. 圆，圆周　　2. 圈子，阶层　　*v.* 环绕，旋转
circumstance	*n.* 1. 环境，条件，情况　　2. [P] 境遇，状况
circuit	*n.* 1. 电路线路　　2. 环行，巡回
citizen	*n.* 1. 公民　　2. 市民，城镇居民
civilization	*n.* 文明，文化
claim	*v.* 1. 宣称　　2. 对……提出要求，索取，夺去　　*n.* 1. 宣称　　2. 索赔
clarify	*v.* 澄清，阐明
classic	*n.* [P] 杰作，名著　　*adj.* 模范的，一流的
classical	*adj.* 古典的，经典的
classify	*v.* 把……分类，把……分级
clerk	*n.* 职员
client	*n.* 1. 委托人　　2. 顾客

climate	*n.* 气候
climb	*v. & n.* 攀爬,爬
clockwise	*adj.* 顺时针方向的　*adv.* 顺时针方向地
cloudy	*adj.* 1. 多云的　2. 模糊的
club	*n.* 1. 俱乐部,夜总会　2. 棍棒,棒球
coach	*n.* 1. 长途公共汽车　2.（铁路）旅客车厢　3. 教练
	v. 训练,主导
coarse	*adj.* 1. 粗的,粗糙的　2. 粗劣的　3. 粗俗的
coast	*n.* 海岸,海滨
code	*n.* 1. 准则,法规　2. 密码,电码,代码
colleague	*n.* 同事,同僚
collection	*n.* 1. 收集,采集　2. 收藏品
collective	*adj.* 集体的,共同的　*n.* 团体,集体
college	*n.* 大学,学院
column	*n.* 1. 柱,圆柱,柱形物　2. 栏,（报刊中的）专栏
combination	*n.* 1. 结合,联合　2. 化合,化合物
combine	*v.* 结合,联合,化合
comfort	*n.* 安慰,舒适　*v.* 安慰,慰问,使舒适
comfortable	*adj.* 舒适的,舒服的,舒坦的
command	*v. & n.* 命令,指挥　*n.* 掌握,运用能力
comment	*n. & v.* 注解,评论
commerce	*n.* 商业,贸易
commercial	*adj.* 商业的,商务的　*n.* 电视广告
commission	*n.* 1. 授权,委托　2. 佣金,回扣　3. 委员会
commit	*v.* 犯（罪）,干（坏事）,使承担义务
committee	*n.* 委员会
commodity	*n.* 商品
communicate	*v.* 1. 传达,传送　2. 交流,通讯,交际
communication	*n.* 1. 传达,通讯,交流　2. [P] 通信系统,交通（工具）
community	*n.* 社区,社会
commute	*v.* 1. 每天往返上下班　2. 定期往返　3. 变换
compact	*adj.* 1. 紧密的　2. 坚定的　3. 简洁的
companion	*n.* 同伴,伴侣
comparable	*adj.* 可与……相比的,敌得上……的
compare	*v.* 比较,对照
compatible	*adj.* 1. 相容的　2. 协调的　3. 一致的
compensate	*v.* 1. 赔偿　2. 报酬　3. 抵补
compete	*v.* 竞争,比赛
competent	*adj.* 有能力的,胜任的
competition	*n.* 竞争,比赛
competitive	*adj.* 竞争的
complain	*v.* 1. 抱怨,发牢骚　2. 投诉

complaint	*n.* 1. 抱怨，诉苦，怨言　　2. 控告，控诉
complete	*adj.* 完整的，完全的，圆满的　　*v.* 完成，使完整
complex	*adj.* 综合的，复杂的　　*n.* 综合体
complicated	*adj.* 复杂的，难懂的
component	*n.* （组）成（部）分，部件，元件
compose	*v.* 1. 组成，构成　　2. 创作（音乐，文学作品），为……谱曲
composition	*n.* 1. 组成，构成，成分　　2. 作文，作品，乐曲　　3. 写作，作曲
compound	*adj.* 化合的，复合的　　*n.* 化合物，复合物
comprehension	*n.* 理解（力）
comprise	*v.* 1. 包含，包括，由……组成　　2. 构成，形成
compromise	*n.* 妥协，折中办法
computer	*n.* 计算机，电脑
concentrate	*v.* 1. 集中，专心　　2. 集合，聚集　　3. 浓缩
concept	*n.* 概念，观念，思想
concern	*n.* 1. 关心，挂念　　2. 关系，关联
	v. 1. 涉及，有关　　2. 关心，挂念
concerning	*prep.* 关于
concert	*n.* 音乐会，演奏会；一致
conclude	*v.* 1. 推断出，推论出　　2. 做出（最后）决定　　3. 结束，终止
conclusion	*n.* 1. 结论，推论　　2. 结束，终结
condition	*n.* 1. 状况，状态　　2. [P] 环境　　3. 条件
conduct	*n.* 行为举止　　*v.* 1. 处理，管理　　2. 指挥　　3. 传导，传（热，电）
conference	*n.* （正式）会议
confess	*v.* 坦白，供认，承认
confidence	*n.* 信任，信心，自信
confident	*adj.* 确信的，自信的
confidential	*adj.* 秘密的，不公开的
confine	*v.* 限制，使局限
confirm	*v.* 1. 证实，肯定　　2. 进一步确定　　3. 批准，确认
conflict	*n.* & *v.* 冲突，抵触，战斗
conform	*v.* 与……一致，符合
confront	*v.* 1. 面对　　2. 遭遇　　3. 对抗
confuse	*v.* 使混乱
congratulate	*v.* 祝贺，向……道喜
congress	*n.* 1. 代表大会　　2. 国会，议会
connect	*v.* 连接，联结，联系
conscious	*adj.* 1. 有意识的，自觉的　　2. 神志清醒的
consequence	*n.* 结果，后果
consequently	*adv.* 所以，因此
conservative	*adj.* 保守的，守旧的，传统的　　*n.* 保守的人，反对进步的人
conserve	*v.* 保持
consider	*v.* 1. 认为，把……看作　　2. 考虑，细想　　3. 关心，考虑到

considerable	*adj.* 1. 相当大的　　2. 值得考虑的
considerate	*adj.* 考虑周到的，体谅的
consideration	*n.* 1. 考虑　　2. 要考虑的事
consist	*v.* 1. 组成，构成　　2. 在于，存在于
constant	*adj.* 1. 不断的，连续发生的　　2. 始终如一的，恒定的　　3. 忠实的，坚定的
constraint	*n.* 1. 强制　　2. 拘束　　3. 压迫感
construction	*n.* 1. 建造，构筑　　2. 建造物，建筑物
consul	*n.* 领事
consulate	*n.* 领事馆
consult	*v.* 1. 请教，向……咨询，找……商量　　2. 查阅，查看
consultant	*n.* 1. 咨询家，求教者　　2. 顾问，专家
consume	*v.* 消耗，花费
consumer	*n.* 消费者，用户
consumption	*n.* 1. 消耗量，消费量　　2. 消耗，消费
contact	*v.* & *n.* 接触，联系，交往
contain	*v.* 包容，容纳
container	*n.* 1. 容器　　2. 集装箱
content	*n.* 1. ［P］内容，（书刊的）目录　　2. 容量，含量 *adj.* 满意的，甘愿的
contest	*n.* 竞争，竞赛，比赛　*v.* 竞赛，比赛，争论
context	*n.* 1. 上下文　　2. 某事之前后关系
continent	*n.* 大陆，洲
continual	*adj.* 不停的，连续的
continue	*v.* 延伸，继续，连续
continuous	*adj.* 连续不断的，不断延伸的
contract	*n.* 合同
contradict	*v.* 同……矛盾，同……抵触
contrary	*adj.* 相反的，对抗的　　*n.* 相反，相反事物，对立面
contrast	*v.* 1. 对比，对照　　2. 形成对比　*n.* 对比，对照
contribute	*v.* 1. 捐献，捐助，贡献　　2. 投稿
control	*v.* & *n.* 1. 控制，支配　　2. 克制，抑制
convenient	*adj.* 方便的，省力的
conversation	*n.* 谈话，会话
convert	*v.* 转变，转化
conversation	*v.* 转变，转化，转换
convey	*v.* 1. 运送，输送，搬运　　2. 传送，传达，表达
convince	*v.* 使确信，使信服
cooperate	*v.* 合作，协作，配合
coordinate	*v.* 调节，协调
cope	*v.* 对付，应付
copyright	*n.* 版权，著作权　*adj.* 有版权的
core	*n.* 1. 果核　　2. 核心，要点

corporation	*n.* 公司
correspond	*v.* 1. 与……一致 2. 相当，相类似
correspondence	*n.* 1. 通行，函电 2. 相当
correspondent	*n.* 1. 通信者 2. 通讯记者 3. 有业务来往者
corresponding	*adj.* 1. 相应的，相当的，对等的 2. 符合的，一致的，相同的
cost	*n.* 成本，费用 *v.* 1. 值 2. 花费 3. 估价
costly	*adj.* 昂贵的，代价高的
council	*n.* 委员会，理事长
count	*v.* 1. 数数，点……的数目 2. 计算，把……算入 *n.* 计数，计算，总数
counter	*n.* 1. 柜台 2. 计数器
couple	*n.* 1. 夫妻 2. 一对，一双，偶 *v.* 连接，结合，耦合
courage	*n.* 勇气，胆识
course	*n.* 1. 课程，教程 2. 过程，进程 3.（一）道（菜）
court	*n.* 1. 法庭，法院 2. 球场 3. 院子
courteous	*adj.* 有礼貌的
craft	*n.* 1. 手艺，技艺 2. 船，航空器，航天器
crash	*n. & v.* 碰，撞，坠落，坠毁 *n.* 破裂声，撞击声
crazy	*adj.* 1. 发疯的，荒唐的 2. 狂热爱好的，着迷的
create	*v.* 1. 创造，创作 2. 引起，产生
creature	*n.* 生物，动物，人
credit	*n.* 1. 信用贷款 2. 信用，信誉 3. 荣誉，赞扬，功劳 4. 学分 *v.* 记入贷方
crew	*n.* 全体船员，全体机组人员，一队（或一班，一组）工作人员
crime	*n.* 罪，罪行，犯罪
criminal	*n.* 犯罪，犯人 *adj.* 犯罪的，刑事的
crisis	*n.* [P crises] 危机，危急关头，决定性时刻
critical	*adj.* 1. 批评的，批判的 2. 决定性的，关键性的
crowd	*n.* 群，人群，群众 *v.* 群集，拥挤，挤满
crucial	*adj.* 1. 极重要的 2. 严重的
crude	*adj.* 1. 简陋的，粗糙的 2. 天然的，未加工的 3. 粗鲁的，粗俗的
cruel	*adj.* 残酷，残忍的
crystal	*n.* 1. 水晶，石英晶体 2. 晶粒 *adj.* 清澈透明的，水晶制的，晶体的
cube	*n.* 1. 立方形，立方体 2. 立方，三次幂
cure	*v.* 1. 治愈，治好 2. 消除，改正 *n.* 1. 治愈，治疗，疗法 2. 药物
curious	*adj.* 好奇的
currency	*n.* 1. 通货，货币 2. 流通，通用
current	*n.* 1.（空气、水等的）流，潮流，流速 2. 电流 *adj.* 1. 现时的，当前的 2. 通行的，流行的
curse	*n. & v.* 诅咒，咒骂
cursor	*n.* 光标

curve	*n.* 曲线，弧线，弯曲　　*v.* （使）弯曲，（使）成曲线
cushion	*n.* 垫子，坐垫
custom	*n.* 1. 习惯，风俗，惯例　　2. ［P］海关，关税
customer	*n.* 顾客，主顾
cycle	*n.* 1. 自行车，摩托车　　2. 循环，周期
	v. 1. 骑自行车，骑摩托车　　2. 循环，做循环运动

D

damage	*v. & n.* 毁坏，损害
damp	*adj.* 潮湿的　　*n.* 潮湿，湿气
danger	*n.* 1. 危险　　2. 危险事物，威胁
dangerous	*adj.* 危险的，不安全的
data	*n.* （datum 的复数）数据，资料
database	*n.* 数据库
deadline	*n.* 1. 截止时间　　2. 界限
deal	*n.* 交易　　*v.* 1. 给予，分给　　2. 处理，对待，论述　　3. 经营
dealer	*n.* 商人；贩子
death	*n.* 死，死亡
debate	*n. & v.* 辩论，争论，讨论
debt	*n.* 债务，欠债
decade	*n.* 十年，十年期
decay	*v.* 1. 腐朽，腐烂　　2. 衰减，衰退，衰落
	n. 1. 腐朽，腐烂　　2. 衰减，衰退
deceive	*v.* 欺骗，行骗
decide	*v.* 1. 决定，拿定主意　　2. 裁决，解决
decision	*n.* 1. 决定　　2. 坚定，果断，决断
declare	*v.* 1. 断言，宣称　　2. 宣布，宣告，声明
decorate	*v.* 装饰，装潢
decrease	*v. & n.* 减小，减少
defeat	*v.* 1. 击败，战胜　　2. 挫败，使落空
	n. 1. 击败，战胜　　2. 战败，失败
defence/defense	*n.* 1. 防御；保卫　　2. 防御物　　3. 辩护，答辩　　4. ［P］防务，防御工事
defend	*v.* 1. 保卫，防守　　2. 为……辩护
define	*v.* 1. 界定，定义　　2. 限定，规定
definite	*adj.* 1. 明确的，确切的　　2. 肯定的
definition	*n.* 定义，释义
degree	*n.* 1. 程度，度数　　2. 学位
delay	*n. & v.* 1. 推迟　　2. 耽误，延误
delegate	*n.* 代表　　*vt.* 委托……为代表；授权
delete	*v.* 取消，删除
deliberately	*adv.* 1. 深思熟虑地　　2. 有目的地
delicate	*adj.* 1. 纤细的，清秀的，鲜美的，柔和的，优美的

	2. 易碎的，纤弱的　　3. 微妙的，棘手的　　4. 灵敏的，精密的
delicious	*adj.* 1. 美味的　　2. 怡人的
delight	*n.* 1. 快乐，高兴　　2. 使人高兴的东西（或人）　　*v.* 使高兴，使欣喜
deliver	*v.* 1. 投递，送交　　2. 发表
delivery	*n.* 交付，递送
demand	*v.* 1. 要求　　2. 需要　　3. 询问，查问
	n. 1. 要求，请求　　2. 需要，需求（量）
democracy	*n.* 1. 民主　　2. 民主国家
demonstrate	*v.* 1. 论证，证明　　2. 演示，显示　　3. 示威
dense	*adj.* 密集的，稠密的，浓密的
density	*n.* 1. 密集，稠密　　2. 密度
dentist	*n.* 牙科医生
deny	*v.* 1. 否认，不承认　　2. 拒绝给予，拒绝（某人）的要求
depart	*v.* 离开，起程，出发
department	*n.* 部门，系科
departure	*n.* 离开，起程，出发
depend	*v.* 依靠，依赖
dependent	*adj.* 依靠的，依赖的
deposit	*v.* 1. 使沉淀，使沉积　　2. 存放，寄存　　3. 储蓄　　4. 交押金
	n. 1. 沉积，沉积物　　2. 定金，押金
depress	*v.* 1. 使沮丧，使消沉　　2. 按下，降低
depth	*n.* 1. 深度　　2. （感情的）深厚，深切
derive	*v.* 1. 取得，得到　　2. 追溯……的起源（来由）
describe	*v.* 形容，描写
description	*n.* 1. 描写，形容　　2. 种类
desert	*n.* 沙漠，不毛之地
	v. 1. 离弃，抛弃　　2. 从……开小差，擅离（职守等）
deserve	*v.* 应受，值得
design	*v.* 设计　　*n.* 图样，图案
desirable	*adj.* 1. 值得向往的，值得拥有的　　2. 称心的，合意的
desire	*v.* 渴望，想望，要求　　*n.* 愿望，欲望，要求
despair	*n.* 绝望　　*v.* 绝望
despite	*prep.* 不管，尽管
dessert	*n.* 甜食，甜点
destination	*n.* 1. 目的地，终点　　2. 目标，目的
destroy	*v.* 1. 破坏，毁灭　　2. 消灭
destruction	*n.* 1. 破坏，毁灭　　2. 消灭
detail	*n.* 1. 细节，详情　　2. 枝节，琐事　　*v.* 详述，详细说明
detect	*v.* 1. 察觉，发现　　2. 侦察
determination	*n.* 决心，决定
determine	*v.* 1. 决定　　2. 查明，确定　　3. 决心
develop	*v.* 1. 发展，开发，研制　　2. （逐渐）显现出，显影　　3. 成长，发育

development	n. 1. 发展，形成，进展，开发，研制　2. 生长，进化　3. 事态发展，新成就，新成果
device	n. 装置，设备，器具，仪器
devote	v. 将……奉献（给），把……专用于
diagnose	v. 诊断
diagram	n. 图解，图表
dial	n. 钟（表）面，标度盘，拨号盘　v. 拨（电话号码），打电话（给……）
dialect	n. 方言，土语，地方话
dialog(ue)	n. 对话，对白
diamond	n. 1. 钻石，金刚石　2. 菱形
dictation	n. 口授，听写
dictionary	n. 词典，字典
differ	v. 1. 不同，相异　2. 与……意见不同
difference	n. 1. 差异　2. 差额　3. （意见的）分歧
different	adj. 1. 差异的，不同的　2. 各种的
difficult	adj. 困难的，艰难的
difficulty	n. 困难，难事，困境
digest	v. 消化，汇编　n. 摘要，文摘
digital	adj. 数字的，数字显示的
dim	adj. 1. 昏暗的　2. 朦胧的，模糊不清的
dimension	n. 1. 尺寸，长（宽、厚、深）度　2. 常做［P］面积，大小，规模
dine	v. 就餐
dinner	n. 1. 正餐，主餐　2. 宴会
diplomat	n. 外交官
direct	adj. 笔直的，直接的，率直的　adv. 直接地，坦率地　v. 1. 把……对准，针对　2. 指示　3. 管理，指导，命令
direction	n. 1. 方向，方位　2. ［常P］用法说明
directly	adv. 1. 直接地，径直地　2. 立即，马上
director	n. 1. 指导者，主管　2. 董事　3. 导演
dirty	adj. 1. 肮脏的　2. 下流的，黄色的　v. 弄脏，玷污
disaster	n. 灾祸，大祸
disc/disk	n. 圆盘，唱片，磁盘
discharge	v. 1. 允许……离开，释放　2. 排除，放出　3. 卸货　n. 1. 获准离开，释放　2. 排除
discipline	n. 1. 纪律　2. 训练，训导　v. 1. 训练，训导　2. 惩罚
discount	n. 1. 折扣　2. 贴现
discussion	n. 讨论，谈论
disease	n. 疾病
disgust	n. 厌恶　v. 使厌恶
disgusting	adj. 令人厌恶的
dismiss	v. 1. 免职，解雇，开除　2. 解散，遣散

display	*n. & v.* 1. 陈列，展览　　2. 显示　　3. 显示器
dispose	*v.* 1. 去掉，丢掉，消除，销毁　　2. 排列，布置 3. 安排（事情），处理（事务）
dispute	*v.* 争论，争吵　　*n.* 争执，争端，争吵
distant	*adj.* 在远处的，远隔的，久远的
distinct	*adj.* 1. 截然不同的　　2. 清楚的，明显的
distinction	*n.* 1. 差别，不同，对比　　2. 区分，辨别
distinguish	*v.* 区别，辨别，分清
distort	*v.* 1. 歪曲，扭曲　　2. 使变形
distribute	*v.* 1. 分发，分送，分配　　2. 分布，散布
district	*n.* 区，地区，行政区
disturb	*v.* 1. 打扰，使不安　　2. 扰乱　　3. 弄乱
divide	*v.* 1. 分，划分　　2. 分配　　3. 隔开　　4. 除
divorce	*n. & v.* 离婚，分离
document	*n.* 公文，文件，文献
domestic	*adj.* 1. 本国的，国内的　　2. 家（庭）的，家用的　　3. 驯养的
dominate	*v.* 1. 支配　　2. 统治　　3. 管辖
dorm(itory)	*n.* （集体）宿舍
double	*adj.* 1. 两倍的　　2. 双的，双重的　　3. 双人的 *v.* 使加倍，把……增加一倍
doubt	*n.* 疑惑，疑问　　*v.* 怀疑，不相信
doubtful	*adj.* 难以预料的
downtown	*adj.* 在商业区的，属于商业区的　　*adv.* 到（在）商业区
dozen	*n.* [P dozens]（一）打，十二个
draft	*n.* 草稿，草案，草图　　*v.* 起草，草拟
dramatic	*adj.* 1. 引人注目的，给人深刻印象的　　2. 戏剧性的 *n.* [P] 表演，演戏
drawing	*n.* 图画，素描（画）
drift	*v.* （使）漂流　　*n.* 漂流
drill	*n.* 1. 钻头，钻床　　2. 操练，演习　　*v.* 1. 钻（孔）　　2. 操练
drown	*v.* 1. 淹死，溺死　　2. 淹没
drug	*n.* 1. 药，药物　　2. [P] 麻醉药品，成瘾性毒品 *v.* [drugged, drugged] 用药麻醉
due	*adj.* 1. 预定的，应到的　　2. 应给的，应得的　　3. 应有的，适当的 4. 应付的，到期的
dull	*adj.* 1. 枯燥的　　2.（色彩等）不鲜明的，晦暗的 3. 阴沉的，（声音）低沉的，沉闷的　　4. 愚钝的，笨的 5. 钝的，不锋利的
duplicate	*adj.* 1. 完全相同的　　2. 副本的　　*v.* 加倍，复制 *n.* 1. 副本　　2. 相同的东西
durable	*adj.* 持久的，耐用的
duration	*n.* 持续，持久，持续时间

duty	*n.* 1. 职务，职责 2. 责任，义务 3. 税
dynamic(al)	*adj.* 1. 动力的，动态的 2. 力学的，动力学的 3. 充满活力的

E

eager	*adj.* 热切的，渴望的
earn	*v.* 挣得，赚得，获得
earnest	*adj.* 认真的，诚恳的
earthquake	*n.* 地震
ease	*n.* 1. 容易 2. 舒适，安逸 *v.* 缓和，减轻
economic	*adj.* 经济（学的）
economical	*adj.* 节约的，节俭的
economy	*n.* 1. 经济 2. 节约，节省
edge	*n.* 1. 边，棱，边缘 2. 刀口，刃 *v.* 徐徐移动，侧着移动
edition	*n.* 版，版本
editor	*n.* 编辑，编者
educate	*v.* 教育，培养，训练
education	*n.* 教育，培养
effect	*n.* 1. 结果 2. 效果，作用，影响
effective	*adj.* 有效的，生效的
efficient	*adj.* 效率高的，有能力的
effort	*n.* 努力
elaborate	*adj.* 1. 复杂的 2. 精心制作的
	v. 1. 详尽阐述，发挥 2. 变得复杂
elder	*adj.* 年龄较大的，年长的 *n.* [P] 长者，长辈
elderly	*adj.* 年长的，近老年的
elect	*v.* 1. 选举，推选 2. 选择
election	*n.* 选举
electric	*adj.* 电动的，电的
electricity	*n.* 电
electronic	*adj.* 电子的
element	*n.* 1. 成分，基本组成部分 2. 要素 3. 元素
elementary	*adj.* 1. 基本的 2. 初级的，基础的
elevator	*n.* 电梯
eliminate	*v.* 1. 消除，根除 2. 排除，淘汰
embarrass	*v.* 使窘迫，使为难
embassy	*n.* 大使馆
emerge	*v.* 1. 浮现，出现，出来
	2.（问题、困难等）发生，显露；（事实、意见等）暴露，被知晓
emergency	*n.* 紧急情况，不测事件，非常时刻
emotion	*n.* 情感，情绪
emphasis	*n.* 强调，重点
emphasize/emphasise	*v.* 强调，着重

employ	*v.* 1. 雇用 2. 用，使用
employee	*n.* 受雇者，雇工，雇员
employer	*n.* 雇用者，雇主
enable	*v.* 使能够，使可能
enclose	*v.* 1. 围住，围起 2. 把……装入信封（或包裹等），封入，附上
encourage	*v.* 鼓励，支持，助长
end	*n.* 1. 最后部分，末尾 2. 终止，结束 3. 端，梢，尽头 4. 目标，目的 5. 死亡，毁灭 *v.* 终止，结束
endless	*adj.* 无止境的，没完没了的
endure	*v.* 1. 忍受，忍耐 2. 持久，持续
energy	*n.* 1. 能，能量 2. 精力，活力
engage	*v.* 1. （使）从事于，（使）忙于 2. 吸引，占用（时间、精力等） 3. 雇用，聘用 4. 使订婚
engine	*n.* 1. 发动机，引擎 2. 机车，火车头
engineer	*n.* 工程师，技师，机械师
engineering	*n.* 工程（学）
enhance	*v.* 1. 增加 2. 提高
enlarge	*v.* 扩大，扩展，放大
enormous	*adj.* 巨大的，庞大的
ensure	*v.* 保证，担保
enterprise	*n.* 企业，事业心
entertain	*v.* 1. 使欢乐，使娱乐 2. 招待，款待 3. 考虑
enthusiasm	*n.* 热情，热心
entire	*adj.* 全部的，整个的
entrance	*n.* 1. 入口，门口 2. 进入，入会，入学
entry	*n.* 1. 进入，入场 2. 入口，大门 3. （参加比赛的）人，（物） 4. （词典、账目等）条目
envelope	*n.* 信封
environment	*n.* 环境，周围状况，自然环境
equal	*adj.* 1. 相等的，同样的 2. 平等的 3. 胜任的 *n.* 同等的人，匹敌者 *v.* 1. 等于 2. 比得上
equip	*v.* (equipped, equipped) 装备，配备
equipment	*n.* 装备，设备，器材
equivalent	*adj.* 1. 相等的，相当的 2. 等量的，等值的 *n.* 相等物，等量，对应词
era	*n.* 时代，纪元，年代
error	*n.* 错误，谬误，差错
escape	*v.* 1. 逃跑，逃脱，逃避 2. （液体或气体）漏出，逸出 *n.* 逃跑，逃脱
especially	*adv.* 1. 尤其，特别 2. 特地
essay	*n.* 文章，短文，散文
essential	*adj.* 1. 必要的，必不可少的 2. 本质的，实质的，基本的

	n. [常 P] 本质，要素，要点
establish	*v.* 1. 建立，创办，设立　　2. 确立，使确认
estate	*n.* 1. 财产　　2. 地产
estimate	*v.* 1. 估计，估价　　2. 评价，判断
	n. 1. 估计，估价　　2. 评价，看法
Europe	*n.* 欧洲
European	*adj.* 1. 欧洲的　　*n.* 欧洲人
evaluate	*v.* 1. 估量，定价　　2. 评价，鉴定
eve	*n.* 前夜，前夕
event	*n.* 1. 事件，大事　　2. 比赛项目
eventually	*adv.* 终于，最后
evidence	*n.* 根据，证据
evident	*adj.* 明显的，明白的
evil	*n.* 1. 邪恶，罪恶　　2. 祸害　　*adj.* 邪恶的，坏的，罪恶的
evolution	*n.* 1. 演变，演化，进化　　2. 进展，发展
exact	*adj.* 确切的，精确的
examination/exam	*n.* 考试，检查
examine	*v.* 1. 检查，调查，仔细观察　　2. 对……进行考查
example	*n.* 1. 例，实例　　2. 范例，榜样
exceed	*v.* 超过，胜过
excellent	*adj.* 优秀的，卓越的，杰出的
exception	*n.* 例外
excess	*n.* 1. 超越，超过　　2. 过量，过剩，过度
	adj. 过量的，额外的，附加的
excessive	*adj.* 过量的，过度的
exchange	*v.* & *n.* 1. 交换，调换　　2.（简短）交谈
excited	*adj.* 激动的，兴奋的
exciting	*adj.* 令人兴奋的，令人激动的
exclude	*v.* 把……排除在外，排斥（可能性）
excuse	*n.* 借口，理由　　*v.* 1. 原谅，宽恕　　2. 免除
execute	*v.* 1. 处死，处决　　2. 实施，执行
executive	*n.* 执行者，行政官　　*adj.* 执行的，行政的
exert	*v.* 1. 运用，行使，发挥，施加　　2. 用（力），尽（力）
exhaust	*v.* 1. 使筋疲力尽　　2. 用尽，耗尽　　*n.* 1. 排气装置　　2. 废气
exhibit	*v.* 展出　　*n.* 展品
exhibition	*n.* 展览（会）
exist	*v.* 存在，生存，生活
existence	*n.* 1. 存在　　2. 生存，生活
exit	*n.* 1. 出口，通道，安全门，太平门　　2. 退场，退出
	v. 退出，离去
expand	*v.* 1. 扩大　　2. 膨胀，扩张
expect	*v.* 预料，等待，期待

expectation	*n.* 期待，预料
expenditure	*n.* 1. 消费　2. 费用
expense	*n.* 费用，花费
expensive	*adj.* 昂贵的，花钱多的
experience	*n.* [U] 经验，感受，体验　　[C] 经历　*v.* 经历，体验
experiment	*n. & v.* 实验，试验
expert	*n.* [C] 专家，能手　*adj.* 熟练的，内行的
explain	*v.* 解释，说明
explanation	*n.* 解释，说明
explode	*v.* 使爆炸，(使)爆发
exploit	*v.* 1. 剥削　2. 利用　3. 开拓，开发，开采
explore	*v.* 1. 探险，勘探　2. 探索，探究
export	*v.* 输出，出口　*n.* [C] 出口（物）
expose	*v.* 使暴露
exposure	*n.* 暴露，揭露，曝光
express	*v.* 1. （用言语）表达，陈述　2. 表示，体现　*n.* 快车
expression	*n.* 1. 词句，措辞　2. 表达，表示，表现　3. 表情
extend	*v.* 1. 延长，延伸　2. 扩大，伸展　3. 致，给予
extensive	*adj.* 广阔的，广泛的
extent	*n.* 程度，范围
external	*adj.* 外部的，外面的
extra	*adj.* 1. 额外的，外加的　2. 特别的　*n.* 额外的事物，另外的收费
extraordinary	*adj.* 非常的，特别的，非凡的
extreme	*adj.* 1. 极度的，极端的　2. 尽头的，末端的　*n.* 极端

F

facility	*n.* 1. [P] 设备　2. 便利，容易
factor	*n.* 因素，要素
faculty	*n.* 1. 才能，能力　2. （大学的）系，科，院 3. （某一专门职业的）全体从业人员
fade	*v.* 1. （使）褪色　2. 衰退；（声音、光线等）变微弱
fail	*v.* 1. 失败　2. 不，未能 3. 评定（学生或考试）不及格，考试不及格　4. 失灵
failure	*n.* 1. 失败　2. 失败的人（或事）　3. 没做到，不履行 4. 失灵，故障
faint	*adj.* 微弱的，微小的　*v.* 晕厥，晕倒
fair	*adj.* 1. 公平的，公正的　2. 相当大的，尚可的　3. 金发的，白皙的 4. 晴朗的　*n.* 1. 定期集市　2. 交易会，博览会
fairly	*adv.* 1. 相当　2. 公正地
faith	*n.* 1. 信任，信心　2. 信仰
faithful	*adj.* 1. 忠诚的，忠实的　2. 如实的
faithfully	*adv.* 1. 忠诚地，忠实地　2. 如实地

fame	*n.* 名声，声望
familiar	*adj.* 1. 熟悉的，通晓的　　2. 日常用的，常见的　　3. 亲近的，随便的
family	*n.* 1. 家，家族（成员）　　2. 家族，氏族　　3. 族，科
famous	*adj.* 著名的
fancy	*n.* 1. 想象力，幻想力　　2. 设想，幻想　　3. 爱好，迷恋
	adj. 1. 根据想象的，空想出来的　　2. 花式的，花哨的
	3. 奇特的，异样的
	v. 1. 想象，设想　　2. 相信，猜想　　3. 喜爱，爱好
fare	*n.*（车、船等）费
farewell	*int.* 再会　　*n.* 离别，告别
fashion	*n.* 1. 方式，样子　　2. 流行式样
fast	*adj.* 1. 快的，迅速的　　2. 牢的，紧的
	adv. 1. 快，迅速地　　2. 紧紧地，牢固地
fasten	*v.* 扎牢，使固定
fatal	*adj.* 1. 命运的，命中注定的，宿命的　　2. 致命的，毁灭性的
	n. 命运
fatigue	*n.* 疲劳，劳累
fault	*n.* 1. 过失，过错　　2. 缺点，毛病　　3. 故障
favo(u)r	*n.* 1. 好感，喜爱　　2. 恩惠，善意的行为，好事
	v. 赞同，偏爱，偏袒
favorable	*adj.* 1. 有利的，顺利的　　2. 赞成的，称赞的
favo(u)rite	*adj.* 特别受喜爱的　　*n.* 特别喜爱的人（或物）
fax/facsimile	*n.* 传真
fear	*n.* 害怕，恐惧　　*v.* 畏惧，害怕，担心
feasible	*adj.* 可行的，可能的，可用的
feature	*n.* 1. 特征，特色　　2. [P] 面貌，相貌
fee	*n.* 费，酬金
feed	*v.*（fed, fed）喂（养），饲（养）
feedback	*n.* 反馈，反应
feel	*v.* 1. 感觉，觉得　　2. 以为，认为　　3. 给人以……感觉　　4. 触，摸
	5.（for）摸索，摸索着寻找
feeling	*n.* 1. 感情　　2. 感觉，知觉
female	*n.* 1. 雌性的动物　　2. 女子　　*adj.* 雌的，女（性）的
fence	*n.* 栅栏，围栏，篱笆
festival	*n.* 1. 节日，喜庆日　　2. 音乐节，戏剧节
festive	*adj.* 节日的，欢乐的
fetch	*v.* 1.（去）拿来　　2. 请来
fever	*n.* 1. 发烧　　2. 一时的狂热
fiber/fibre	*n.* 纤维
field	*n.* 1. 田野　　2. 运动场　　3.（电或磁）场　　4. 领域，范围
fierce	*adj.* 1. 凶猛的，残酷的　　2. 狂热的，极度的　　3. 猛烈地，激烈的
fight	*v. & n.*（fought, fought）战斗，搏斗，斗争，打架

figure	*n.* 1. 数字　　2. 外形，轮廓　　3. 人物　　4. 体形，风姿　　5. 插图
file	*n.* 1. 档案，卷宗　　2. 文件，文档
	v. 1. 把……归档　　2. 提出（申请等）　　3. 排成纵队行进
fill	*v.* 装满，使充满
filter	*v.* 过滤　　*n.* 过滤器
final	*adj.* 1. 最后的，最终的　　2. 决定性的
finance	*n.* 财政，金融
financial	*adj.* 财政的，金融的
finding	*n.* 1. 发现（物）　　2. [P]调查（或研究）的结果
firm	*n.* 商行，公司　　*adj.* 1. 结实的，坚固的　　2. 坚定的，坚决的
fit	*v.* 1. （使）适合，合身，合适　　2. （使）配合　　3. 安装
	adj. 1. 适合的，恰当的　　2. 健康的，强健的
fix	*v.* 1. 固定，安装　　2. 决定，确定　　3. 修理，安排
flash	*n.* 闪光，闪烁　　*v.* 1. 闪光，闪烁　　2. 飞驰，掠过　　3. 闪现，闪耀
flat	*n.* 公寓，公寓套房　　*adj.* 1. 平的，平坦的　　2. 扁平的，平展的
flavour	*n.* 风味
flexible	*adj.* 1. 易弯曲的，柔韧的　　2. 灵活的
flight	*n.* 1. 空中旅行　　2. 航班，班机　　3. 飞行，飞翔
flood	*n.* 洪水，水灾　　*v.* 淹没，使泛滥
flow	*v.* 1. 流（动）　　2. 垂，飘拂　　*n.* 流动
fluent	*adj.* 流利的，流畅的
fly	*n.* （flew, flown）苍蝇
	v. 1. 飞，飞行　　2. 驾驶（飞机），空运　　3. 飘扬　　4. 飞跑，飞逝
focus	*v.* 使聚集，使集中
	n. 1. 焦点　　2. （注意、活动、兴趣等的）中心，集中点
fog	*n.* 雾
fold	*v.* 折叠　　*n.* 褶（痕）
folk	*n.* 人们　　*adj.* 民间的
follow	*v.* 1. 跟随　　2. 接着　　3. 结果是　　4. 沿着……行进
	5. 遵照，采用，仿效
following	*adj.* 接着的，下列的
fond	*adj.* 1. (of) 喜爱的，喜欢的　　2. 溺爱的，痴情的
fool	*n.* 蠢人　　*v.* 欺骗，愚弄
foolish	*adj.* 愚蠢的
forbid (forbade, forbidden)	*v.* 不许，禁止
force	*v.* 强迫，迫使
	n. 1. 暴力，武力　　2. 力（量），力气　　3. [常 P]军队，部队
foreign	*adj.* 1. 外国的，在外国的　　2. 对外的，涉外的　　3. 外来的，异质的
foreigner	*n.* 外国人
forget (forgot, forgotten)	*v.* 忘记，遗忘
forgive	*v.* 原谅，饶恕，宽恕

(forgave, forgiven)	
fork	*n.* 1. 餐叉　　2. 耙　　3. 分叉，岔口
form	*n.* 1. 形式，形状　　2. 表格　　*v.* 形成，构成，组成
formal	*adj.* 1. 正式的　　2. 礼仪上的　　3. 形式的
format	*n.*（常）版式　　*v.* 格式化
former	*adj.* 在前的，以前的　　*n.* 前者
formula	*n.* 1. 公式　　2. 配方
forth	*adv.* 向前，往外
fortnight	*n.* 两星期
fortunate	*adj.* 幸运的，侥幸的
fortunately	*adv.* 幸运地，幸亏
fortune	*n.* 1. 命运，运气　　2. 财产
forward	*adv.* 1. 向前　　2. 向将来，往后
	adj. 1. 向前的，前进的　　2. 前部的　　*v.* 转交，转运
found	*v.* 创立，创办，创建
foundation	*n.* 1. 基础　　2.［P］地基　　3. 建立，设立，创办
	4. 基金会　　5. 根据
fountain	*n.* 喷泉
fox	*n.* 狐狸，狡猾的人
frame	*n.* 1. 框子，框架　　2. 构架　　*v.* 框住
framework	*n.* 1. 框架，架构，结构　　2. 体系
frank	*adj.* 坦白的，直率的，真诚的
free	*adj.* 1. 自由的，无拘束的　　2.（of, from）无……的
	3. 空闲的，未被占用的　　4. 免费的　　*v.* 使自由，解放
freedom	*n.* 自由
freeze(froze, frozen)	*v.* 冰冻，结冰
frequency	*n.* 1. 屡次，频繁　　2. 频率，出现率
frequent	*adj.* 时常发生的，频繁的
freshman	*n.* 新手，新生
fridge	*n.*（refrigerator 的略语）冰箱
friendly	*adj.* 友好的，友谊的
friendship	*n.* 友谊，友好
frighten	*v.* 使惊恐，吓唬
front	*adj.* 前面的，前部的　　*n.* 1. 前面，前部　　2. 前线，战线　　*v.* 面对
frustrate	*v.* 1. 使受挫　　2. 破坏　　3. 使挫败
fry	*v.* 油煎，油炸
fuel	*n.* 燃料　　*v.* 给……加燃料（油）
fulfil(l)	*v.* 1. 履行，实现　　2. 满足，使满意
function	*n.* 1. 功能，技能，作用　　2. 职务，职责
	v. 1. 运行，起作用　　2. 行使职责
fund	*n.* 1.［P］资金　　2. 基金，专款　　3. 储备，贮存
fundamental	*adj.* 基本的，根本的，基础的　　*n.*［P］基本原则，原理

funeral	*n.* 葬礼，丧礼
funny	*adj.* 1. 滑稽的，可笑的　2.［口］反常出格的，古怪的
fur	*n.* 1. 柔毛　2. 毛皮　3. 裘皮衣
furniture	*n.*［U］家具
further	*adv.*（far 的比较级）1. 在更大程度上，进一步地　2. 而且，此外　3. 更远，再往前地
	adj. 1. 更多的，另外的　2. 更远的　*v.* 促进，推进
furthermore	*adv.* 而且，此外
future	*n.* 1. 将来，未来　2. 前途，前景　*adj.* 将来的，未来的

G

gain	*v.* 1. 获得　2. 增加　3. 受益，得益　4.（钟、表等）走快
	n.［C］1. 增进，增加　2. 收益
gap	*n.*［C］1. 缺口，裂口　2. 间隔，间隙　3. 差距
garage	*n.* 1. 车库　2.（常兼汽车修理、销售业务的）加油站
gather	*v.* 1. 聚集，集合　2. 收集，采集　3. 逐渐增加，逐渐获得　4. 猜想，推测
gay	*adj.* 1. 快乐的　2. 色彩鲜艳的
gene	*n.* 遗传因素，基因
general	*adj.* 1. 总的，普遍的　2. 一般的，普通的　3. 通用的　*n.* 将军
generally	*adv.* 一般地，通常，大体上
generate	*v.* 1. 使产生，使发生　2. 引起
generation	*n.* 1.［C］一代（人、产品）　2.［U］产生，发生
generous	*adj.* 1. 慷慨的，大方的　2. 宽厚的，宽宏大量的
genius	*n.*［P geniuses］［U］天才，天赋　［C］天才人物
gentle	*adj.* 1. 和蔼的，温和的，不粗俗的　2. 轻柔的，徐缓的　3. 不陡的，坡度小的
genuine	*adj.* 1. 真心的　2. 坦诚的
geography	*n.*［U/C］地理（学）
geometry	*n.* 几何（学）
gesture	*n.*［U/C］1. 姿势，手势　2.（外交等方面的）姿势，表示
giant	*n.* 巨人　*adj.* 巨大的
glance	*v.* 看一眼，扫视　*n.*［C］一瞥，扫视
global	*adj.* 全球的，世界的
globe	*n.* 1. 地球，世界　2. 地球仪　3. 球体
glorious	*adj.* 1. 壮丽的，辉煌的　2. 光荣的
glory	*n.*［U］光荣，荣誉
glove	*n.*［C］手套
glow	*n.* 光亮，光辉　*v.* 发光，发热
goal	*n.*［C］1. 球门　2. 得分进球　3. 目标，目的
gold	*n.*［U］金，黄金　*adj.* 金（制）的，金色的
golden	*adj.* 1. 金的，金制的　2. 金色的，闪金光的，发亮的　3. 极好的，兴盛的

goods	*n.* 货物，商品
goose	*n.* ［P geese］［C］鹅
govern	*v.* 1. 统治，治理，管理　　2. 支配，影响
government	*n.* 1. ［C］政府　　2. ［U］治理，管理，支配
graceful	*adj.* 优美的，优雅的，得体的
grade	*v.* 分等，分级
	n. ［C］1. 等级，级别　　2. 成绩，分数　　3.（学校的）年级
gradual	*adj.* 逐渐的，逐步的
gradually	*adv.* 逐渐地，逐步地
graduate	*n.*（大学）毕业生，研究生　　*v.* 毕业
grain	*n.* ［C］谷粒，谷物　　［C］颗粒，细粒
gram/gramme	*n.* ［C］克
grammar	*n.* 语法（书）
grand	*adj.* 1. 宏伟的，壮丽的　　2. 重大的，主要的　　3. 豪华的
grant	*n.* 拨款　　*v.* 授予，同意，准予
graph	*n.* ［C］图表，曲线图
graphic	*adj.* 1. 图的　　2. 生动的
grasp	*v. & n.* 1. 抓紧，抓牢　　2. 理解，领会
grass	*n.* ［U］草
grateful	*adj.* 感激的，感谢的
gratitude	*n.* ［U］感激，感谢
grave	*n.* ［C］坟墓　　*adj.* 1. 严重的　　2. 严肃的，庄重的
great	*adj.* 1. 大的，极大的　　2. 伟大的　　3. 美妙的，好极的
greedy	*adj.*（greedier, greediest）1. 贪食的，嘴馋的　　2. 贪婪的　　3. 渴望的
greenhouse	*n.* 温室，玻璃暖房
greet	*v.* 1. 问候，迎接，招呼　　2.（以特定方式）接受，对……做出反应 　　3. 呈现在……前
grey/gray	*adj.* 灰色的　　*n.* 灰色
grocer	*n.* 食品杂货商
gross	*adj.* 1. 总的，毛的　　2. 严重的，显著的
ground	*n.* 1. 地，地面，土地　　2. 场地，场所　　3. 理由，根据
grow	*v.*（grew, grown）1. 生长，成长　　2. 种植，栽种　　3. 变得，成为 　　4. 增长，发展
growth	*n.* 1. 增长，增加　　2. 增长量　　3. 生长，发展
guarantee	*n. & v.* 保证，担保
guard	*v.* 1. 守卫，保卫　　2.（against）防止，防范 *n.* ［C］警卫员，看守，卫兵
guidance	*n.* 指引，指导，领导
guide	*n.* 1. 导游，向导　　2. 指南，手册 *v.* 1. 给……导游，给……领路　　2. 指导
guilty	*adj.* 1. 内疚的　　2. 有罪的
gym(nasium)	*n.* ［C］体育馆，健身房

H

halt	*n.* & *v.* 停住，停止
handle	*n.* [C] 柄，把手 *v.* 1. 处理，应付，对待 2. 操作
handsome	*adj.* 1.（男子）漂亮的，英俊的 2.（女子）端庄健美的，好看的
handwriting	*n.* 笔迹，笔法
hang	*v.* 1.（hung, hung）悬挂，吊 2.（hanged, hanged）吊死，绞死
harbo(u)r	*n.* [C] 海港，港口
hardly	*adv.* 几乎不，简直不
hardship	*n.* [U] 艰难，困苦
hardware	*n.* 1.[总称] 金属器件（或构件），五金制品 2.（计算机的）硬件
harm	*n.* & *v.* 伤害，损害，危害
harmful	*adj.* 有害的
harvest	*n.* [C] 收获，收割，收成 *v.* 收割，收获
haste	*n.* 急速，急忙
hatred	*n.* [U/C] 憎恶，憎恨，仇恨
heading	*n.* 标题
headline	*n.* [C] 1. 大字标题 2.[P] 新闻提要
headquarters	*n.* [C] 1. 司令部，指挥部 2. 总部
health	*n.* [U] 健康（状况）
healthy	*adj.* 1. 健康的，健壮的 2. 有益健康的
heat	*v.* 加热，使变热 *n.* 1. 热，炎热，暑热 2. 体温，热度 3. 激动，热烈，激烈
heel	*n.* [C] 脚后跟，踵
height	*n.* [U/C] 1. 高，高度，身高 2.[P] 高处，高地
hello/hullo	*int.*（唤起注意，回答电话）喂 *n.* 问候
helpful	*adj.* 1. 给予帮助的，肯帮助的 2. 有益的
hence	*adv.* 1. 因此，所以 2. 今后，从此
hero	*n.* [P heroes] [C] 1. 男主角，男主人公 2. 英雄
heroic	*adj.* 英雄的；英勇的
hesitate	*v.* 犹豫，踌躇，迟疑不决
hide	*v.*（hid, hidden）1. 把……藏起来，躲藏，（被）隐藏 2. 隐瞒，遮掩
highlight	*v.* 1. 以强烈光线照射 2. 强调 *n.* 1. 最明亮的部分 2. 最重要的部分
highly	*adv.* 高度，极，非常
highway	*n.* [C] 公路
hint	*n.* [C] 1. 暗示，示意 2.[P] 建议，提示 *v.* 暗示
hire	*v.* & *n.* 租用，雇用
hit	*v.*（hitting, hit, hit）1. 打，击，击中 2. 碰撞 *n.* 1. 击中 2. 成功而风行一时的事物
hi-tech	*n.* 高新技术

hold	v. (held, held) 1. 拿着，握住，托住　　2. 是保持某种状态 3. 抑制，约束，控制　　4. 容纳，装得下，包含 5. 举行（会议，会谈等），主持，庆祝（节目） 6. 拥有，持有，保持　　7. 认为，想，相信 n. 掌握，控制，约束
honest	adj. 诚实的，正直的，老实的
honor	n. (U.S. honor) [U] 光荣，荣誉 v. 1. 给……以荣誉　　2. 向……表示敬意　　3. 尊敬
hono(u)rable	adj. 诚实的，正直的，尊敬的
hope	n. & v. 希望，期望
hopeful	adj. 有希望的
horizon	n. [C] 1. 地平线　　2. [P] 眼界，见识
horror	n. [U/C] 1. 恐怖　　2. 憎恶
horsepower	n. [C][单复同] 马力
hospitable	adj. 好客的
hostile	adj. 敌对的，敌意的，不友善的
household	n. [C] 家庭，户　　adj. 家庭的，家常的，普通的
humble	adj. 1. 谦逊的，谦虚的　　2. 地位（或身份）低下的，恭顺的
humorous	adj. 幽默的，诙谐的
humour	n. (U.S. humor) [U] 幽默，诙谐
hunger	n. [U] 饿，饥饿　　[C] (for) 渴望
hungry	adj. (hungrier, hungriest) 饥饿的，感到饿的
hunt	n. & v. 1. 打猎，猎取　　2. 搜寻，寻找
hurry	v. (hurried, hurried) 匆忙，赶紧，催促　　n. [U] 急忙，匆忙
hurt (hurt, hurt)	v. 1. 使受伤，弄痛，伤害　　2. 伤……的感情　　3. 危害，损害 n. 伤害，伤痛

I

ideal	adj. 理想的，完满的　　n. [C] 理想
identical	adj. 相同的；相等的
identification (ID)	n. [U] 1. 识别，鉴别　　2. 身份
identify	v. (identified, identified) 1. 认出，鉴定　　2. 认为……等同于
idle	adj. (idler, idlest) 1. 空闲的，闲着的　　2. 懒散的，无所事事的 v. 虚度，懒散，无所事事
ignore	v. 不顾，不理，忽视
illegal	adj. 违规的，非法的
illustrate	v. 1. 说明，阐明　　2. 给……作插图说明
illustration	n. [U] 说明，图解　　[C] 例证，插图
image	n. [C] 1. 像，形象　　2. 映像，图像
imagine	v. 1. 现象，设想　　2. 料想，猜想
imitate	v. 1. 模仿，仿效　　2. 仿制，仿造
imitation	n. 模仿，仿效

immediate	*adj.* 1. 立即的，即刻的　　2. 直接的，最接近的
immigrant	*n.* [C] 移民，侨民
immigrate	*v.* （从外地）移居，移民
impatient	*adj.* 不耐烦的，急躁的
implication	*n.* [U/C] 含义，暗示，暗指
imply	*v.* (implied, implied) 暗示；意味着
import	*v. & n.* 进口，输入　　*n.* [P] 进口商品
importance	*n.* [U] 重要（性）
important	*adj.* 1. 重要的，重大的　　2. 有势力的，有地位的
impose	*v.* 1. 把……强加于　　2. 征（税等）
impossible	*adj.* 不可能的，办不到的
impress	*v.* 1. 给……深刻的印象，使铭记　　2. 印，压印
impression	*n.* [C] 1. 印象，感想　　2. 印记，压痕
improve	*v.* 改进，改善，提高
improvement	*n.* [U/C] 1. 改进，增进　　2. 改进之处
incident	*n.* [C] 1. 发生的事　　2. 事件，事变
incline	*v.* 1. （使）倾斜　　2. （使）倾向于　　*n.* [C] 斜坡，斜面
include	*v.* 包括，斜面
inclusive	*v.* 包括的，包含一切的
income	*n.* [U/C] 收入，所得，收益
increase	*v. & n.* 增加，增长，增强
independence	*n.* [U] 独立，自主，自立
independent	*adj.* 独立的，自主的
index	*n.* [C] [P indexes] 1. 索引　　2. 指数，指标 *v.* 为……编索引，把……编入索引
indicate	*v.* 1. 标示，指示，指出　　2. 表明，暗示
individual	*adj.* 1. 个别的，单独的　　2. 独特的　　*n.* [C] 个人，个体
industrial	*adj.* 工业的，产业的
industry	*n.* [U] 1. 工业，产业　　2. 勤劳，勤奋
inevitable	*adj.* 不可避免的，必然（发生）的
infect	*v.* 传染，感染
infectious	*adj.* 感染的，传染的
infer	*v.* (inferred, inferred) 推论，推断
inference	*n.* [U] 推论，推测
inferior	*adj.* （等级、身份等）低下的，下级的
infinite	*adj.* 无限的，无穷的，无边无际的
influence	*n.* [U/C] 影响　　[U] 感化力　　[U] 势力，权势 *v.* 影响，感化
inform	*v.* 1. 通知，报告　　2. 告发，检举
information	*n.* [U] 1. 消息，情报，资料　　2. 通知，告之　　3. 信息
initial	*adj.* 开始的，最初的　　*n.* [C] 首字母
initiative	*n.* [U] 1. 主动性　　2. 首创精神

injection	n. [U/C] 注射，注入
injure	v. 伤害，损害，损伤
injury	n. [P injuries] [U/C] 1. 伤害，损害　　2. 受伤处
inner	adj. 1. 内部的，里面的　　2. 内心的
innocent	adj. 1. (of) 清白的，无罪的　　2. 幼稚的，无知的 　　　3. 无害的，没有恶意的
input	n. [U] 输入　　[U/C] 投入的资金（或物资）
inquiry/enquiry	n. 1. 打听，询问　　2. 调查，查问
insect	n. [C] 昆虫，虫
insert	v. 1. 插入，嵌入　　2. 刊登　　n. 嵌入物
insight	n. [U] 洞察力，观点
insist	v. 1. (on, upon) 坚持，坚决认为，强调　　2. 坚决主张，坚决要求
inspect	v. 检查，视察
inspection	n. [U] 检查，调查
inspire	v. 1. 鼓舞　　2. 激起　　3. 给……以灵感
instal(l)	v. 安装（机器、设备等）
installment	n. [C]（分期付款的）一期付款
instance	n. [C] 例子，实例，事例
instant	n. [C] 瞬间，顷刻　　adj. 1. 立即的，即刻的　　2. 紧急的，急迫的 　　　3.（食品）速溶的，方便的
instead	adv. 1. 作为替代　　2. 反而，却
instinct	n. [U] 本能，天性　　[C] 直觉
institute	n. [C] 1. 学会　　2. 研究所，学院
institution	n. 1. 设立，制定　　2.（学校、医院等）公共（社会福利）机构 　　　3. 学会，协会
instruct	v. 1. 教，指导　　2. 指示，命令　　3. 通知
instruction	n. 1. 教学，教导　　2. [常P] 命令，指示，用法，说明
instrument	n. 1. 仪器，器械，工具　　2. 乐器
insult	v. 侮辱，辱骂　　n. [U/C] 侮辱，凌辱
insurance	n. 保险，保险金，保险费
insure	v. 1. 给……保险　　2. 保证，确保
integrate	v. 1. 合而为一，使一体化　　2.（使）综合
intellectual	n. [C] 知识分子　　adj. 智力的，理智的
intelligence	n. [U] 1. 智力，智慧　　2. 情报，消息
intelligent	adj. 聪明的，明智的
intend	v. 想要，打算，计划
intense	adj. 1. 强烈的，剧烈的　　2. 认真的，热情的
intention	n. [U/C] 意图，目的
interact	v. 相互作用，相互影响
interaction	n. [U/C] 相互作用，相互影响
interest	n. [U] 兴趣，关注，趣味　　[C] [常P] 利益，利害关系 　　[C] [常P] 利息，利率　　v. 使感兴趣，引起……关注

interesting	*adj.* 有趣的，令人关注的
interested	*adj.* 感兴趣的
interfere	*v.* (with, in) 1. 干涉，介入　　2. 妨碍，干扰
interference	*n.* [U] 1. 干涉，介入　　2. 阻碍，干扰
interior	*adj.* 1. 内部的　　2. 内地的，国内的　　*n.* [U] 1. 内部　　2. 内地
intermediate	*adj.* 中间的，居中的
internal	*adj.* 1. 内的，内部的　　2. 国内的　　3. 内政的
international	*adj.* 国际的，世界（性）的
internet	*n.* 国际互联网
interpret	*v.* 1. 解释，说明　　2. 口译，翻译
interpretation	*n.* [U] 1. 解释，说明　　2. 口译，翻译
interrupt	*v.* 1. 打断，打扰　　2. 中止，阻碍
interval	*n.* [C] 1. 间隔，间距　　2. 幕间（或工间）休息
interview	*n.* [C] 1. 接见，会见　　2. 面谈，面试，采访　　*v.* 接见，会见，采访
introduce	*v.* 1. 介绍　　2. 引进，传入
introduction	*n.* 1. [U/C] 介绍　　2. [C] 引进，传入　　3. [C] 引言，导论
invade	*v.* 1. 侵入，侵略　　2. 侵犯　　3. 侵袭
invent	*v.* 1. 发明，创造　　2. 捏造，虚构
invest	*v.* 投资，投入
investigate	*v.* 调查，调查研究
investigation	*n.* [U/C] 调查
investment	*n.* [U] 投资，[C] 投资额
invisible	*adj.* 看不见的，无形的
invitation	*n.* [U] 邀请，招待　　[C] 邀请书，请柬
invite	*v.* 邀请，聘请
invoice	*n.* [C] 发票，发货单
involve	*v.* 1. 使陷入，使卷入，牵涉　　2. 包含，含有
irrevocable	*adj.* 1. 无可挽救的　　2. 不能撤销的
island	*n.* [C] 岛，岛屿
isolate	*v.* 使隔离，使孤立
issue	*n.* [C] 1. 问题，争论点　　2. 发行，（书刊的）期号　　*v.* 发行，颁布，出版
item	*n.* [C] 1. 条，条款，项目　　2. （新闻等的）一条，一则
itinerary	*n.* 旅行计划

J

jealous	*adj.* 1. 妒忌的，羡慕的　　2. 猜忌的
jeans	*n.* 牛仔裤，紧身裤
jet	*n.* 1. 喷气式飞机，喷气发动机　　2. 喷嘴，喷射口　　3. 喷射，喷流　　*v.* 喷出，射出
joint	*n.* 1. 接头，接合处　　2. 关节　　*adj.* 联合的，连接的，合资的
journal	*n.* 1. 日报，杂志，期刊　　2. 日志，日记

journalist	*n.* 新闻工作者
journey	*n.* 旅行，行程
judge	*n.* 1. 法官，审判员　　2. 裁判员，评判员，鉴定人
	v. 1. 审判，判决　　2. 裁决，评定　　3. 断定，判断
judg(e)ment	*n.* 1. 审判，判决　　2. 判断　　3. 判断力　　4. 看见，意见，评价
junior	*adj.* 1. 年少的，较年幼的　　2. 资历较浅的，等级较低的
	n. 1. 年少者　　2. 等级较低者，晚辈
just	*adv.* 1. 刚才，方才　　2. 只是，仅仅　　3. 正好，恰恰正是　　4. 勉强地
	adj. 1. 正义的，公正的　　2. 恰当的，应得的
justice	*n.* 1. 正义，公正　　2. 司法，法律制裁
justify	*v.* 证明……正当（或有理、正确），为……辩护

K

keen	*adj.* 1. 锋利的，刺人的　　2. 激烈的，强烈的　　3. 敏锐的，敏捷的
	4. 热心的，渴望的
keyboard	*n.* 键盘
kilogram(me)/kilo	*n.* 千克，公斤
kilometre/kilometer	*n.* 千米，公里
kind	*n.* 种类　　*adj.* 1. 友好的，亲切的　　2. 和蔼的，仁慈的
kindness	*n.* 1. 仁慈，好意　　2. 仁慈（或好心）的行为
kitchen	*n.* 厨房
knock	*v.* 1. 敲，打　　2. 碰撞，撞击　　*n.* 敲击
knowledge	*n.* [C] 1. 知识，学问　　2. 知道，了解

L

label	*n.* 标签，标记　　*v.* 1. 贴标签于　　2. 把……称为
labo(u)r	*n.* 1. 劳动，努力　　2. 劳工，工人
laboratory/lab	*n.* 实验室
lack	*v. & n.* 缺乏，不足，没有
ladder	*n.* 梯子
land	*n.* 1. 陆地，地面　　2. 土地，田地　　3. 国家，国土
	v. （使）靠岸，（使）登陆，（使）着陆
language	*n.* 语言
later	*adv.* 1. 后来　　2. 过一会儿
latter	*adj.* 1. 后者的　　2. 后一半的，末了的
laugh	*v.* 笑　　*n.* 笑，笑声
laughter	*n.* 笑，笑声
launch	*v.* 1. 发射，投射　　2. 使（船）下水　　3. 发动，发起
	n. 发射，（船）下水
laundry	*n.* 1. 洗衣店，洗衣房　　2. 已洗好的衣服，待洗的衣服
law	*n.* 1. 法律　　2. 法制　　3. 规律，法则，定律
lawyer	*n.* 律师

lay	*v.* (laid, laid) 1. 置放，放下　　2. 铺，砌，敷设　　3. 设置，布置
layout	*n.* 安排，设计，布局，陈设
lead	*v.* 1.（为……）带路，引导　　2. 领导，引导，指引　　3.（to）导致，通向 　　4. 领先　　*n.* 1. 指导，领导，领先　　2. 铅
leader	*n.* 领袖，领导者
leadership	*n.* 领导
leak	*v.* 1. 漏，渗　　2. 泄露，走漏 *n.* 1. 漏洞，裂缝　　2. 泄露，漏出量
lean	*v.* (leaned, leant) 1. 斜，倾斜　　2. 靠，屈身　　3. 依靠，倚
leap	*v.* (leapt, leapt) 跳，跃　　*n.* 1. 跳跃　　2. 飞跃，跃进
learn	*v.* 1. 学，学习，学会　　2. 获悉，发现，得知　　3. 记住
learner	*n.* 学习者
learning	*n.* 1. 知识，学问　　2. 学习
least	*adj.*（little 的最高级）最少的，最小的　　*adv.* 最少，最小
lecture	*n.* & *v.* 演讲，讲课
legal	*adj.* 1. 法律（上）的　　2. 合法的，法定的
leisure	*n.* 1. 空闲时间，闲暇　　2. 悠闲，安逸
lend	*v.* (lent, lent) 把……借给，出借，贷
length	*n.* 1. 长，长度，距离　　2. 一段，一节
lest	*conj.* 唯恐，免得
level	*n.* 1. 水平面，水平线　　2. 水平，等级　　*adj.* 平的，水平的
liable	*adj.* 1. 易于……的，有……倾向的　　2. 可能的
liberate	*v.* 1. 解放，使获自由　　2. 释放，放出
liberation	*n.* 解放
liberty	*n.* 1. 自由　　2. 许可，准许　　3. 冒昧
library	*n.* 1. 图书馆，藏书室　　2. 藏书
license/licence	*n.* 1. 许可，特许　　2. 许可证，执照 *v.* 发许可证给……，批准，许可
lie	*v.* (lay, lain) 1. 躺　　2. 平放　　3. 位于　　4. (lied, lied) 说谎 *n.* 谎话，假话
lifetime	*n.* 一生，终身
lift	*v.* 1. 提，抬，举，吊，（尤指向上）移动　　2. 提高，提起 　　3.（off）（飞机、火箭等）起飞，发射 *n.* 1. 提，抬，举，吊，上升　　2.［英］电梯 =［美］elevator
lightning	*n.* 闪电
likely	*adj.* 可能的，有希望的　　*adv.* 很可能
likewise	*adv.* 1. 同样，照样　　2. 也，又
limit	*n.* 1. 限度，限制　　2.［pl］范围　　*v.* 限制，限定
limited	*adj.* 有限的
line	*n.* 1. 线，绳　　2. 排，行　　3. 路线，航线
link	*v.* 连接，联系　　*n.* 1. 环，节　　2. 联系，纽带
lip	*n.* 嘴唇

list	*n.* 表，目录，名单　　*v.* 把……编列成表，列举
literature	*n.* 1. 文学，文学作品　　2. 文献，图书资料
lively	*adj.* 1. 充满活力的，活泼的　　2. 逼真的，栩栩如生的
living	*adj.* 活（着）的，有生命的　　*n.* 生计，生活
load	*v.* 装，装载，装货　　*n.* 负荷，负担，装载量
loan	*n.* 1. 贷款　　2. 暂借
local	*adj.* 1. 地方性的，当地的　　2. 局部的
locate	*v.* 1. 找出，查明，探明　　2. 把……设置在，使……坐落于
location	*n.* 位置，场所
logic	*n.* 逻辑（学），逻辑性
logical	*adj.* 逻辑的，符合逻辑的
lonely	*adj.* 1. 孤独的，寂寞的　　2. 荒凉的，人迹稀少的
loose	*adj.* 松的，宽松的
lorry	*n.* ［英］运货汽车，卡车
lose	*v.* (lost, lost) 1. 失去，丢失　　2. 迷失，使迷路　　3. 输掉
loss	*n.* 1. 遗失，丧失　　2. 损失，减少，亏损　　3. 失败，输掉
lovely	*adj.* 1. 可爱的，秀美的　　2. 令人愉快的，美好的
loyal	*adj.* 忠诚的，忠心的
luck	*n.* 1. 运气　　2. 好运，幸运
lucky	*adj.* 幸运的，侥幸的
luggage	*n.* ［C］行李
lung	*n.* 肺脏，肺

M

magazine	*n.* ［C］杂志，期刊
magic	*n.* ［C］魔法，魔术　　*adj.* 有魔力的，魔术的
magnificent	*adj.* 壮丽的，宏伟的
maintain	*v.* 1. 维持，保持　　2. 维修，保养　　3. 坚持，主张
maintenance	*n.* ［U］1. 维持，保持　　2. 维修，保养　　3. 坚持，主张
major	*adj.* （无比较等级）较大的，主要的
	n. ［C］主修科目，专业学生　　*v.* (in) 主修，专攻
majority	*n.* ［U］多数，大多数
male	*adj.* （无比较等级）男（性）的，雄的　　*n.* ［C］男的，雄性动物
mall	*n.* 购物中心，商场
manage	*v.* 1. 管理，经营，处理　　2. 设法对付，设法做到，勉力完成
management	*n.* ［U］管理
manager	*n.* ［C］经理，管理人，业务员
mankind	*n.* ［U］人类
manner	*n.* 1. ［C］方式，方法　　2. 态度，举止　　3. ［P］礼貌，规矩
manual	*adj.* （无比较等级）手工的，体力的　　*n.* ［C］手册，指南
manufacture	*v.* 制造，加工　　*n.* 1. ［U/C］制造　　2. 制造业　　3. 制造品，产品
margin	*n.* ［C］1. 页边空白，边缘　　2. 余地，余裕

mark	*n.* 1.［U/C］痕迹，斑点　　2. 符号，记号　　3. 标签，商标 　　4.（考试等的）分数 *v.* 1. 做记号于，标明　　2. 给（试卷等）打分
market	*n.* 1.［C］市场，集市　　2. 销路，需求
marriage	*n.*［U/C］结婚，婚姻
marry	*v.*（married，married）娶，嫁，（和……）结婚
marvellous (US. marvelous)	*adj.* 奇迹般的，惊人的，了不起的
mask	*n.* 1.［C］面具，面罩，口罩　　2. 假面具，伪装 *v.* 1. 戴面具，化装　　2. 掩饰，伪装
mass	*n.* 1.［C］众多，大量　　2. 团，块，堆　　3.［P］群众，民众　　4. 质量
master	*n.* 1.［C］（男）主人，雇主　　2. 能手，名家，大师　　3.［M-］硕士 *v.* 精通，掌握
match	*n.* 1.［C］比赛，竞赛　　2. 对手，敌手　　3. 火柴 *v.*（和）相配，（和）相称
material	*n.* 1.［U/C］材料，原料　　2. 素材，资料 *adj.*（无比较等级）物质的，实体的
mathematics	*n.*［also math（s）］［U］数学
matter	*n.* 1.［C］事情，问题　　2. 麻烦，毛病　　3.［U］物质 *v.* 要紧，有关系
mature	*adj.* 1. 成熟的　　2. 成年人的　　*v.*（使）成熟
maximize	*v.* 1. 使达到最大或最高限度　　2. 充分重视
maximum	*n.*（also max）［P maxima］［C］最大限度，最大量，顶点 *adj.*（无比较等级）最高的，最大的
mean	*v.* 1. 表示……的意思　　2. 意指，意味着　　3. 意欲，打算 *adj.* 1. 自私的，吝啬的　　2. 卑鄙的
meaning	*n.*［U/C］意义，意思
means	*n.*［C］方法，手段
measure	*v.* 量，测量　　*n.* 1.［U］分量，尺寸　　2.［C］［P］措施，办法
mechanical	*adj.* 1. 机械的　　2. 机械学的，力学的　　3. 机械似的，呆板的 　　4. 手工操作的
mechanism	*n.* 机械装置；机制
medal	*n.*［C］奖章，勋章，纪念章
medical	*adj.* 1. 医学的，医疗的　　2. 内科的
medicine	*n.* 1.［U/C］内服药　　2.［U］医学，内科学
medium	*adj.* 中等的，适中的 *n.* 1.［P 通常 media］［C］媒介物，传导体　　2. 中间，适中
memorandum	*n.*（also memo）［C］［P memoranda］备忘录
memorial	*adj.* 纪念的，追悼的　　*n.* 纪念碑，纪念堂，纪念仪式
memory	*n.* 1.［U/C］记忆（力）　　2. 回忆　　3.［U］纪念　　4. 存储（器）
mend	*v.* 修理，修补
mental	*adj.* 1. 精神的，思想上的　　2. 智力的，脑力的

mention	*v.* 提及，说起　　*n.* [U] 提及，说起
menu	*n.* 菜单
merchant	*n.* [C] 商人，零售商
mercy	*n.* [U] 慈悲，仁慈，宽容
mere	*adj.* 1. 仅仅的，只不过的　　2. 纯粹的
merely	*adv.* 仅仅，只不过
merit	*n.* [U] 优点
merry	*adj.* 欢乐的，愉快的
message	*n.* 1. 信息，文电　　2. 启示，要旨
metal	*n.* [U/C] 金属
meter	*n.* 计，仪表
method	*n.* [C] 方法，办法
microphone	*n.* [C] 扩音器，话筒
microscope	*n.* 显微镜
mild	*adj.* 1. 和缓的　　2. 温和的　　3. 温暖的，暖和的
mile	*n.* [C] 英里
military	*adj.* 军事的，军用的
mill	*n.* 1. 磨坊，碾磨机　　2. 制造厂，工厂
millimetre (US. millimeter)	*n.* 毫米
million	*num.* [C] 百万，百万个（人或物）　　*n.* [C][P] 许多，无数
mind	*n.* 1. [U/C] 头脑，精神，理智　　2. 注意力，心思 *v.* 1. 介意，反对　　2. 注意，留心
mine	*pron.* [I 的物主代词] 我的　　*n.* 1. 矿，矿山　　2. 地雷，水雷 *v.* 开采（矿物）
minimum	*n.* [C][P minima] 最低限度，最少量 *adj.* （also min）最低的，最小的
minister	*n.* 部长，大臣
minor	*adj.* 1. 较小的，较少的　　2. 较次要的
minority	*n.* 1. [C] 少数　　2. 少数派　　3. 少数民族
minus	*adj.* 负的，减去的　　*prep.* 减（去）
miracle	*n.* [C] 奇迹，令人惊奇的人
miserable	*adj.* 痛苦的，悲惨的，可怜的
mislead	*v.* (misled, misled) 使误入歧途
missing	*adj.* 丢失的，缺少的，失踪的
mission	*n.* 1. [C] 使命，任务　　2. 代表团，使团
misunderstand	*v.* (misunderstood, misunderstood) 误解，误会
mix	*v.* 1. （使）混合，掺和　　2. 混淆，搞混
mixture	*n.* [U/C] 混合；混合物
mobile	*adj.* 1. 移动式的，活动的　　2. 流动的，机动的
mode	*n.* [C] 方式，样式
model	*n.* 1. [C] 模型　　2. 模仿，典型　　3. 样式，模式　　4. 模特儿

moderate	*adj.* 1. 温和的，稳健的　　2. 有节制的，适度的
modern	*adj.* 现代的，新式的
modest	*adj.* 1. 适中的，不过分的　　2. 谦虚的，谦恭的
modification	*n.* 1. [U/C] 修改　　2. 修饰　　3. 减少，缓和
modify	*v.* (modified, modified) 1. 缓和，减轻　2. 修改，更改　3. （语法上）修饰
moisture	*n.* [U] 潮湿
moment	*n.* [C] 片刻，瞬间，时刻
monitor	*n.* 1. [C]（学校的）班长　　2. 监听器，监视器，检测器 *v.* 1. 监听，监视　　2. 检测（放射性污染物）
monthly	*adj.* 每月的，每月一次的　　*adv.* 每月，每月一次　　*n.* [C] 月刊
monument	*n.* [C] 纪念碑
mood	*n.* 1. [C] 心情，情绪　　2. 语气
moral	*adj.* 1. 道德（上）的　　2. 有道德的　　*n.* [C] 寓意
mortgage	*n.* 抵押贷款
motion	*n.* 1. [U]（物体的）运动　　2. [C] 手势，眼色，示意动作 　　3. [C] 提议，动议
motivate	*v.* 1. 使有动机，激起　　2. 激发……的积极性
motive	*n.* [C] 动机，目的
motor	*n.* [C] 发动机，电动机
mount	*v.* 1. 登上　　2. 安放，安装　　*n.* [C][M-]（用于山名前）山，峰
mountain	*n.* [C] 山，[P] 山脉
mouse	*n.* [P mice] 1. [C] 鼠　　2. 鼠标
movement	*n.* 1. [U/C] 动，活动，运动　　2. 移动，迁移
multiple	*adj.* 复合的，多样的，多重的，多部的　　*n.* [C] 倍数
multiply	*v.* (multiplied, multiplied) 1. 增加，繁殖　　2. 乘，使相乘
municipal	*adj.* 都市的，市政的
murder	*v.* & *n.* [U] 谋杀，凶杀
muscle	*n.* [U/C] 肌肉
museum	*n.* [C] 博物馆
musician	*n.* [C] 音乐家，乐师
mutual	*adj.* 1. （无比较等级）相互的，彼此的　　2. 共同的，共有的
mysterious	*adj.* 1. 神秘的　　2. 难以理解的
mystery	*n.* 1. [U/C] 神秘　　2. 神秘的事物

N

nail	*n.* [C] 1. 钉子，钉状物　　2. 指甲，爪　　*v.* 钉，钉牢
naked	*adj.* 1. 光秃的，裸露的　　2. 赤裸裸的，不掩饰的
namely	*adv.* 即，就是
narrow	*adj.* 狭窄的
nation	*n.* [C] 国家，民族
national	*adj.* 1. 国家的，全国的　　2. 民族的
nationality	*n.* 国籍，民族

native	*adj.* 本地的，本国的
natural	*adj.* 1. 自然的，天然的，天生的　　2. 自然如此的，正常的
naturally	*adv.* 1. 当然，自然地　　2. 天然地，天生地
nature	*n.* [U] 大自然，自然界　　[U/C] 性质，天性
navigation	*n.* 1. 航海术，航空术　　2. 航海，航空，导航，领航
navy	*n.* 海军
neat	*adj.* 1. 整洁的，爱整洁的　　2. 利索的，简洁的
necessarily	*adv.* 必定，必然地，当然
necessary	*adj.* 1. 必要的，必需的　　2. 必然的
	n. [常 P] 必需品
necessity	*n.* [U] 必要（性），（迫切）需要　　[C] 必需品
negative	*adj.* 1. 否定的　　2. 反面的，消极的　　3. 负的，阴性的
	n. [C] 1. 底片　　2. 负数
neglect	*v.* 1. 忽视，忽略　　2. 疏忽，玩忽
negotiate	*v.* 1. 商定　　2. 谈判
neighbour	*n.* [C] 1. 邻居　　2. 邻近的人（或物），邻国
neighbourhood	*n.* [U] 1. 地段，地区，四邻　　2. 邻近地区，附近
nerve	*n.* [C] 神经　　[U] 勇气，胆量
nervous	*adj.* 1. 神经紧张的，情绪不安的　　2. 神经系统的，神经性的
network	*n.* [C] 1. 网，网状物　　2. 网络，网状系统　　3. 广播网，电视网
neutral	*adj.* 1. 中立的　　2. 中性的
nevertheless	*adv.* 仍然，不过　　*conj.* 然而，不过
newsletter	*n.* 通讯，简讯
noble	*adj.* 1. 高尚的，宏伟的　　2. 贵族的，高贵的
nod	*v.* (nodded, nodded) 1. 点（头），点头表示，点头同意
	2. 打瞌睡，打盹　　*n.* [C] 1. 点头，点头同意　　2. 瞌睡，打盹
noise	*n.* [C] 声音，响声　　[U] 喧哗声，噪声
noisy	*adj.* 嘈杂的，喧闹的
normal	*adj.* 1. 正常的，平常的　　2. 正规的，标准的
normally	*adv.* 通常的，正常地
northern	*adj.* 北方的，北部的
note	*n.* [C] 1. 便条　　2. 记录，笔记　　3. 注解，按语　　4. 票据，钞票
	v. 1. 记录，记下　　2. 注意，留意
notebook	*n.* 笔记本
notice	*v.* 注意到，察觉到　　*n.* 1. [U] 注意，察觉　　2. [C] 通知，通告
nowadays	*adv.* 现今，现在
nuclear	*adj.* 1. 核子的，核能的，核武器的　　2. 核心的，中心的
numerous	*adj.* 众多的，许多的
nurse	*n.* [C] 1. 护士　　2. 保姆，保育员
nursery	*n.* 1. 托儿所，保育室　　2. 苗圃
nut	*n.* 1. 干果，果仁，坚果　　2. 螺母，螺帽

O

obey	*v.* 服从，听从
object	*n.* 1. 物体，实物　　2. 目的，目标　　3. 对象　　4. 宾语 *v.* (to) 反对，不赞成
objection	*n.* [U] 反对，异议
objective	*n.* [C] 目标，目的　　*adj.* 客观的，真实的
obligation	*n.* [U] 义务，职责
oblige	*v.* 1. 迫使　　2. 施恩惠于，帮……的忙　　3. 使感激
observe	*v.* 1. 注意到，觉察到　　2. 观察，观测　　3. 说，评论　　4. 遵守，奉行
obtain	*v.* 获得，得到
obvious	*adj.* 显然的，明显的
occasion	*n.* [C] 1. 时刻，时候，场合　　2. 重大（或特殊）活动，盛会 3. 时机，机会
occasional	*adj.* 偶尔的，间或发生的
occupation	*n.* 1. 工作，职业　　2. 占领，占据
occupy	*v.* 1. 占，占用，占领　　2. 使忙碌，使从事
occur	*v.* (occurred, occurred) 1. 发生；存在，出现　　2. 被想起，被想到
ocean	*n.* [C] 洋，海洋
offence	*n.* (US. offense) [U] 冒犯，得罪，违反
offend	*v.* 1. 冒犯，得罪，违反　　2. 使厌恶，使不舒服
offer	*v.* 给予，提供，提出　　*n.* [C] 提供（物），提议
officer	*n.* [C] 1. 军官，警官　　2. 官员，高级职员
official	*n.* [C] 官员，行政人员　　*adj.* 官员的，官方的，正式的
omit	*v.* (omitted, omitted) 1. 省略，删节　　2. 遗漏，疏忽
online	*adj.* （网络）在线的，网上的
operate	*v.* 1. 作业，工作，运转，运行　　2. 操作，操纵，控制，使用（机器等） 3. 经营，管理　　4. （对……）动手术
operation	*n.* 1. [U] 操作，运转　　2. [C] 经营，业务　　3. [U] 运算　　4. [C] 手术
operator	*n.* [C] 1. 操作员　　2. 话务行报务员
opinion	*n.* [U/C] 意见，看法，主张
opponent	*n.* [C] 敌手，对手，反对者
opportunity	*n.* [U/C] 机会，时机
oppose	*v.* 反对，反抗
opposite	*prep. & adv.* 在对面　　*adj.* 1. 对面的　　2. 相反的，对立的 *n.* [C] 对立面，对立物
optimal	*adj.* 最适宜的，最理想的
oral	*adj.* 1. 口头的　　2. 口的，口用的
order	*n.* 1. 命令，嘱咐　　2. 订购，订货　　3. 次序，顺序 4. 整齐，有条理　　5. 治安，有秩序 *v.* 1. 命令，嘱咐　　2. 定购，点（饭菜等）
ordinary	*adj.* 通常的，普通的平庸的，平淡的
organization	*n.* (also organisation) [C] 1. 团体，机构　　2. 组织

· 186 ·

organize	v. (also organise) 组织
orient	n. 东方　adj. 1. 东方的　2. 珍贵的　v. 定方位
orientation	n. 东方，方位
origin	n. 1. 起源，来源，起因　2. [P] 出身，血统
original	adj. 1. 起初的，原来的　2. 独创的，新颖的
outcome	n. [U] 结果
outlet	n. [C] 1. 出路，出口　2. 电源插座
outline	n. [C] 1. 外形，轮廓，略图　2. 大纲，概要 v. 1. 描……的外形　2. 概述
outlook	n. [C] 1. 观点，见解　2. 展望，前景
output	n. [C] 1. 产量　2. 输出，输出功率
outstanding	adj. 突出的，杰出的，显著的
overcome	v. (overcame, overcome) 战胜，克服
overload	n. 超载，过载　v. 使超载
overlook	v. 1. 俯瞰，眺望　2. 看漏，忽略　3. 宽容
oversea(s)	adv. 在（或向）海外，在（或向）国外 adj. （在）海外的，（在）国外的
overweight	adj. 超重
owe	v. 1. 欠　2. 应该把……归功于，应感激
own	adj. 自己的　v. 有，拥有
owner	n. [C] 物主，所有人
ownership	n. [U] 所有（权），所有制

P

pace	n. [C] （一）步，步速
Pacific	adj. [P-] 太平洋的　n. [the P-] 太平洋
pack	v. 1. 捆扎，把……打包　2. 使……挤在一起，塞满　n. [C] 包，小盒
package	n. [C] 包裹，包装
packet	v. 打包；打行李　n. [C] 包；捆；行李
pain	n. 1. 痛，疼痛　2. 痛苦，悲痛　3. [P] 辛苦，苦心
paint	n. [U] 油漆，颜料　v. 1. 油漆　2. 绘画
painter	n. [C] 1. 画家　2. 油漆匠
painting	n. [C] （一幅）画　[U] 绘画，绘画艺术
pale	adj. 1. 苍白的，灰白的　2. 浅色的，淡的
palm	n. [C] 手掌，掌状物
pamphlet	n. 小册子
panel	n. [C] 1. 专门小组　2. 面，板　3. 控制板，仪表盘
paragraph	n. [C] （文章的）段落，节
parallel	n. [C] 1. 可相比拟的事物，相似处　2. 平行线，平行面 adj. 平行的，类似的
parameter	n. [C] 参数
parcel	n. [C] 包裹，包装

parliament	*n.* [C] 议会，国会
participant	*n.* [C] 参与者，参加者
participate	*v.* 参与，参加
particular	*adj.* 1. 特定的，某一的　2. 特殊的，特别的，特有的 3.（过分）讲究的，挑剔的　*n.* [常 P] 详情，细目
particularly	*adv.* 特别，尤其
partly	*adv.* 在一定程度上，部分地，不完全地
partner	*n.* [C] 1. 伙伴，同伙　2. 合伙人，股东　3. 搭档，同伴　4. 配偶
passenger	*n.* [C] 乘客，旅客
passion	*n.* [U/C] 1. 激情，热情　2. 酷爱
passive	*adj.* 被动的，消极的
passport	*n.* [C] 护照
patience	*n.* [U] 忍耐，耐心
patient	*adj.* 忍耐的，有耐心的　*n.* 病人
pattern	*n.* [C] 1. 型，模式，样式　2. 花样，图案
pause	*v. & n.* 暂停，中止
pay	*v.* 1. 付款，支付，交纳　2. 付出代价 3. 给予（注意等），致以（问候等）　*n.* 工资，薪金
payment	*n.* [U/C] 1. 支付，付款　2. 支付的款项
peace	*n.* [U] 1. 平静，安宁　2. 和平，和谐
pear	*n.* [C] 梨
peculiar	*adj.* 1. 奇怪的，古怪的　2. 特殊的，独特的
perceive	*v.* 1. 感觉，感知　2. 认识到，意识到，理解
percent	*n.*（单复同）百分之一
perfect	*adj.* 1. 完美的，完满的，完好的　2. 完全的，十足的 *v.* 使完美，改善
perform	*v.* 1. 做，履行　2. 演出，表演
performance	*n.* [C] 演出，表演　[U] 履行，执行　[U] 工作情况，表现
period	*n.* [C] 1.（一段）时间，时期，时代　2. 学时，课时　3. 句号，句点
permanent	*adj.* 永久（性）的，固定（性）的
permissible	*adj.* 可允许的，可原谅的
permission	*n.* [U] 允许，许可，准许
permit	*v.*（permitted，permitted）允许，许可，准许　*n.* 许可证，执照
persist	*v.* 1.（in）坚持不懈，执意　2. 持续，存留
personal	*adj.* 1. 个人的，私人的　2. 亲自的　3. 针对个人的，有关私人的
personnel	*n.* [总称] 人员，员工
persuade	*v.* 1. 说服，劝服　2. 使相信
petrol	*n.* [U] [英] 汽油
phase	*n.* [C] 1. 阶段，时期　2. 面，方面
phenomenon	*n.* [P phenomena] [C] 现象，迹象
philosopher	*n.* [C] 哲学家
philosophy	*n.* [U] 1. 哲学，人生哲学　2. 主旨

photograph/photo	*n.* [C] 照片，相片
phrase	*n.* [C] 短语，词组，用语
physical	*adj.* 1. 身体的，肉体的 2. 物理（学）的 3. 物质的，有形的 4. 自然的，按自然规律的
physics	*n.* （无复数）物理，物理学
pick	*v.* 1. 挑选，选择 2. 采摘
picnic	*n.* [C] 郊游野餐，户外用餐
pile	*n.* [C] 一堆，一叠 *v.* （把……）堆积
pill	*n.* [C] 药丸
pilot	*n.* [C] 1. 飞行员 2. 引航员，舵手 *v.* 1. 驾驶（飞机等） 2. 为（船舶）引航
pioneer	*n.* [C] 1. 先驱者 2. 开拓者
plan	*n.* [C] 1. 计划，打算 2. 平面图，示意图 *v.* （planned，planned）计划，给……制订计划
plastic	*n.* [常 P] 塑料，塑料制品 *adj.* 塑料（制）的，可塑的
plate	*n.* [C] 1. 盆子，盘子 2. 平板，薄板 *v.* 覆镀
platform	*n.* [C] 1. 台，平台，讲台 2. 站台，月台
pleasant	*adj.* 令人愉快的，讨人喜欢的
please	*adv.* 请 *v.* 使高兴，使满意
pleased	*adj.* 高兴的，愉快的
pleasure	*n.* [U] 愉快，满足 [C] 乐事，乐趣
plentiful	*adj.* 丰富的，多的
plenty	*n.* 丰富，大量
plot	*n.* [C] 1. （秘密）计划，密谋 2. 情节 3. 小块地皮，小块土地 *v.* （plotted，plotted）1. 密谋，计划 2. 绘制，标绘
poem	*n.* 诗
poet	*n.* 诗人
point	*n.* [C] 1. 尖，尖端 2. 点，小数点 3. 条款，细目 4. 分数，得分 5. 要点，论点，观点 *v.* （at，to）指，指向，表明
poison	*n.* [U/C] 毒物，毒药 *v.* 放毒，毒害
pole	*n.* [C] 1. 柱，杆 2. 地极，磁极，电极
police	*n.* （单复同）警察局，警察
policeman	*n.* [P policemen] [C] 警察
policy	*n.* [U/C] 1. 政策，方针 2. 保险单
polish	*v.* 1. 磨光，擦亮 2. 使优美，润饰 *n.* 擦光剂，上光蜡
polite	*adj.* 1. 有礼貌的，客气的 2. 有教养的，文雅的
political	*adj.* 政治的
politics	*n.* 1. （用作单数）政治，政治学 2. （用作复数）政纲，政见
poll	*n.* [C] 1. 民意测验 2. 投票 3. （选票）计数
pollute	*v.* 弄脏，污染
pollution	*n.* [U] 污染

pond	n. [C] 池塘
pool	n. [C] 1. 水池　　2. 合资经营，联营　　v. 合资经营，联营
popular	adj. 1. 流行的，通俗的，大众的　　2. 广受欢迎的，有名的
population	n. [U/C] 人口
port	n. [C] 港口
portable	adj. 便于携带的，手提式的，轻便的
portion	n. [C] 一部分，一份
position	n. [C] 1. 位置　　2. 职位，职务　　3. 姿势，姿态　　4. 见解，立场
positive	adj. 1. 确实的，有事实根据的　　2. 确信的，有把握的　　3. 明确的，断然的　　4. 肯定的，表示赞成的　　5. 正（极）的，阳性的
possess	v. 占有，拥有
possibility	n. [U] 可能性　　[C] 可能发生的事
possible	adj. 1. 可能的，做得到的　　2. 合理的，可允许的
possibly	adv. 尽可能地，也许
post	v. 1. 贴出　　2. 宣布，公告　　3. 投寄，邮寄　　n. [C] 1. （支）柱，标杆　　2. 邮政　　3. 职位，岗位
postage	n. [U] 邮资
postcard	n. [C] 明信片
poster	n. [C] 海报，标语
postman	n. [P postmen] [C] 邮递员
postpone	v. 推迟，延期
potential	adj. 潜在的，可能的　　n. [U] 潜力，潜能
pound	n. [C] 1. 磅　　2. 英镑　　v. 1. （连续）猛击，（猛烈）敲打　　2. 捣碎
pour	v. 1. 灌，倒，注　　2. 倾斜，流出
poverty	n. [U] 贫穷，贫困
power	n. [U/C] 1. 权力，政权　　2. 力量，能力　　3. 功率　　4. 动力，电力　　5. [数学] 幂，乘方
powerful	adj. 强大的，有力的，有权的
practical	adj. 实际的，实用的
practice	n. (also practise) [U] 1. 练习，实习　　2. 实践，实际　　3. 业务，开业
praise	v. 赞扬，歌颂，表扬，称赞　　n. 1. [U] 称赞，赞美　　2. [C] 赞美的话
pray	v. 1. 请求，恳求　　2. 祈祷，祈求
precaution	n. [U] 预防，防备，警惕
preceding	adj. 在先的，在前的，前面的
precious	adj. 珍贵的，贵重的
precise	adj. 精确的，准确的
predetermine	v. 预先决定
predict	v. 预言，预测
prefer	v. 更喜欢，宁愿
preference	n. (for, to) [C] 1. 更加喜爱，偏爱　　2. 优先（权）

prejudice	*n.* [U/C] 偏见，成见
preliminary	*adj.* 预备的，初步的
prepare	*v.* 准备，预备
preposition	*n.* [C] 介词
prescribe	*v.* 指示；开处方
prescription	*n.* [C] 1. 指示　　2. 处方
presence	*n.* [U] 1. 出席，在场　　2.（某物的）存在
present	*adj.* 1. 出席的，到场的　　2. 现在的，目前的
	n. 1. 现在，目前　　2. 礼物，赠品
	v. 1.（赠送），呈献　　2. 介绍，陈述　　3. 提出，呈交
preserve	*v.* 1. 保护，维持　　2. 保存，保藏　　3. 腌制
president	*n.* [C] 总统，校长，会长，主席
press	*v.* 1. 压，按　　2. 压榨，压迫　　3. 催促，逼迫
	n. [U/C] 1. 报刊，出版社，通讯社　　2. 压榨机　　3. 压，按
pretend	*v.* 假装，装扮
pretty	*adj.* 漂亮的，秀丽的　　*adv.* 相当地，颇
prevail	*v.* 流行，盛行
prevent	*v.* 预防，防止
previous	*adj.* 先，前，以前的
price	*n.* [C] 1. 价格，价钱　　2. 代价　　*v.* 标价，定价
pride	*n.* 1. 自豪，得意　　2. 引以为自豪的人或物　　3. 自满，骄傲，傲慢
	v. 使自豪，使自夸
primary	*adj.* 1. 最初的，初级的　　2. 首要的，主要的，基本的
prime	*adj.* 1. 首要的，主要的　　2. 最好的，第一流的
	n. [U] 1. 青春，壮年　　2. 全盛时期
primitive	*adj.* 1. 原始的，早期的　　2. 简单的，粗糙的
principal	*adj.* 最重要的，主要的　　*n.* [C] 1. 负责人，校长　　2. 资本，本金
principle	*n.* [C] 原理，原则
print	*v.* 1. 印刷，出版　　2. 用印刷体写
	n. [U/C] 1. 印刷，印刷品　　2. 印刷字体
prior	*adj.* 1.（时间、顺序）在前的，在先的　　2. 比……重要的，优先的
priority	*n.* [U] 1. 优先　　2. 在前
prison	*n.* [C] 监狱
prisoner	*n.* [C] 囚徒
private	*adj.* 1. 私人的，个人的　　2. 秘密的，私下的
prize	*n.* [C] 鉴赏，奖金，奖品　　*v.* 珍视，珍惜
probably	*adv.* 大概，或许，很可能
problem	*n.* [C] 1. 问题，疑难问题　　2. 思考题，讨论题
procedure	*n.* [U/C] 程序，手续，步骤
proceed	*v.* 进行，继续下去
process	*n.* [U/C] 1. 过程，进程　　2. 工序，制作法　　3. 工艺　　*v.* 加工，处理
procession	*n.* [C] 队伍，队列

produce	*v.* 1. 生产，制造，产生　　2. 显示，出示　　*n.* [U] 产品，农产品
product	*n.* [C] 1. 产品，产物　　2. 乘积
production	*n.* [U] 生产，产量　　[C] 产品，作品
profession	*n.* [C] 职业
professional	*adj.* 职业的，专业的　　*n.* [C] 自由职业者，专业人员
professor	*n.* [C] 教授
proficient	*adj.* 精通的，熟练的
profit	*n.* [U/C] 利润，收益，益处　　*v.* 1. 有益于，有利于　　2. (by, from) 得到，获益
profitable	*adj.* 1. 可赚钱的　　2. 有好处的，有益的
programme	*n.* [C] 1. 节目，节目单　　2. 计划，规划，大纲　　3. 程序　　*v.* 编制程序
progress	*v. & n.* 前进，进步，紧张
progressive	*adj.* 1. 进步的，先进的　　2. 前进的
prohibit	*v.* 禁止，不准
project	*n.* [C] 1. 方案，计划　　2. 工程　　3. 项目　　*v.* 1. 投射，放映　　2. （使）伸出　　3. 设计，规划
promise	*v.* 1. 允许，允诺，答应　　2. 有……可能，有希望　　*n.* [C] 承诺，诺言　　[U] 希望，出息
promote	*v.* 1. 促进，发扬　　2. 提升，提拔　　3. 增进，助长
prompt	*v.* 促使，推动　　*adj.* 敏捷的，及时的，迅速的
pronoun	*n.* 代（名）词
pronounce	*v.* 1. 发音　　2. 宣布，宣判
pronunciation	*n.* [U/C] 发音，发音方法
proof	*n.* 1. [U/C] 证据，证明　　2. 校样，样张
proper	*adj.* 1. 适合的，恰当的　　2. 合乎体统的，正当的　　3. 固有的，特有的
property	*n.* [U] 财产，资产，所有物　　[C] 性质，特性
proportion	*n.* 1. [U/C] 比例　　2. 部分，份儿　　3. 均衡，相称
proposal	*n.* [U/C] 提议，建议
propose	*v.* 1. 提议，建议　　2. 提名，推荐
prospect	*n.* [U/C] 前景，展望，前途
prospectus	*n.* 1. [C] 招生简章　　2. 厂商介绍
prosperity	*n.* [U] 兴旺，繁荣
prosperous	*adj.* 繁荣的，昌盛的
protect	*v.* 保护，保卫
protest	*n. & v.* 抗议，反对
proud	*adj.* 1. 骄傲的，妄自尊大的　　2. (of) 自豪的，得意的
prove	*v.* 1. 证明，证实　　2. 检验，鉴定　　3. 结果是，原来是
provide	*v.* (with, for) 供给，提供
provided	*conj.* 假如，若是
province	*n.* [C] 1. 省　　2. 领域，范围
provision	*n.* 1. 供应　　2. (for, against) 准备，预备　　3. 条款，规定

192

	4. [P] 给养，口粮
psychological	*adj.* 心理的，心理学的
public	*n.* 公众，民众
	adj. 1. 公共的，公用的　　2. 公众（事务）的　　3. 公开的，公然的
publication	*n.* [U/C] 1. 出版物　　2. 出版，发行　　3. 公布，发表
publish	*v.* 1. 出版，刊印　　2. 公布，发表
pull	*v. & n.* 拉，拖　　*n.* 拉力，牵引力
punctual	*adj.* 准时的，正点的
punish	*v.* 惩罚，处罚
pupil	*n.* [C] 1. 学生，小学生　　2. 瞳孔
purchase	*v.* 买，购买　　*n.* [C] 购买的物品
pure	*adj.* 1. 纯的，纯洁的　　2. 完全的，十足的
purpose	*n.* [U/C] 1. 目的，意图　　2. 用途，效果
purse	*n.* [C] 钱包
pursue	*v.* 1. 追赶，追踪　　2. 追求，从事
puzzle	*v.* （使）迷惑，（使）为难　　*n.* [C] 1. 难题，谜　　2. 迷惑

Q

qualified	*adj.* 合格的
qualify	*v.* (qualified, qualified) 1. （使）具有资格，证明合格　　2. 限制，限定
quality	*n.* [U/C] 质量，品质，特性
quantity	*n.* [U] 量，数量　　[U/C] 大量
quarantine	*n.* 检疫
quarrel	*v.* 争吵，争论　　*n.* [C] 争吵，口角
quarter	*n.* [C] 1. 四分之一　　2. 季，季度　　3. 一刻钟　　4. [P] 居住区
quit	*v.* (quitted, quitted; quit, quit) 1. 离开，退出　　2. 停止，放弃，辞职

R

race	*n.* 1. [C] （速度上的）比赛　　2. 人种，种族
	v. 1. 全速行进　　2. （使）比赛速度，竞赛
radar	*n.* [C] 雷达
raise	*v.* 1. 举起，提升，提高　　2. 增加　　3. 饲养，养育
	4. 引起，惹起　　5. 提出，发起
random	*adj.* 1. 随便的　　2. 无目的的
range	*n.* 1. 幅度，范围　　2. 距离　　3. 一系列　　4. （山）脉
	v. 1. 排列成行　　2. 延伸，绵延　　3. （在某范围内）变动，变化
rank	*n.* [C] 1. 军衔　　2. 地位，社会阶层　　3. 排，横列
	v. 1. 分等级，把……分类　　2. 列入
rapid	*adj.* 快的，迅速的
rarely	*adj.* 1. 稀有的，难得的，珍奇的　　2. 稀薄的，稀疏的
rate	*n.* 1. 率，速度，比率　　2. 等级　　3. 价格，费
	v. 1. 估价　　2. 评级，评价

ratio	*n.* [C] 比，比率
raw	*adj.* 1. 未煮过的，生的　　2. 未加工过的　　3. 神速无知的，未经训练的
ray	*n.* [C] 光线
reach	*v.* 1. 抵达，达到　　2. 伸手够到，触到　　*n.* 能达到的范围
react	*v.* 1. 反应，起作用　　2. 反动，起反作用
readily	*adv.* 容易地
realistic	*adj.* 现实（主义）的
reality	*n.* [U] 现实，实际　　[C] 真实
realize	*v.* (also realise) 1. 认识到，体会到　　2. 实现
reasonable	*adj.* 1. 合理的，正当的　　2. 通情达理的，讲道理的　　3. 公道的，公平的
recall	*v.* 1. 回忆，回想　　2. 撤销，收回
receipt	*n.* [C] 收据，收条　　[U] 收到，接到
receive	*v.* 1. 收到，接到　　2. 遭受，受到　　3. 接待，接见
recent	*adj.* 新近的，近来的
recently	*adv.* 最近，新近
reception	*n.* 1. [U]（旅游的）接待处　　2. 接待　　3. 招待会　　4. 接收，接受，接收效果
receptionist	*n.* [C] 招待员
recognition	*n.* [U] 1. 认出，识别　　2. 承认
recognize	*v.* (also recognise) 1. 认出，识别　　2. 承认
recommend	*v.* 1. 推荐，介绍　　2. 劝告，建议
recommendation	*n.* 1. 推荐　　2. 建议，劝告
record	*n.* 1. 记录，记载　　2. 最高纪录，最佳成绩　　3. 履历，经历　　4. 唱片 *v.* 1. 记录，登记　　2. 录音
recorder	*n.* 1. 记录员　　2. 录音机
recover	*v.* 1. 收回，挽回　　2. 重新获得，重新找到　　3. 恢复，痊愈
reduce	*v.* 1. 减少，缩小　　2. 简化，还原
refer	*v.* (referred, referred) 参考，查阅，查询
reference	*n.* [U/C] 1. 提及，涉及　　2. 参考，参考书目　　3. 证明书（或人），推荐信（或人）
refine	*v.* 精炼，精制，提纯
reflect	*v.* 1. 反射　　2. 反映，表现　　3. 反省，细想，考虑
reflection	*n.* [C] 映像，倒影　　[U] 反省，沉思
reform	*n. & v.* 改革，改造，改良
refresh	*v.* （使）精神振作，（使）精力恢复
refreshment	*n.* [P] 点心，饮料
refrigerator	*n.* (also fridge) [C] 冰箱，冷藏库，冷冻机
refundable	*adj.* 可归还的，可偿还的
refuse	*v.* 拒绝，谢绝
regard	*v.* 1. 把……看作为，认为　　2. 尊重　　3. 考虑，注重，留意 *n.* [P] 敬意，致意，问候
regardless	*adj.* 不留心的，不注意的　　*adv.* 无论如何，不管怎样

region	n. [C] 1. 地区，区域 2. 范围
register	n. [C] 登记，注册 v. 1. 登记，注册 2. 把（邮件）挂号
regret	v. (regretted, regretted) & n. 遗憾，懊悔，抱歉
regular	adj. 1. 有规律的，有规则的 2. 整齐的，匀称的 3. 正规的，正式的 4. 经常的，习惯性的
regulate	v. 1. 使有条理，整理 2. 调整，调节
regulation	n. [C] 规章，规则 [U] 管理，控制 [U] 调整，调节
reinforce	v. 增强
reject	v. 1. 拒绝，排斥，抵制，驳回 2. 舍弃 3. 退掉
relate	v. 1. 叙述，讲述 2. 联系，关联
relation	n. 1. 关系，联系 2. 亲属，亲戚
relative	adj.（无比较等级）1. 相对的，比较的 2. 有关系的，相关的 n. 亲属，亲戚
relax	v.（使）松弛，放松
release	v. 1. 释放，解放 2. 发表，发行
reliable	adj. 可靠的
relief	n. [U] 1.（痛苦等的）减轻，解除 2. 救援，救济
relieve	v. 1. 减轻，解除 2. 救济，救援
religion	n. [U/C] 宗教，信仰
religious	adj. 1. 宗教的 2. 信宗教的，虔诚的
reluctant	adj. 不情愿的，勉强的
rely	v.（relied, relied）依靠，依赖
remain	v. 1. 剩下，余留 2. 留待，尚须 3. 仍然是，依旧是 n. [常 P] 1. 残余，余额 2. 遗迹
remark	n. [C] 评语，议论，意见 v. 1.（on）评论，谈论 2. 注意到，察觉
remarkable	adj. 1. 显著的，值得注意的 2. 异常的，非凡的
remedy	n. [C] 1. 补救方法，治疗措施 2. 药品 v. 1. 纠正，补救 2. 治疗，医治
remember	v. 1. 记住，记得 2. 代向……致意，代向……问好
remind	v.（of）提醒，使想到
remote	adj. 遥远的，偏僻的，疏远的
remove	v. 1. 排除，清除，去掉 2. 搬迁，移动，运走
renew	v. 1. 更新，续（约） 2. 重新开始，重建
rent	v. 租，租赁 n. [U/C] 租金
replace	v. 1. 替换，取代 2. 把……放回原处
reply	v. & n. 回答，答复
represent	v. 1. 描述，表示 2. 代表，代理 3. 象征，体现
representative	n. [C] 代表，代理人 adj. 典型的，有代表性的
republic	n. [C] 共和国
reputation	n. [U/C] 名气，名声，名望
request	v. & n. 请求，要求
require	v. 1. 需要 2. 要求，命令

rescue	*v.* & *n.* 营救，援救
research	*n.* & *v.* 研究，调查
resemble	*v.* 像，类似
reserve	*v.* 1. 保留，储备　　2. 预定，预约 *n.* ［U/C］储备（物），储藏量，储备金
reset	*v.*（reset, reset）重放，重调
residence	*n.* ［C］住宅，住处
resident	*n.* ［C］居民，定居者　　*adj.* 居住的
resist	*v.* 1. 抵抗，反抗　　2. 忍住，抵制
resolution	*n.* ［U/C］1. 决心，决定　　2. 坚定，刚毅　　3. 解决
resort	*n.* ［C］胜地
resource	*n.* 1. ［P］资源，财力　　2. 应对办法，对策
respect	*v.* 尊敬，尊重　　*n.* 1. 尊敬，尊重　　2. ［P］敬意，问候
respective	*adj.* 各自的，各个的
respectively	*adv.* 1. 个别地　　2. 各自地
respond	*v.* 1. 回答，答复　　2. 响应，反应
response	*n.* ［U/C］1. 回答，答复　　2. 反应，响应
responsibility	*n.* ［U］责任，责任心　　［C］职责，义务
responsible	*adj.* 1. 需负责任的，承担责任的　　2. 有责任感的，负责可靠的 　　3. 责任重大的，重要的
restaurant	*n.* ［C］餐馆，饭店
restrain	*v.*（from）1. 抑制，遏止　　2. 阻止，控制
restrict	*v.* 限制，约束
result	*n.* ［U/C］结果，成果，成绩 *v.* 1. 导致，结果是　　2. 起因于，因……而造成
resume	*v.*（中断后）重新开始，恢复　　*n.* 简历
retain	*v.* 保持，保留
retire	*v.* 1. 退休　　2. 退却，撤退　　3. 就寝
retreat	*v.* 撤退，退却
reveal	*v.* 1. 展现，显示，揭示　　2. 揭露，泄露，透漏
reverse	*v.* 颠倒，倒转　　*n.* ［U］相反，反转，颠倒　　［C］背面，反面 *adj.* 相反的，倒转的
review	*n.* ［U/C］1. 评论　　2. 回顾　　3. 复习　　*v.* 1. 回顾　　2. 复习
revise	*v.* 1. 修订，订正，校正　　2. 复习
revolution	*n.* 革命
revolutionary	*adj.* 1. 革命的　　2. 大变革的　　*n.* 革命者
reward	*n.* ［C］报酬，赏金，奖赏　　*v.* 1. 酬劳，奖赏　　2. 报答
ridiculous	*adj.* 可笑的，荒谬的
ripe	*adj.* 1. 熟的，成熟的　　2. 时机成熟的
rise	*v.* 1. 升起，上升　　2. 起立，起床　　3. 上涨，增高 *n.* 1. 上涨，增高　　2. 起源，发生
risk	*n.* 冒……的危险　　*n.* ［U/C］冒险，风险

rival	*n.* [C] 竞争对手，敌手　　*adj.* 竞争的　　*v.* 与……竞争
roast	*v.* 烤，炙，烘
rob	*v.* (robbed, robbed) 1. 抢劫，盗取　　2. 非法剥夺
robot	*n.* [C] 机器人
roll	*v.* 1. 滚动，滚落，翻落　　2. （使）摇摆，（使）摇晃　　3. 碾，轧
	n. [C] 1. 一卷，卷状物　　2. 面包卷　　3. 名单，名册
rough	*adj.* 1. 粗糙的　　2. 粗略的，大致的　　3. 粗野的，粗暴的
route	*n.* [C] 路，路线
routine	*adj.* 例行的，日常的，常规的
	n. [C/U] 例行公事，惯例，惯常的程序
royal	*adj.* （无比较等级）王室的，皇家的
rubbish	*n.* [U] 1. 垃圾，废物　　2. 废话
rude	*adj.* 1. 粗鲁的，不礼貌的　　2. 粗糙的，粗陋的
ruin	*v.* （被）毁灭，（被）毁坏
	n. 1. [U] 毁灭，灭亡，没落　　2. [P] 废墟，遗址
rural	*adj.* 农村的

S

safe	*adj.* 1. 安全的，平安的　　2. 牢靠的，可靠的　　*n.* 保险箱
safety	*n.* 1. 安全，保险　　2. 安全设备，保险设置
salary	*n.* 薪金，薪水
sale	*n.* 1. 出卖，卖　　2. 贱卖，廉价出售　　3. [P] 销售额
salesman	*n.* 售货员，推销员
sample	*n.* 样品，式样，实例，标本　　*v.* 抽样（试验或调查）
satisfaction	*n.* 1. 满足，满意　　2. 乐事，快事
satisfactory	*adj.* 令人满意的
satisfy	*v.* 使满意
save	*v.* 1. 救，满足　　2. 储蓄，保存，保留　　3. 节省，节约，省去
saving	*n.* 1. 节省，节约　　2. [P] 储蓄金，存款
scale	*n.* 1. 刻度，标度　　2. [P] 天平，磅秤　　3. 比例（尺）　　4. 规模范围
scan	*v.* (scanned, scanned) 1. 细看，审视　　2. 扫描　　3. 浏览
scarce	*adj.* 1. 缺乏的，不足的　　2. 稀少的，罕见的
scarcely	*adv.* 几乎不，简直没有，勉强
scare	*n.* 惊恐，恐慌　　*v.* 惊吓，受惊，使恐惧
scatter	*v.* 1. 散开，驱散　　2. 撒，撒播
scenery	*n.* 1. 风景，景色　　2. 舞台布景
scenic	*adj.* 景色好的
schedule	*n.* 时间表，日程安排表　　*v.* 安排，排定
scheme	*n.* 1. 计划，方案　　2. 阴谋　　3. 系统，组合，配合
scholarship	*n.* 1. 奖学金　　2. 学问，学识
science	*n.* 1. 科学　　2. 学科
scientific	*adj.* 科学（上）的，科学性的

scientist	n. 科学家
search	v. & n. 搜索，寻找，探查
secret	adj. 秘密的，机密的　　n. 秘密
secretary	n. 1. 秘书　　2. 书记　　3. 部长，大臣
section	n. 1. 章节　　2. 部分　　3. 部门，科　　4. 截面，剖面
secure	adj. 安全的，牢固的，可靠的　　v. 使安全，保全
security	n. 1. 安全　　2. 担保，抵押
seek	v.（sought，sought）寻找，探索，追求
select	v. 选择，挑选　　adj. 精选的，挑选出来的
selection	n. 1. 选择，挑选　　2. 选集，精品选
selective	adj. 选择的，有选择能力的
seminar	n. 学术讨论会
senior	adj. 1. 较年长的，年高的　　2. 资格较老的，地位较高的，高年级的
sense	n. 1. 感官，官能　　2. 感觉　　3. 观念，意识，辨识力　　4. 意义，意思　　v. 感觉到，意识到
sensible	adj. 明智的，合情合理的
sensitive	adj. 1.（to）敏感的，神经过敏的　　2. 灵敏的
separate	adj. 分离的，分开的　　v. 分离，分开
sequence	n. 1. 连续，接续，一连串　　2. 次序，顺序
series	n. 1. 一系列，连续　　2. 系列（丛书，产品）
serious	adj. 1. 严肃的，庄重的　　2. 重大的，严重的，危急的　　3. 认真的，当真的
servant	n. 仆人
serve	v. 1. 服务，尽责　　2. 招待，伺候，端上（食物等）
service	n. 1. 服务，效劳，帮助，用处　　2. 公共设施，（公共设施的）运转　　3. 维修，保养　　4. 政府部门，服务性事业　　v. 维修，保养
settle	v. 1. 安放，安顿　　2. 定居　　3. 解决，调停　　4. 安排，料理
settlement	n. 1. 解决，协议　　2. 居留地
severe	adj.（severer, severest）1. 严厉的，严格的　　2. 严峻的，艰难的
shade	n. 1. 荫，阴暗　　2. 遮光物，罩　　v. 遮蔽，遮光
shadow	n. 1. 阴影，荫，影子　　2. 暗处
shame	n. 1. 羞耻，羞愧　　2. 耻辱，丢脸　　3. 带来耻辱的人（或事物），倒霉的事
share	v. 1. 分配，均分　　2. 分享，分担，共有　　n. 1. 一份，份额　　2. 股东
shareholder	n. 股东
shelter	n. 1. 掩蔽处，躲避处　　2. 掩蔽，保护　　v. 掩蔽，躲避，庇护
shift	v. 1. 替换，改变　　2. 移动，转移　　n. 1. 替换，转变　　2. 班，轮班
shipment	n. 装船，装运
shortage	n. 不足，缺少
shortcoming	n. 短处，缺点
shortly	adv. 1. 立刻，不久　　2. 简短地，简慢地

shower	*n.* 1. 阵雨，暴雨　　2. 淋浴，淋浴器　　3. 一阵，一大批
sightseeing	*n.* 观光，游览
sign	*n.* 1. 标记，符号，（招）牌　　2. 踪迹，征召，迹象
	v. 签（名），署（名）
signal	*n.* 信号，暗号　　*v.* 发信号，用信号联系
signature	*n.* 签名，署名，签字
significance	*n.* 1. 意思，含义　　2. 重要性，重大
significant	*adj.* 1. 相当数量的，不可忽略的　　2. 重要的，意义重大的
	3. 意味深长的
similar	*adj.* 相似的，类似的
simultaneous	*adj.* 同时的
sincere	*adj.* （sincerer, sincerest）诚实的，真诚的
sincerely	*adv.* 由衷地，真心地
site	*n.* 场所，地点
situation	*n.* 1. 形式，局面　　2. 处境，状况　　3. 位置，地点
sketch	*n.* 1. 描述，速写　　2. 略图，草图　　3. 概述，纲要
	v. 素描，速写，画草图
skill	*n.* 1. 技能，技巧，技艺　　2. 熟练，能力
skilled	*adj.* 熟练的，有本领的
skillful	*adj.* 有技术的，娴熟的
smooth	*adj.* 1. 光滑的，平滑的，平整的　　2. 平稳的，平静的，顺利的
	3. 流畅的，和谐悦目的
smuggle	*v.* 走私
snack	*n.* 1. 小吃　　2. 快餐
social	*adj.* 1. 社会的　　2. 交际的，社交的
society	*n.* 1. 社会，（社会）阶层　　2. 社团，协会　　3. 社交界
software	*n.* 软件
soil	*n.* 泥土，土壤　　*v.* 弄脏，（使）变脏
sole	*adj.* 单独的，唯一的，仅有的
solid	*adj.* 1. 固体的　　2. 实心的　　3. 结实的，牢固的，可靠的　　*n.* 固体
solution	*n.* 1. 解答，解决（办法）　　2. 溶解，溶液
solve	*v.* 解决，解答
sophisticated	*adj.* 1. 老于世故的，老练的　　2. 精密的，尖端的
sorrow	*n.* 悲哀，悲痛
sort	*n.* 种类，类别，品种　　*v.* 把……分类，整理
source	*n.* 1. 源，根源，源头　　2. 来源，出处
southern	*adj.* 南方的，南部的
souvenir	*n.* 纪念品
spacecraft	*n.* 宇宙飞船
span	*n.* 1. 一段时间　　2. 跨距，跨度
special	*adj.* 特殊的，专门的
specialist	*n.* 专家

specialize	v. 1. 专政，专门从事 2. 专门化，专营
specific	adj. 1. 明确，具体的 2. 特定的，特有的
specification	n. 1. 详细说明 2. ［常 P］规格，规范
specimen	n. 样本，样品，标本
spectator	n. 观众
speech	n. 1. 演说，讲话 2. 说话，言语
sphere	n. 1. 球（体） 2. 范围，领域
spill	v.（split, split）（使）溢出，（使）洒落
spirit	n. 1. 精神，心灵 2. 勇气，志气 3.［P］情绪，心情 4.［P］酒精，烈酒
splendid	adj. 1. 灿烂的，壮丽的，辉煌的 2. 极好的
split	v.（split, split）1. 切开，劈开，撕裂 2. 分裂，分离
spoil	v.（spoilt, spoilt/spoiled, spoiled）1. 损坏，破坏 2. 宠坏，溺爱
sponsor	v. 1. 发起，主办 2. 倡议，赞助 n. 发起者，主办者
spot	n. 1. 斑点，污渍 2. 地点，场所 v. 认出，发现
spread	v.（spread, spread）& n. 1. 张开，伸展，扩展 2. 散布，传播，蔓延
square	n. 1. 正方形，方块 2. 广场 adj. 1. 正方形的，方的 2. 平方的 v. 求平方，求……的面积
stable	adj. 稳定的，稳固的，固定的 n. 厩，牛（或羊）棚
staff	n. 全体职员，全体人员. 为……配备人员
stage	n. 1. 舞台，戏剧 2. 阶段，时期
standard	n. 标准，规格，水平 adj. 标准的
starve	v. 1.（使）挨饿，（使）饿死 2. 渴望
state	n. 1. 状态，情况 2. 国家 3. 州 v. 陈述，说明
statement	n. 1. 说明，声明 2. 报单
station	n.（车）站，所，局
statistics	n. 1. 统计（学） 2. 统计数字
statue	n. 塑像，雕像
status	n. 地位，身份
steep	adj. 陡峭的，陡直的
stick	n. 棍，棒，手杖 v.（stuck, stuck）1. 刺，戳，扎 2. 粘贴，粘住，钉住
stiff	adj. 1. 硬的，僵直的 2. 拘谨的，生硬的
stimulate	v. 刺激，激励
stipulate	v. 记明，规定
stir	v. 1. 搅拌，搅动 2. 微动，移动 3. 激励，打动 4. 惊动，搅乱 5. 引起，煽动
stock	n. 1. 备料，库存，现货 2. 股票，公债 v. 储备，贮存
stove	n.［C］炉子，火炉
straight	adj. 1. 直的，挺直的 2. 整齐的，有条理的 3. 正直的，坦率的 adv. 直接，径直
strategy	n. 战略，策略

strength	*n.* 力量，实力
strengthen	*v.* 加强，巩固
stress	*n.* 1. 压力，紧张，应力　2. 着重，强调　3. 重音　*v.* 强调，着重
stretch	*v.* 拉伸，伸展　*n.* 伸展，扩张
strict	*adj.* 1. 严格的，严厉的　2. 严谨的，精确的
structure	*n.* 结构
stuff	*n.* 原料，材料，东西，物品　*v.* 把……塞满，把……塞进
subject	*n.* 1. 主题，题目　2. 学科，科目　3. 主语
	adj. 易遭……的，受……支配的　*v.* 使遭受，使服从
submission	*n.* 1. 服从　2.（文件等的）提交
submit	*v.* 1.（使）服从，（使）屈服　2. 呈交，提交
substance	*n.* 1. 物质，材料　2. 实质，本质　3. 要旨，实质性的东西
substantial	*adj.* 1. 客观的，大量的　2. 牢固的，坚实的，结实的　3. 实在的
substitute	*n.* 代用品，替补　*v.* 代替，接替
suburb	*n.* 市郊，郊区
subway	*n.* 1. 地铁　2. 地道
succeed	*v.* 1. 成功　2. 继承，接替
success	*n.* 成就，成功
suffer	*v.* 1. 经受，遭受，蒙受　2. 受痛苦，受疼痛，受苦难，患病
	3. 受损害，受损失
sufficient	*adj.* 足够的，充分的
suggest	*v.* 1. 建议，提议　2. 使想起，意思是，暗示
suggestion	*n.* 建议，意见，暗示
suit	*v.* 1. 合适，适中，中……的意　2. 相称，相当
	n. 1.（一套）外装　2. 起诉，诉讼
suitable	*adj.* 合适的，适宜的
sum	*n.* 1. 总数，总和　2. 金额，款子　3. 算术题　*v.* 合计，总计
summarise/ ~ze	*v.*（作）概括，（作）总结
summary	*n.* 总结，摘要，概要
superficial	*adj.* 1. 肤浅的，浅薄的　2. 表面的，外表的
superior	*adj.* 1. 较好的，优良的　2. 较多的，较大的
	3. 较高的，上级的，有优越感的　*n.* 上级，长官
supplement	*v.* 增补，补充
	n. 1. 增补（物），补充（物）　2.（报刊等的）增刊，副刊
supply	*v.* 供给，供应，提供　*n.* 供应（量）
support	*v.* 1. 支撑，支承　2. 支持，拥护　3. 供养，维持
	n. 1. 支持，支承　2. 供养，赡养
suppose	*v.* 1. 料想，猜想，假定，认为　2.［用于祈使句］让，设
surgery	*n.* 外科
surprise	*v.* 使诧异，使惊奇
	n. 1. 惊奇，诧异　2. 令人惊奇的事物，意想不到的事物
surroundings	*n.* 周围的事物，环境

survey	*v.* & *n.* 1. 俯瞰，眺望 2. 测量，勘测 3. 全面审视，调查
survive	*v.* 1. 幸免于，幸存 2. 比……活得长
suspect	*v.* 怀疑，疑有 *n.* 犯罪嫌疑人，可疑分子
suspicion	*n.* 怀疑，略有所知
suspicious	*adj.* 怀疑的
swallow	*v.* 吞，咽 *n.* 燕子
sweater	*n.* 运动衣，套头衫，毛衣
sweep	*v.* (swept, swept) 1. 扫，清扫 2.（风）吹，（浪）冲 3. 扫过，掠过
swing	*v.* (swung, swung) 1. 摇摆，摇荡，挥动 2. 转身，转向 *n.* 1. 秋千 2. 摇摆，摆动，挥动
switch	*n.* 1. 开关，电闸 2. 转变，转换 *v.* 转变，转换
sword	*n.* 剑，刀
symbol	*n.* 1. 象征，标志 2. 符号，代号
sympathy	*n.* 同情，同情心
symphony	*n.* 交响乐
symptom	*n.* 症状
synthetic	*adj.* 1. 合成的，人造的 2. 综合（性）的
system	*n.* 1. 系统，体系 2. 制度，体制
systematic	*adj.* 系统的

T

tablet	*n.* 药片
tackle	*n.* 用具 *v.* 解决，处理
talent	*n.* 1. 才能，天资 2. 人才
tank	*n.* 1. 箱，罐，槽 2. 坦克
target	*n.* 1. 靶子 2. 目标，对象
tax	*n.* 1. 税（款） 2. 负担 *v.* 对……征税
technical	*adj.* 技术的，工艺的
technique	*n.* 1. 技术，技能 2. 技巧，手艺
technology	*n.* 技术，工艺
telescope	*n.* 望远镜
temperature	*n.* 1. 温度，体温 2. 发烧
temporary	*adj.* 暂时的，临时的，一时的
tempt	*v.* 1. 吸引，引起……的兴趣 2. 引诱，诱惑
tend	*v.* 1. 趋向，倾向 2. 照管，护理
tendency	*n.* 去向，趋势，倾向
tender	*adj.* 1. 温柔的 2. 嫩的，和平的 3. 脆弱的，敏感的 *v.* 投标
terminal	*n.* 1. 终点（站），末端 2. 终端 *adj.* 末端的，终点的，极限的
terrible	*adj.* 1. 可怕的，骇人的 2. 很糟的，极坏的 3. 极度的，厉害的
territory	*n.* 1. 领土，版图 2. 领域，范围
theory	*n.* 1. 理论，原理 2. 学说
thorough	*adj.* 彻底的，完全的

thought	*n.* 1. 思想 2. 思考，思维，思想活动 3. 想法，见解
thoughtful	*adj.* 1. 沉思的，思考的 2. 体贴的，关心的
threat	*n.* 1. 威胁，恐吓 2. 凶兆，征兆
threaten	*v.* 1. 威胁，恐吓 2. 预示（危险）快要来临，是……的征兆
tolerate	*v.* 容忍，忍受，容许，宽恕
topic	*n.* 题目，话题，主题
total	*n.* 总数，总计 *adj.* 总的，全部的 *v.* 合计，总数达
tough	*adj.* 1. 强壮的，坚强的，能吃苦耐劳的 2. （肉等食物）老的 3. 坚韧的，牢固的 4. 困难的，艰苦的
tour	*n. & v.* 旅行，旅游，观光
tourist	*n.* 旅游者，观光者，游览者
trade	*n.* 1. 贸易，商业，交易，交换 2. 行业，职业 *v.* 进行交易，做买卖，交换
trademark	*n.* 商标
tradition	*n.* 传统，惯例
traffic	*n.* 交通，交通量
transaction	*n.* 交易
transfer	*v.* (transferred, transferred) & *n.* 1. 迁移，转移 2. 转让，过户 3. 调动，转职，转学
transform	*v.* 1. （使）变形，（使）转变 2. 改造，改善，改革
transit	*n.* 1. 通行 2. 运输
translate	*v.* 翻译
transparent	*adj.* 1. 透明的 2. 显然的，明显的
transport	*v.* 运输，运送 *n.* 1. 运输，运送 2. 运输工具
trap	*n.* 陷阱，圈套 *v.* 诱捕，使中圈套
travel	*v. & n.* 旅行，游历
tray	*n.* 盘，托盘，碟
treasure	*n.* 1. 金银财宝，财富 2. 珍品，珍藏品 *v.* 珍爱，珍视，珍藏
treat	*v.* 1. 对待，看待 2. 处理 3. 医疗，医治 4. 款待，请（客）
treaty	*n.* 条约，协定
tremendous	*adj.* 巨大的，极大的，非常的
trend	*n.* 趋向，趋势，倾向
trial	*n.* 1. 讯问，审讯 2. 试用，试验
triangle	*n.* 三角（形）
trick	*v.* 欺诈，哄骗 *n.* 1. 诡计，花招 2. 窍门，诀窍 3. 恶作剧，戏弄 4. 戏法，把戏
trip	*n.* 旅行，行程 *v.* (tripped, tripped) 绊倒，失误
trust	*v.* 1. 信托，信赖，相信 2. 委托，托付 3. 信心，希望 *n.* 信任，信赖
truth	*n.* 1. 真相，实情 2. 忠实性，真实性 3. 真理
tuition	*n.* 学费
tutor	*n.* 1. 教师 2. （大学的）导师

type	*n.* 1. 类型，种类，品牌　　2. 铅字　　*v.* 打字
typewriter	*n.* 打字机
typical	*adj.* 1. 典型的，有代表性的　　2.（品质、性格等方面）特有的，独特的
typist	*n.* 打字员

U

ultimate	*adj.* 1. 最后的，最终的　　2. 根本的，基本的
umbrella	*n.* 伞，雨伞
underground	*adj.* 1. 地（面）下的　　2. 秘密的，不公开的
	adv. 1. 在地（面）下　　2. 秘密地，不公开地　　*n.* 地铁
underline	*v.* 1. 在……下面划底线　　2. 强调
understanding	*n.* 1. 理解（力）　　2. 谅解，协议　　*adj.* 有理解力的，通情达理的
undertake	*v.* 1. 承担，担任　　2. 许诺，保证　　3. 着手做，从事
undo	*v.* 1. 解开，松开　　2. 取消，消除
undoubtedly	*adv.* 无疑，必定
uneasy	*adj.* 1. 心神不安的，忧虑的　　2. 不安宁的，令人不安的
unexpected	*adj.* 想不到的，意外的
unfair	*adj.* 1. 不公正的，不公平的　　2. 不正当的，不正直的
unfortunately	*adv.* 不幸地，可惜的是　　*n.* 制服，军服
	adj. 相同的，一律的，一贯的
uniform	*n.* 制服，军服　　*adj.* 相同的，一律的，一贯的
union	*n.* 1. 工会，协会，联盟　　2. 结合，联合，合并
unique	*adj.* 1. 唯一的　　2. 独特的，独一无二的
unit	*n.* 1. 单元，单位　　2. 部件，元件，装置
unite	*v.*（使）联合，（使）团结
united	*adj.* 1. 统一的　　2. 联合的
universal	*adj.* 1. 普通的，全体的，共同的　　2. 通用的，万能的
universe	*n.* 宇宙，万物，世界
university	*n.*（综合性）大学
unlike	*adj.* 不像　　*prep.* 不同于，不似
unnecessary	*n.* 不必要的，无用的
unprecedented	*adj.* 空前的，无前例的
unusual	*adj.* 1. 不正常的，少有的　　2. 与众不同的，独特的
upset	*v.* 1. 打乱，扰乱　　2. 使……心烦意乱，使（身体、肠胃等）不适
	3. 打翻，推翻
urge	*n.* 强烈的欲望，迫切的要求，冲动
	v. 1. 鼓励，激励　　2. 催促，力劝
urgent	*adj.* 急迫的，紧要的，紧急的
usage	*n.* 用法
used	*adj.* 1. 惯常的，习惯于……的　　2. 用过的，旧的
usual	*adj.* 通常的，平常的，惯常的
usually	*adv.* 通常

utility	*n.* 1. 功用，效用　　2. 公用事业
utilize	*v.* 利用

V

vacation	*n.* 休假，假期
vain	*adj.* 1. 徒劳的，无效的，不成功的　　2. 自负的，爱虚荣的
valid	*adj.* 1. 有效的　　2. 有根据的
validity	*n.* 1. 确实性　　2. 效力
valley	*n.* 1. 山谷，溪谷　　2. 流域
valuable	*adj.* 贵重的，有价值的　　*n.* ［常 P］贵重物品［尤指首饰］
value	*n.* 1. 价值　　2. 有用性，重要性　　3. ［P］价值观念，标准
	v. 1. 尊重，重视，珍视　　2. 评估，估价
vanish	*v.* 消失，逐渐消散
variable	*adj.* 易变的，可变的　　*n.* 变量
variety	*n.* 1. 变化，多样化　　2. 品种，变种　　3. 种种，多种多样
various	*adj.* 1. 不同的，各种各样的　　2. 不止一个，许多的　　3. 多方面的，多种的
vary	*v.* 改变，（使）变化
vegetable	*n.* 蔬菜，植物　　*adj.* 蔬菜的，植物的
vehicle	*n.* 1. 交通工具，车辆　　2. 传播媒介，工具，手段
venture	*n.* 冒险（行动）；（为赢利而投资其中的）企业
	v. 1. 冒险（行事）　　2. 敢于，大胆表示
verify	*v.* 1. 核实，查对　　2. 证明，证实
version	*n.* 1. 版本　　2. 译本，译文　　3. 说法，描述
versus	*prep.* 对，相对
vertical	*adj.* 垂直的，竖的
via	*prep.* 经由，经过，通过
victim	*n.* 牺牲品，受害者
victory	*n.* 胜利，成功
video	*n.* 录像（机）　　*adj.* 1. 电视的，视频的　　2. 录像的
view	*n.* 1. 看法，见解，观点　　2. 观察，视域，眼界　　3. 景色，风景
	v. 1. 看待，考虑，估量　　2. 观察，看
village	*n.* 乡村，村庄，村
violence	*n.* 1. 暴力（行为），强暴（行为）　　2. 猛然，剧烈，强烈
violent	*adj.* 1. 暴力引起的，强暴的　　2. 猛烈的，剧烈的，强烈的
virtual	*adj.* 事实上，实际上的
virtually	*adv.* 实际上，事实上
virtue	*n.* 1. 美德，德行　　2. 优点，长处
virus	*n.* 病毒
visa	*n.* 签证
visible	*adj.* 看得见的，可见的，有形的
vision	*n.* 1. 想象（力），幻想，幻觉　　2. 视力，视觉　　3. 目光，眼力
visual	*adj.* 视觉的，看得见的，形象化的

vital	*adj.* 1. 生死攸关的，致命的　　2. 极其重要的，必不可少的 　　　3. 有生命的，充满生机的
vivid	*adj.* 1. 鲜艳的　　2. 生动的，栩栩如生的
vocabulary	*n.* 1. 词汇（量）　　2. 词汇（表）
volt	*n.* 伏（特）
voltage	*n.* 电压
volume	*n.* 1. 卷，册，书卷　　2. 体积，容积，容量　　3. 音响，响度
vote	*n.* 1. 票，选票　　2. 投票，选举，表决 *v.* 投票，选举，表决
voyage	*n.* 航海，航行，旅行，航程　　*v.* 航海，航行，旅行

W

wage	*n.* ［常 P］工资　　*v.* 进行，从事，开展
wake	*v.* （woke, woken) 1. 醒，醒来　　2. 唤醒，弄醒 　　　3. 使认识（或意识）到，激起，引起，唤起
walkman	*n.* 随身听
wander	*v.* 1. 徘徊，漫步，闲逛　　2. 走神，（神智）恍惚
warn	*v.* 警告，告诫
waste	*v.* 浪费，消耗　　*n.* 1. 浪费，消耗　　2. 废料，弃物 *adj.* 1. 废的，丢弃的，无用的　　2. 荒芜的
watch	*n.* 1. 表　　2. 看管，监视　　*v.* 1. 注视，观看　　2. 看守，监视
wealth	*n.* 1. 财富，财产　　2. 丰富，大量
weapon	*n.* 武器，兵器
wear	*v.* 1. 穿着，戴着，佩戴　　2. 穿破，磨损，用旧　　3. 蓄，留（须、发等）
website	*n.* 网址
weekly	*adj.* 每周的，一周一次的　　*adv.* 一周一次地　　*n.* 周报，周刊
weep	*v.* （wept, wept) 哭泣，流泪
weigh	*v.* 1. 称（……的重量）　　2. 认真考虑，权衡
weight	*n.* 1. 重量，体重　　2. 砝码，秤砣　　3. 重要性，重大价值
welfare	*n.* 福利，福利救济
western	*adj.* 西方的，西部的
whisper	*v. & n.* 低语，耳语，私语，密谈
widespread	*adj.* 遍及广大范围的，流传很广的
wild	*adj.* 1. 野的，野生的，未驯化的　　2. 未开化的，原始的，野蛮的 　　　3. 难以约束的，不受控制的，放荡的
willing	*adj.* 愿意的，乐意的，心甘情愿的
win	*v.* （won, won) 1. 获胜，赢　　2. （经过努力）赢得，获得，取得
wipe	*v. & n.* 擦，抹，揩
wire	*n.* 金属丝，电线
wisdom	*n.* 1. 智慧，明智　　2. 学问
wit	*n.* 智力，才智
withdraw	*v.* （withdrew, withdrawn) 1. 收回，取回，提取　　2. 撤退，撤销，退出

	3. 撤回所说的话（或所做的事）
withdrawal	n. 1. 提款　2. 撤销
withstand	v.（withstood，withstood）经受，承受，抵住
witness	n. 1. 目击者，见证人　2. 证据，证言
	v. 1. 目击，目睹　2.（为……）作证，证明
wonder	v. 1.（对……）感到惊讶，感到诧异　2.（对……）感到疑惑，觉得好奇，想知道　n. 1. 惊奇，惊异　2. 奇迹，奇事，奇观
wonderful	adj. 1. 令人惊奇的，奇妙的　2. 精彩的；绝妙的，了不起的
worry	v.（使）烦恼,（使）发愁,（使）担心　n. 担心，发愁，忧虑
worse	adj. 更坏的，更差的　adv. 更坏，更差
worst	adj. 最坏的，最差的　adv. 最坏，最差
worship	n. & v. 1. 崇拜，崇敬　2. 敬奉，信奉
worth	adj. 1. 值……钱，相当于……价值　2. 值得，具有……价值　n. 价值，作用
worthwhile	adj. 值得（做）的
worthy	adj. 1. 值得的，配得上的　2. 有价值的，可尊敬的
wound	n. 创伤，伤口　v. 伤害
wrap	v.（wrapped，wrapped）包，裹，缠绕　n. 披肩，围巾
wrist	n. 腕，腕关节

Y

yearly	adj. 每年的，一年一度的　adv. 每年，一年一次地
yield	v. 1. 生产，出产　2. 产生（效果、收益等），带来　3. 让出，放弃　4.（使）屈服,（使）顺从,（使）投降　n. 出产，产量，收益
youth	n. 1. 年轻，青春，青（少）年时代　2. 男青年，小伙子　3.［总称］（男女）青年们

Z

zone	n. 地区，区域，地带

专业词汇表

a demand bill	见票即付的汇票，即期汇票
a guide to international direct dialing	国际直拨电话指南
a laser printer	激光打印机
abbreviations（used in the dictionary）	缩写，缩写词
accounts payable	应付账
accounts receivable	应收账
acknowledgement of order	确认订单
actual stuff	现货
advertising agent	广告代理商
agriculture policy	农业政策

annual report	年终报告，年度报告
antenna	天线
appeal body	上诉机构
application letter	申请函
assurance company	保险公司
astronaut	太空人，宇航员
authorized signature	授权签字
average income	平均收入
balance of international payment	国际收支平衡
best-seller	畅销品
board of directors	董事会
bound level	约束水平
broadband technology	宽带技术
business management	企业管理
buy in installments	分期付款购买
calculator	计算器
campus-wide area network	校园网络
cancel an account	注销账户
capital accumulation	资本积累
capital stock	股本
carry on business	营业
cartridge	墨盒
cash price	现金价格
casual price	临时费用
character	字符
circuit	电路，线路
class of business	业务范围，业务种类
closing price	收盘价
closing words	结束语
code	代码
collection letter	催款函
command	指令，命令
common business abbreviation	商务常用缩写
common stock	普通股
communication process	交流过程
commodity supply volume	商品供应量
company home office	公司本部
competitive mechanism	竞争机制
complaint letter	投诉函
computer language	计算机语言
confirmation	确认订单
connecting to the internet	网络连接

credit card	信用卡
currencies of the world	世界货币
currency banking science	货币学
current account	往来账户，活期存款账户
current deposit	活期存款
current money	通用货币
current prices of stock	证券行市
customs duties	关税
customs formalities	海关手续
customs tariff	关税率
cyber business	网上贸易
cyber café	网吧
cyber space	网络空间
cyber world	网络世界
data processing	数据处理
dial-in access	拨号上网
digital computer	数字计算机
disc, disk	磁盘
display unit	显示装置
download	下载
e-commerce	电子商务
e-currency	电子货币
economic law	经济法
electronic bulletin board	电子公告板
electronics	电子学
emerging industry	新兴产业
encryption technology	加密技术
entertainment and sports	娱乐和体育
equipment management	设备管理
explanatory note	注释
exploring your computer	浏览计算机
factory price, manufacturer's price	出厂价
feasibility report	可行性报告
feedback and evaluation	反馈与评价
financial management	财务管理
fixed deposit	定期储蓄
fixed price	固定价格
food security	食品安全
foot an account	结账
free article	免税品
free delivery	免费邮递
free publicity	免费宣传

full payment	全额付款
full return	全额退款
gas purifier	煤气净化器
general policy condition	保险单一般规定
general surgery	普通外科
giving quotation	开价
government and public affairs	政府和公众事物
government bonds	政府债券
graphic designer	美术设计员
gross income, gross earnings	总收入，总收益
group baggage	团体行李
harbor entrance	海港入口
height above sea level	海拔高度
high rate saving	高息储蓄
home market	国内市场
human resource management	人力资源管理
human rights, rights of man	人权
identity card	身份证
income and expenditure, receipts and expenditure, input and output	收入和支出
income tax	所得税
information material	情报资料
information media	情报载体（指书刊、电影、广播、电视、磁带等）
information science	情报学
information storage	情报贮存
inland trade, home trade, domestic trade, internal trade, interior trade	国内贸易
inline progressing	内处理
integrated circuit	集成电路
intellectual property rights	知识产权
international business law	国际商法
International Development Association, IDA	国际开发协会
international Monetary Found, IMF	国际货币基金组织
international public relations	国际公共关系
international situation	国际形势
international trade	国际贸易
international waters	国际水域
investigative report	调查报告
investment in non-productive project	非生产性计划投资
iron and steel industry	钢铁工业
irrevocable credit	不可撤销信用证
job processing	作业处理

keyboard	键盘
language conversion program	语言转换程序
large capacity storage	大容量存储器
latency time	等待时间
legal problem	法律问题
letter shift	字母移位
library	库，程序库
limited company	有限公司
line advance	换行
liquid crystal display	液晶显示器
log-in	注册，登记
log-off	注销
luminance	亮度
machine language	机器语言
magnetic storage	磁存储器
magnetic tape	磁带
management information system	管理信息系统
maritime resource	海洋资源
maritime transportation insurance	海洋运输保险
market access	市场转让
market price	市场价
marketing management	营销管理
marriage certificate	结婚证书
maximum price, ceiling price	最高价
means of liquidity	流动资金
mechanization of farming	农业机械化
miner's lamp, safety lamp	矿灯，安全灯
minimum price	最低价
Ministry of Civil Affairs	民政部
Ministry of Communications	交通部
Ministry of Construction	建设部
Ministry of Culture	文化部
Ministry of Finance	财政部
Ministry of Foreign Trade and Economic Co-operation	对外贸易经济合作部
Ministry of Health	卫生部
Ministry of Information Technology and Telecommunications	信息产业部
Ministry of Justice	司法部
Ministry of Labor and Social Security	劳动和社会保障部
Ministry of Land and Natural Resources	国土资源部
Ministry of Personnel	人事部
Ministry of Public Security	公安部

Ministry of Railways	铁道部
Ministry of State Security	安全部
miscarriage of justice	审判不当，误判
Ministry of Supervision	监察部
Ministry of Water Resources	水利部
Money order, postal order	汇票，汇单
monthly payment	月付款
mutual non-aggression	互不侵犯
mutual respect for sovereignty and territorial integrity	互相尊重主权和领土完整
mutual understanding and mutual accommodation	互谅互让
national boundary	国界
national highway	国道
national income	国民收入
national public servant	国家公务员
natural calamity	自然灾害
net income	纯收益，净收入
net price	净价，实价
news media	新闻媒体
night shift	夜班
non-interference in each other's internal affairs	互不干涉内政
nonretroactive character	不溯既往性
on account	赊账
on-line research service	在线搜索服务
only valid in this country	国内有效
open market	公开市场
opening price	开盘
operating cost	生产费用，营业成本
operating expense	营业费用
operating instruction	操作指南
operations management	生产管理
optical character reader	光符阅读机
optical scanner	光扫描器
organized tour	组团旅游
original accumulation	原始积累
overhead cost	营业间接成本
overhead expense	间接费用，管理费用
package design	包装设计
paid vacation	带薪假期
paper measure	纸张规格
parcel list	包裹单
passenger cabin	客舱
passive asset	固定资产

patent article	专利品
payment in arrears, outstanding payment	拖欠贷款
peaceful coexistence	和平共处
permanent worker	长期工，固定工
personal computer	个人计算机
personal property	个人财产
personnel agency	职业介绍所
personnel testing	员工考核
petition for a reprieve	缓刑起诉书
physical geography	自然地理
piece price, unit price	单位价格，单价
piecework	计件工作
plastic surgery hospital	整形外科医院
platform bridge	天桥
pleasure trip	游览，漫游
port of registry	船籍港
postage paid	邮资已付
power on	接通电源
preferential price	优惠价
presiding judge	庭长，首席法官
price control	物价管制，价格控制
price fall	价格下降
price fixing	限价，限定价格
price free on board	船上交货价
price freeze	价格冻结
price index	物价指数
printed matter	印刷品
processing unit	处理部件
public health nurse	保健护士
public lavatory	公共厕所
public notice	公告
public prosecutor	公诉人，检察官
public telephone	公共电话
purchase price	买价，进货价格
quality assurance	质量保护
quality determination	质量鉴定
quality specification	质量标准
queer transaction	不正当交易
radio beacon	无线电导航台
radio engineering, radio-technology	无线电技术
radio frequency	无线电广播频率
radio receiver, radio set, receiving set, wireless	收音机

radio station	广播站
radio transmission	无线电广播频率
railway system, railway network	铁路系统
raise a loan	借款，筹款
raise funds	筹款
real estate	不动产
refund, repayment	归还，调换证券
registered office, head office	总公司，总店，总部
registered trademark	注册商标
registration form	登记表
release on bail	保释
release on parole	假释
repeal rescission	撤销（判决）
research and analysis	研究与分析
resident physician	住院医生
residential hotel	公寓旅馆
retail price	零售价
return ticket	往返票，双程票
right-angled triangle	直角三角形
rise in price	价格上涨
risk management	风险管理
role of departments	部门职能
rule of three	比例法
sacrifice sale	亏本出售
sale by auction	拍卖
sale for cash	现金交易
sale price	卖价，销售价格
sales letters	推销信
sales representative	销售代表
sampling public opinion	公众意见抽样调查
scanning control register	扫描控制寄存器
sealed container	密封集装箱
seasonal demand	季节性需求
secondary market	二级市场
selector	选择器，选择符
self-service cafeteria	自助餐厅
sentinel	标记
separator	分隔符
sequence	序列，顺序
sequential	顺序的
serial	串行的，连续的
service request	服务器请求

settle account	结账
settled income	固定收入
share broker	股票经纪人
share holder	股东
shared memory	共享存储器
shift	移位
shift of responsibility	推卸责任
shifting charge	搬运费，装卸费
side benefit	附带条件
side condition	限制条件，副条件
side effect	副作用
side wind	间接影响
signal	信号
simulation	模拟
simulator	模拟器，模拟程序
single instruction execute	单指令执行
social and cultural agencies	社会与文化机构
software	软件，软设备
sort	分类，排序
sorter	分类人员，分类机，分类程序，排序程序
speaker	扬声器，话筒
standard interface	标准接口
stock exchange	证券交易所
stock investment	股票投资
stock market	证券市场
stock transfer	股份转让
storage	存储器
switch	开关
symbolic language	符号语言
system compatibility test	系统兼容测试
table expense	伙食费
table of price	价格表
table top computer	台式计算机
take stock	盘货，点清存货
taking notes	记录留言
target return	目标利润
tax bureau	税务局
tax loophole	税法漏洞
tax-free	免税的
technical know-how transfer	技术转让
technology-intensive	技术密集的
teleprinter	电传打字机

terminal area distribution	终端区域分布处理
terminal unit	终端设备
the global environment and international business	跨国企业和全球环境
through train	直达列车
ticket agency	售票代理处
time sharing	分时
time wage	计时工资
timer	时钟，精密计时器
timing	定时
to load	装入，寄存，写入，加载
to process	处理
to raise to the power of five	使乘五次方
to store	存储器
to update	更新
track	磁道
tracking program	跟踪程序
trade mark	商标
transducer	传感器，翻译机
translator writing system	翻译程序编写程序
transportation business	运输业
trial period	试用期
trustee fee	托管费
typewriter output routine	打字机输出程序
ultimate production	总产量
umbrella project	大型项目
underwriting contract	证券包销合同
unified brand	统一商标
upper case	大写字母
use area	用户区
user file directory	用户文件目录
using multiple monitors	使用多功能监视器
vending machine	自动售货机
video display unit	视频显示器
vocational bureau	职业介绍所
voice data processing system	声音数据处理系统
voice mail for all staff	教工语言信箱
volume of trade	贸易额
warrant money	保证金
watered stock	掺水股
wholesale dealer	批发商
wholesale market	批发市场
wholesale price	批发价

work force	劳动力
working capital	流动资金
working condition	工作条件
working storage	工作存储器
World Bank	世界银行
writing contract	书面合同
writing report	书面报告
yearly budget	年度预算
yearly income	年度收入
zero economic growth（ZEG）	经济零增长
zero balance	收支平衡

附录 B "实战演练"参考答案

第 1 章

1. 并列句   2. 并列句   3. 简单句   4. 并列句   5. 复合句
6. 并列句   7. 简单句   8. 简单句   9. 复合句   10. 复合句

第 2 章

1. [答案]　D
   [译文]　到下个月你来看我时，我将已完成了我的学期论文。
   [注解]　by the time 表示在某个时间之前，从句中有表示将来时的短语 next month，故主句用将来完成时。
2. [答案]　is equipped
   [译文]　这家医院配备了现代化的设施，是该国最好的医院之一。
   [注解]　关系代词 which 指医院，与 equip 之间是被动关系，故应填入 is equipped.
3. [答案]　have become
   [译文]　在过去的几年里，交通问题越来越严重。
   [注解]　in the past few years 表示动作的持续性，故谓语动词应填入 have become。
4. [答案]　A
   [译文]　数年来在显微镜的帮助下，医生们挽救了数百万人的生命。
   [注解]　for years 表示"数年来"说明时间延续到现在，并可能还会延续下去，因此应用现在完成时。
5. [答案]　have made
   [译文]　没有人可以否认我们在过去二十年所取得的巨大成就。
   [注解]　句中时间状语 in the past twenty years 是现在完成时的标志，其构成是 have/has + 过去分词，故应用现在完成时。
6. [答案]　were sent
   [译文]　在昨天晚上的事故中受伤的人被送到最近的医院治疗。
   [注解]　the people 与 send 之间为被动关系，应用被动语态；又因为时间状语为 last night 是过去时，所以用过去被动语态。
7. [答案]　will have found
   [译文]　到下个月底，我们就会找到解决这个技术难题的好方法。
   [注解]　本题考查时态。by the end of next month 决定了所填处为将来时，并且到

那时已经完成，故用将来完成时。

8. [答案] D
   [译文] 自从我来这里就一直住在这宿舍，因为这儿价格便宜。
   [注解] 句中状语 ever since 表示"（从那时起就）一直怎样"的意思，显然主句应用现在完成进行时。

9. [答案] were/had been told
   [译文] 警察被告知等进一步接到命令后再采取行动。
   [注解] 后半句已经说明等他们接到命令后再行动，而 tell 后面没有宾语，因此，须用被动语态。

10. [答案] was questioned
    [译文] 父亲想知道为什么他儿子上周被警察提审。
    [注解] 此题同前题情况基本相同，也是被动语态。

11. [答案] B
    [译文] 自十年前从安东技术学院毕业至今，他一直就在这家公司工作。
    [注解] since 引导的时间状语从句通常用一般过去时，主句中常用现在完成时或现在完成进行时。

12. [答案] will have produced
    [译文] 到今年年底，这家工厂将生产出 20 000 部手机。
    [注解] by the time 或 by the end of 常表示某一时刻或某一动作发生之前，句中谓语动作已经完成，同时句中另一时间为今年，故用将来完成时。

13. [答案] was（being）elected
    [译文] 上周选举主席时，俱乐部全体会员都出席了。
    [注解] 句中 the chairman 和 elect 之间构成被动关系，而时间状语 last week 决定时态为一般过去时，因此要用一般过去时的被动语态。

14. [答案] D
    [译文] 尽管在面试前他做了充分的准备，但他仍没回答上来一些重要的问题。
    [注解] 本题中从句的谓语动作 prepare 发生在主句的谓语动作 failed 之前，因此，从句谓语动作 prepare 就应是发生在过去的过去，故应用过去完成时。

15. [答案] are asked
    [译文] 在飞机起飞前，所有的乘客都被要求系上安全带。
    [注解] 句中主语 passengers 与谓语动词 ask 之间是被动关系，故应用被动式；又因此句陈述的是一般事实，故时态为一般现在时。

16. [答案] will find
    [译文] 毫无疑问，在不久的将来，我们会找到解决这些技术问题的有效方法。
    [注解] 句中 in the near future 为介词短语作时间状语，表示将来的时间，故谓语动词应用将来时形式，即 will find。

17. [答案] D
    [译文] 汽车出了故障，停在路边，司机试着修理它。

[注解] 题目是由 and 连接的两个并列句，前后句的时态应保持一致，后句用的是一般过去时，故前句也应为一般过去时。

18. [答案] are not allowed
    [译文] 按照规定，读者不允许把字典带出阅览室。
    [注解] 因 readers 与 allow 之间是被动关系，故应填入 are not allowed。

19. [答案] had been produced
    [译文] 到去年底，那家汽车工厂已经生产出近 100 万辆小汽车。
    [注解] by the end of 后接过去的某一段时间，一般与过去完成时连用，故答案为 had been produced。

20. [答案] C
    [译文] 明天你到达上海的时候，我已经出发去了重庆。
    [注解] 本题考查将来完成时的用法，其标志是从句经常由 by the time 等结构来引导，主句一般用 will/shall + have done 形式，显然本题的正确答案为 C。

21. [答案] would be built
    [译文] 村民们告诉我们，一年以后这条河上将建一座桥。
    [注解] 在宾语从句中主句用一般过去时，从句也应该用表示过去的时态。根据从句中的时间状语 in a year 可知，这里应该用过去将来时，因此答案为 would be built。

22. [答案] C
    [译文] 下周的这个时候我将度假，也许那时我正躺在美丽的沙滩上。
    [注解] 本题考查了将来进行时的用法，将来进行时用来表示将来的某一时刻正在进行的动作，其结构是 shall/will be + doing 形式，故 C 正确。

23. [答案] had joined
    [译文] 吉姆告诉我他两年前已经参军了。
    [注解] 做本题时需抓住关键词 before。仔细审题之后我们知道，before 一般与过去时连用，经初步判断此处应该是过去的过去，应填过去完成时来表现参军的动作发生在"告诉我"之前。

24. [答案] A
    [译文] 因为今天一整天不停地接待来访者，琳达感到非常疲劳。
    [注解] 根据题意可以判断，这里应该用完成时的某种形式。从题中的关键词 today 不难看出，这里应该使用现在完成进行时。

25. [答案] will have taken
    [译文] 大多数学生到毕业前会拿到 60 个学分。
    [分析] by the time 通常与完成时连用，由于学生还未毕业，所以要用将来完成时表示将来某一时刻之前业已完成的动作。

26. [答案] C
    [译文] 大多数正在英国游览的人总是抱怨那里的食物和天气。
    [注解] 本题阐述的是通常发生的情况，因此用一般现在时，显然可以先排除 B

和 D。A 项表达有明显错误，故答案为 C。

27. [答案] be discovered
    [译文] 尽管警察努力侦查，但事故的起因也许永远不会被发现。
    [注解] 事故的起因与"发现"是被动关系，故填 discover 的被动形式。

28. [答案] had been waiting/had waited
    [译文] 他被告知那位陌生人已经等了他两个小时。
    [注解] 题目中的 for 2 hours 表示时间段，根据对题意的不同理解，用过去完成进行时和过去完成时均可。

29. [答案] would try
    [译文] 警察承诺将竭尽全力调查此事。
    [注解] 根据题意，宾语从句中缺少谓语成分，而主语的时态又为过去时，因而从句须用过去将来时。

30. [答案] C
    [译文] 学生们在这个月底将会完成他们的论文。
    [注解] 本题主要考查将来完成时。by the end of this month 表示一段时间，一般与完成时连用。根据题意可知，这里是阐明将来发生的情况，故应该用将来完成时。will have done 为将来完成时的结构，表示将来某事已经发生的情况，因此 C 为正确选项。

第 3 章

1. [答案] were
   [译文] 如果我是你的话，我是不会错过明早的工作面试的。
   [注解] if 引导的表示现在情况的虚拟条件，从句中的 be 动词应用 were 来表示。

2. [答案] paid
   [译文] 是这位经理该注重对顾客服务的质量的时候了。
   [注解] 在"It's high（about）time..."的固定句型中，句型意为"是……的时候了"。从句中的谓语动词应用过去时来表示。

3. [答案] A
   [译文] 任何人申请驾照都要进行测试。
   [注解] 在表示命令、要求、请求、建议时，从句的谓语动词应用 should + 动词原形构成，should 可省去。故 A 为正确。

4. [答案] would have saved
   [译文] 他要是听取了律师的意见，就会为自己省去好多麻烦。
   [注解] 由于条件从句中谓语动词时态为过去完成时，故主句应该用 would + 现在完成时的结构，说明与过去事实相反的情况。

5. [答案] D
   [译文] 该公司的代表要求修改协议的部分内容。
   [注解] 在表达愿望、要求、请求、命令、建议等动词后的宾语从句中，谓语动词

结构为 should + 动词原形，should 可省去。

6. [答案]　would have been

   [译文]　那男孩通过了期末考试，但如果他再多花点时间学习的话，成绩应该会更好。

   [注解]　由于从句中的谓语用的是过去完成时，因此主句中应用 would + 现在完成时结构，表示对过去发生的事情的假设。

7. [答案]　A

   [译文]　他自己在网上只需点几下鼠标就能查找信息，真是再好不过了。

   [注解]　在 advisable, appropriate, desirable, essential, important, impossible, necessary, proper 等形容词之后的 that-引导的从句中谓语动词要使用"should + 动词原形"的形式，其中 should 可以省略。其一般形式为：It is/was + 引导虚拟语气的词 + that 从句。

8. [答案]　C

   [译文]　早知道他病得这么厉害我就不会告诉他真相了。

   [注解]　if 引导的表示过去情况的虚拟条件，主语谓语用 would have + 过去分词，从句用 had + 过去分词。此句中从句省去了连词 if，故应用倒装结构。

9. [答案]　C

   [译文]　如果没有他们的帮助，我们就不能及时地完成任务。

   [注解]　此句表示与过去事实相反的假设。主句谓语动词结构为 could + have done，故从句谓语动词应是 had done。

10. [答案]　D

    [译文]　自动取款机已经好几天不能用了，它应该在上周就被修好的。

    [注解]　此句表示对过去事实的假设，故主句应该用 should + have done 由于主语和动词之间是被动关系故应用被动语态。

11. [答案]　B

    [译文]　如果他上个星期五离开的话，他应该已经到达巴黎了。

    [注解]　此句的从句结构表示与过去事实相反，故用 had + 过去分词，由于省去了 if 所以从句部分就应倒装。

12. [答案]　C

    [译文]　我认为早该到了采取严厉措施来制止污染的时候了。

    [注解]　it's high time that 为固定句型。意思为"早该是什么的时候了"，从句中的谓语动词用过去时表示虚拟。

13. [答案]　B

    [译文]　公司的经理坚决要求公司的所有的员工都必须遵守新的安全规则。

    [注解]　由表示命令、建议、要求等意义的动词引导的宾语从句。从句用 should + 动词原形表示。should 常被省略。

14. [答案]　A

    [译文]　我昨天本来想给你打电话，但是我没有你的电话号码。

    [注解]　本句表示与过去事实相反的虚拟，从句应用 had + 过去分词，而主句是

一个用过去时表示的陈述语气，说明过去的一个事实。

15. [答案] C

    [译文] 如果汤姆听了你的劝告，就不会犯如此严重的错误了。

    [注解] 本句考查虚拟语气的用法。主句用的是"情态动词+现在完成时态"，说明是对过去发生的事的假设，因此从句应该用过去完成时。

16. [答案] C

    [译文] 每次我有问题时，都会在线交流寻求帮助。

    [注解] as if 意为"好像，似乎"；just as 意为"正像，正当……的时候"；so far 意为"到现在为止"；every time 意为"每次"，此处用作连词，相当于 when。

17. [答案] A

    [译文] 每周一早上，当置身于我的小办公室时，我都希望是在一家跨国公司工作。

    [注解] wish 后面所跟的宾语从句要用虚拟语气。本句用过去进行时"were doing..."，表示对现在状态的虚拟。

18. [答案] C

    [译文] 如果那时候他接受了我的建议，他就会得到所应聘的工作了。

    [注解] 因为主句用了 would have done，表示对过去发生之事的假设，因此从句应使用过去完成时，表示对过去的虚拟。

19. [答案] B

    [译文] 如果我们有更多时间和金钱的话，就能参观更多地方了。

    [注解] 对过去事实进行假设时，主句用"情态动词+完成时态"，从句用过去完成时态。

20. [答案] D

    [译文] 如果 Jack 早知道真实的情况，他就会制定一个不同的计划。

    [注解] 主句所用的谓语动词 would have made 为虚拟形式，可以推断出从句的谓语形式应为 D。

第 4 章

1. [答案] C

    [译文] 在新能源汽车设计方面，他们依然有一些难题需要攻克。

    [注解] 此处考察不定式作定语，have sth. to do。

2. [答案] A

    [译文] 有时候创业就像是做一个艰难的决定，不管你的主意有多好。

    [注解] 此题考查非谓语动词作主语的用法。选项中只有不定式和动名词可以做主语，C 是动词原形可以排除掉，B 和 D 表示被动，根据题意应该表示主动，故选 A。

3. [答案] surprising

    [译文] 新款的手提包主要由年轻女性购买是不足为奇的。

    [注解] It is + *adj.* + that 句型中，that 后面的句子是真正的主语，由此可知此处需

填 surprise 的形容词形式，表示事物的性质用 surprising。

4. [答案]　dealing
   [译文]　一个全新的关于处理城市空气污染的主意吸引了公众的广泛关注。
   [注解]　此题考查动名词作同位语的用法。

5. [答案]　A
   [译文]　如果你的车每年在我们这儿作保养，我们可以保证所有配件的质量。
   [注解]　此题考查 have sth. done 的用法，意为"让、叫、使、请别人做某事"。

6. [答案]　B
   [译文]　本门课程选取三本案例分析用书，涵盖了世界各地的各种商业活动。
   [注解]　本题考察现在分词作状语的用法，covering 的逻辑主语是 course，"课程涵盖了世界各地的各种商业活动"表示主动，用现在分词。

7. [答案]　turned
   [译文]　他要求应聘者在面试过程中将手机关闭。
   [注解]　此题考查 have sth. done 的用法，意为"让、叫、使、请别人做某事"。have her cell phone turned，要她把手机关掉。

8. [答案]　helping
   [译文]　青年志愿者们乐于在日常生活中帮助老年人。
   [注解]　此题考查非谓语动词中动名词的用法，英语中一些动词后面只能接动名词作宾语，如 enjoy，mind, consider, finish, admit 等。

9. [答案]　to transfer
   [译文]　我们已经同意把部分业务移交给一个新雇主。
   [注解]　此题考查非谓语动词中动词不定式的用法，英语中一些动词后面只能接不定式作宾语，如 agree, ask, plan, want, hope, promise, expect, manage, afford, tend, pretend, intend 等。

10. [答案]　D
    [译文]　因毒品引发的医疗事故已在那个国家引起了高度重视。
    [注解]　本题考察的是非谓语动词作定语的用法。本句已经有了谓语动词 have attracted，cause 这一动词位于 medical accidents 后，只能作定语修饰它，cause 的逻辑主语就是所修饰的名词 medical accidents。"医疗事故"和"引起"之间是被动关系，故用过去分词。

11. [答案]　A
    [译文]　公司的销售部致力于产品销售和创造利润。
    [注解]　此题考查 be engaged in 的用法。它的意思是"从事于，致力于"，介词后面用动名词作宾语。

12. [答案]　C
    [译文]　如果你期望雇员使用新技术，那可能就需要再培训。
    [注解]　本题考察的是 expect 的用法。expect sb. to do sth.，期望某人去干某事。根据句意，选 C。

13. [答案] B
    [译文] 调查显示，近六分之一的儿童在与人交流方面有困难。
    [注解] 本题考察 have difficulty (in) doing sth. 的用法，意为"在某方面有困难"，故选 B。

14. [答案] imported
    [译文] 从马来西亚进口的货物主要是钢铁和医疗设备。
    [注解] 过去分词作定语。句中 import 位于 products 后作定语，其逻辑主语就是 products，"产品"和"进口"之间是被动的关系，故用过去分词。

15. [答案] studying
    [译文] 上大学的时候，他与教授相识并且向教授学习到了很多知识。
    [注解] 本题考查非谓语动词做状语的用法。从题干可以看出，study 前有 while，逗号后是主句，说明前半句是一个由 while 引出的时间状语。while 后没有主语，表示所要填的 study 一词的逻辑主语就是主句的主语 he，he 和 study 之间是主动关系，故用现在分词。

16. [答案] C
    [译文] 由于遭受了经济危机带来的巨大损失，该公司去年倒闭了。
    [注解] 本题考查非谓语动词作状语的用法。being suffered 是现在分词一般式的被动形式，表示被动动作与谓语动词所表示的动作同时发生；to suffer 是动词不定式，表将来，通常放在句首作目的状语；suffered 是过去分词，表示被动与完成；having suffered 是现在分词主动式的完成时态，表示主动和完成，作原因状语，符合题意，应该选 C。

17. [答案] C
    [译文] 这家公司给出 5% 的折扣作为网上销售的促销手段。
    [注解] 本题考查不定式作定语的用法。一些名词后面常用不定式作定语，如 way, chance, time 等。

18. [答案] to work
    [译文] 有人告诉我史密斯先生拒绝在人事部门工作。
    [注解] 此题考查非谓语动词中动词不定式的用法，英语中一些动词后面只能接不定式作宾语，如 refuse, learn, agree, ask, plan, want, hope, promise, expect, manage, afford, tend, pretend, intend 等。

19. [答案] having
    [译文] 消费者对家用 3D 电视越来越不感兴趣，部分原因是因为不得不戴上特别的眼镜才能观看。
    [注解] 本题考查非谓语动词作状宾语的用法。because of 是一个介词短语，后面应该用动名词作宾语。

20. [答案] published
    [译文] 根据昨天发布的一份报告，越来越多的年轻人参与到社区活动中。
    [注解] 考查非谓语动词的用法。过去分词 published 作 report 的后置定语，表示

被动。

21. [答案]　encouraged

    [译文]　受到朋友的极大鼓舞，杰克已经报名参加歌唱比赛。

    [注解]　本题考查过去分词作状语的用法。本句主语是 Jack，Jack 受到鼓舞，表示被动，故用过去分词。

22. [答案]　A

    [译文]　网络时代之前，我们常常通过旅行社订票度假。

    [注解]　used to do sth. 表示过去常常做某事，be/get used to doing 表示现在常常做某事。根据题意，选 A。

23. [答案]　C

    [译文]　一般来说，在一个陌生的国度开始新的生活对于一个上了年纪的人来说是需要勇气的。

    [注解]　本题考查动词不定式的用法。在 It takes/took... for sb. to do sth. 或 It takes/took sb. some time/courage to do sth. 句型中，it 是形式主语，真正的主语是动词不定式。

24. [答案]　finding

    [译文]　这些科学家对短期记忆是如何转化成长期记忆的很感兴趣。

    [注解]　be interested in 为固定搭配，意为对……感兴趣，后面跟动名词作宾语。

25. [答案]　to inform

    [译文]　销售经理要求下属每周通报销售情况。

    [注解]　ask sb. to do sth.，要求某人做某事。

26. [答案]　C

    [译文]　我很抱歉由于装运延误给你们造成了很多麻烦。

    [注解]　本题考查不定式的用法。be sorry 后往往接 that 从句或不定式，所以选项 A 和 B 排除掉；选项 C to have caused 是不定式完成时态的主动形式，表示主动和完成（由于装运延误造成了很多麻烦在先，此动作已完成，抱歉在后）；to be caused 是不定式一般时的被动语态，表示被动，所表示的动作与谓语动词同时发生或发生在其后。根据题意应选 C。

27. [答案]　B

    [译文]　在拐角处右转，你会看到通往古城楼的小路。

    [注解]　此题考查非谓语动词作定语的用法。在"通往……的路"中，用现在分词 leading 作定语修饰"路"。

28. [答案]　solving

    [译文]　在进行了数百次的实验之后，他们终于成功地解决了问题。

    [注解]　介词后接动名词作宾语。

29. [答案]　C

    [译文]　今年，人力资源部连同其他部门会将预算减至两百万。

    [注解]　此题考查 have 的固定搭配。have sth. done，使……被做，或请人做某

226

事；have sb. do，让某人去做某事；have sb. doing sth. 让某人在做某事。本题中"预算"和"减少"之间是被动关系，故选 C。

30. [答案] B
    [译文] 虽然史密斯小姐对待她的助理很苛刻，但是他仍然乐意为其工作。
    [注解] enjoy doing sth.，乐意做某事。enjoy 后只跟动名词，故选 B。

31. [答案] to keep
    [译文] 法律要求公司对所有金融往来交易做好记录。
    [注解] 此题考查 require 的用法，require sb. to do sth. 的被动态为 sb. be required to do sth.，故用不定式 to keep。

32. [答案] applying
    [译文] 在申请工作旅游签证之前，你应该阅读关于英语工作旅游文件的相关信息。
    [注解] before 此处是介词，介词后面跟动名词，所以用 applying。

33. [答案] interested
    [译文] 会议上我提了一些建议，但是似乎没有人感兴趣。
    [注解] 此题考查固定搭配，be interested in 是一个固定搭配，表示"对……感兴趣"。

34. [答案] A
    [译文] 会议上正在被讨论的提案对于我们部门来说非常重要。
    [注解] 本题考察非谓语动词做定语的用法。本句中已有谓语动词 is，discuss 位于 proposal 之后，作定语修饰 proposal。"提案"和"讨论"之间是被动关系，后面还有一个时间状语 now，表示正在进行，即提案正在被讨论，所以用现在分词一般式的被动形式（being discussed）。

35. [答案] conducted
    [译文] 根据最近进行的调查，去年 52% 的美国商务人士通过互联网进行出差预定。
    [注解] 考查非谓语动词的用法。according to 是一个介词短语，后面往往只能接名词短语作宾语或接宾语从句。题中是一个名词短语，所以 conduct 只能用非谓语动词形式。survey 和 conduct 之间是被动关系，后面还有一个时间状语 recently，表示被动动作已完成，所以用过去分词 conducted。

36. [答案] injured
    [译文] 据报道，受伤人员在事故后被立刻送往医院。
    [注解] 此题考查非谓语动词作定语的用法。injure 位于 people 之前，作定语，表示被动，（被）受伤的人员，所以用过去分词 injured。

37. [答案] to accept
    [译文] 由于我们的商务计划没有说服银行，所以银行拒绝接受我的贷款申请。
    [注解] refuse to do sth.，拒绝做某事。

38. [答案] D

[译文]　她不知道如何在公共场合用英语把自己的想法表达清楚。

[注解]　本题考查"疑问词+不定式"的用法。在"which, why, what, how+不定式"的结构中, which, what 往往充当不定式的宾语, 表示内容, 此题中 to express her ideas 有了宾语 her ideas, 所以 which, what 应排除掉。why, how 往往充当不定式的状语, why 表原因, how 表方式, 根据上下文意思来判断, 应该是表示"如何", 所以选 how。

39. [答案]　A

[译文]　马克在这家公司已经工作三年了, 他对生意谈判很有经验。

[注解]　本题考察非谓语动词作状语的用法。根据句子结构, 后半部分为一个完整的句子, 中间无任何连词, 因此可判断句子的前半部分为动词的非谓语动词形式作状语, B 和 C 可排除掉。分词短语在句中作状语时, 其逻辑主语应该是主句的主语 Mark, Mark 和 work 之间是主动关系, Mark 在公司工作三年后在生意谈判方面才变得有经验, 应该用现在分词完成形式的主动语态, 所以选 A。

40. [答案]　to make

[译文]　不允许员工在办公室打私人电话。

[注解]　allow sb. to do sth.（允许某人做某事）变成被动语态后还是接不定式, 所以填 to make。

41. [答案]　putting

[译文]　店员把商品上架之前给它们标价。

[注解]　before 此处是介词, 介词后面跟动名词, 所以用 putting。

42. [答案]　correcting

[译文]　我对您迅速纠正我银行账户的错误表示感谢。

[注解]　介词 in 后的动词应该用动名词, 所以用 correcting。

43. [答案]　brought

[译文]　应该采取措施避免由不公平竞争所带来的负面影响。

[注解]　本句考查过去分词作定语的用法。bring 的过去分词为 brought。

44. [答案]　C

[译文]　我认为行万里路去游览长城是值得的。

[注解]　本题考查固定搭配 be worth doing（值得做某事）, 所以用动名词 traveling。

45. [答案]　C

[译文]　这个项目的失败使得经理惊讶得几乎说不出话来。

[注解]　此题考查非谓语动词作状语的用法。先排除 B, 因为 B 是谓语动词形式, 不可作状语。A 是不定式被动形式, 放在句首作目的状语, 但本题应为原因状语, A 不符合。shock 的逻辑主语是主句主语 manager, manager"受到惊吓"应该用过去分词, 所以选 C。

46. [答案]　B

[译文]　汽车业投入了大量资金用于市场营销, 以此吸引年青客户。

[注解]　不定式 to attract 表示目的, 作目的状语。

47. [答案] informed
    [译文] 我们必须通知经理有关广告活动的事。
    [注解] 词组 keep sb. informed of sth. 意思是"通知某人某事"。

48. [答案] winning
    [译文] 这位新大学毕业生对获得总经理助理职位有信心。
    [注解] be confident of，对……有信心。of 为介词，后接动名词作宾语。

49. [答案] left
    [译文] 剩下如此短的时间，我们不可能完成这个复杂的实验。
    [注解] 本题考察的是"with + 宾语 + 分词"的结构。在本句中，with 后的宾语 time 是动词 leave 的逻辑主语，"时间"和"剩下"是被动关系，所以填过去分词 left。

50. [答案] D
    [译文] 即使我对她的建议的看法让她不舒服，我也不后悔告诉她这一想法。
    [注解] 此题考查 regret 的用法。regret 后既可接动名词，表示后悔做过某事，也可接不定式，表示遗憾去做某事。根据题意，应选 D。类似的动词有 remember/forget 等词。

51. [答案] B
    [译文] 当认识到没有多少提升的机会时，我不久就厌烦了我的工作。
    [注解] 此题考查非谓语动词作状语的用法。分词和不定式都可作状语，A 为不定式形式，放在句首时常作目的状语，这显然与本题逻辑上不符合。realize 的逻辑主语是 I，两者为主动关系，应该用现在分词表主动，故选 B。C、D 两选项中的分词与主语 I 构成的是被动关系，不合题意。

52. [答案] C
    [译文] 科学家们应该被告知他们研究领域的最新发展。
    [注解] 此题考查 keep 的用法：keep + 宾语 + 宾语补足语（doing/done）。如果是主动，就用现在分词；如果是被动，就用过去分词。根据题意，应该为"被告知"，所以用过去分词 informed。

53. [答案] written
    [译文] 在孩提时代他就读过马克·吐温所写的大部分书。
    [注解] 此题考查非谓语动词作定语的用法。根据题意，books 和 write 之间是被动关系，故用过去分词。

54. [答案] selling
    [译文] 史密斯先生考虑在搬到北京之前把他的房和车卖了。
    [注解] 此题考查 consider 的用法。consider 后往往接名词或动名词。根据题意，应填 selling。

55. [答案] boring
    [译文] 报告太枯燥了，教室里的许多学生都睡着了。
    [注解] 本题考查分词做表语的用法。现在分词作表语，表示主语的特点；过去

分词作表语，表示主语的状态。本句是说报告枯燥、乏味，故用 boring。bored 指人感到厌烦。

56. [答案]　lost
　　[译文]　在警察的帮助下，这位妇女在一个不眠之夜后终于找到了她丢失的孩子。
　　[注解]　本题考查分词做定语的用法。过去分词 lost 表示"丢失的"，根据题意，此处应填过去分词。

57. [答案]　A
　　[译文]　秘书看墙上的钟时，才发现已是午夜了。
　　[注解]　此题考查非谓语动词作状语的用法。先排除 B，因为 B 是谓语动词形式，不可作状语。分词和不定式都可作状语，C 项为不定式形式，放在句首时常作目的状语，这显然与本题逻辑上不符合。look up 的逻辑主语应该是句子的主语 the secretary，二者为主动关系，所以正确答案为 A。

58. [答案]　B
　　[译文]　第一本英语作为外语的教科书在十六世纪就出版了。
　　[注解]　此题考查非谓语动词作定语的用法。本题已有谓语动词 came out，write 作定语修饰 textbook，textbook 和 write 之间是被动关系，故用过去分词。

59. [答案]　introduced
　　[译文]　信不信由你，当西红柿首次引入到欧洲时，人们认为它是有毒的。
　　[注解]　根据句子结构，后半部分为一个完整的句子，中间无任何连词，因此可判断句子的前半部分为动词的非谓语动词形式作状语。introduce 的逻辑主语应该为句子的主语 tomato，它们之间是被动关系，故应填 introduced。

60. [答案]　seeing
　　[译文]　我记得以前在某处见过你，但是我说不出确切的地方了。
　　[注解]　此题考查 remember 的用法。remember 后既可接动名词，表示"记得做过某事"，也可接不定式，表示"记得去做某事"。根据题意，应填 seeing。类似的动词有 forget，regret 等词。

61. [答案]　to discuss（不定式做真正的宾语）
　　[译文]　我认为在问题解决之前，和他讨论此事是不必要的。
　　[注解]　不定式短语作宾语时，如后面有宾语补足语，往往把不定式宾语放在宾语补足语后，而用 it 作形式宾语，常见的句型为"主语 + 谓语动词（think/find/consider...）＋形式宾语 it ＋形容词（easy/difficult/necessary/important...）＋不定式 to do"。

62. [答案]　D
　　[译文]　被邀请到开幕式上讲话是我巨大的荣幸。
　　[注解]　It's one's honor to do sth. 表示"某人非常荣幸做某事"。本句中的 it 是形式主语，不定式做真正的主语，又因为这里是"被邀请"到开幕式上来讲话，所以要用不定式的被动语态，故选 D。

63. [答案] B

[译文] 昨天晚上我正要睡着时，突然听到了敲门声。

[注解] hear sb. do sth. 表示"听到某人做某事（动作已经完成）"；hear sb. doing sth. 表示"听到某人正在做某事（动作正在进行）"。根据题意应该选 B。

64. [答案] D

[译文] 将在北京召开的这次会议注定要取得巨大的成功。

[注解] 本题考查非谓语动词做定语的用法。conference 与 hold 之间是被动关系，并且有一个时间状语 next week 表示是下周将要召开的会议，所以要用不定式的被动态，故选 D。

65. [答案] working

[译文] 工程师花了整整一个晚上的时间来研究新设备。

[注解] 本题考查 spend 的用法：spend time/money on sth.，花时间（金钱）在某事上；spend time/money (in) doing sth.，花时间（金钱）做某事。work on 是动词词组，其动名词形式是 working on。

66. [答案] suggesting

[译文] 调查组递交了一份报告，建议进行改革。

[注解] 本题考查分词短语做状语的用法。suggest 的逻辑主语是 the research group，两者是主动关系，应该用现在分词做状语。

67. [答案] asked

[译文] 当被问到新型产品广告促销活动的效果时，经理说它非常成功。

[注解] 本题考查分词短语做状语。ask 的逻辑主语是 the manager，根据题意，应为"被问到"，二者为被动关系，所以应填过去分词 asked。

68. [答案] D

[译文] 由于没有找到合适的工作，他决定放弃在这座城市找事做。

[注解] 本题考查非谓语动词作状语的用法。failed 是过去分词，表示被动或完成；being failed 是现在分词一般式的被动式，表示被动动作与谓语动词所表示的动作同时发生；to fail 是动词不定式，表示将来，通常放在句首作目的状语；having failed 是现在分词主动式的完成时态，表示主动和完成，作原因状语，符合题意，应该选 D。

69. [答案] A

[译文] 议案已被接受，我们必须决定何时开工。

[注解] 考查分词独立结构的用法。分词做状语时，其逻辑主语通常是句子的主语，当分词的逻辑主语与句子的主语不一致时，就必须带上自己的逻辑主语，构成分词独立结构，其构成是"名词或代词（主格）＋分词（如果是主动关系，就用现在分词；如果是被动关系，就用过去分词）"。根据题意，proposal 和 accept 之间是被动关系，所以用过去分词，选 A。

70. [答案] A

[译文] 警察一直盯着电脑屏幕以分辨罪犯的脚印。

[注解] 本题考查 keep 的用法：keep sb./sth. doing；keep sb./sth. done；keep sb./sth.＋adj。本句中，eyes 和 fix 在逻辑上是被动关系，所以选 A。

71. [答案] not to speak

[译文] 护士告诉来访者不要大声说话以免打扰到病人。

[注解] tell sb.（not）to do，不定式的否定式作动词 tell 的宾语补足语。

72. [答案] Impressed

[译文] 年轻人良好的求职条件给他们留下了不错的印象，他们在自己的公司给了他一份工作。

[注解] 本题考查过去分词做状语的用法。由于 impress 与 they 之间是被动关系，所以用 impressed。

73. [答案] launching

[译文] 当中国成功发射第一颗人造卫星时我们很激动。

[注解] succeed（in）doing sth. 是固定搭配，意为"成功做某事"，所以填动名词 doing。

74. [答案] interested

[译文] 很遗憾地告诉你，我们不再生产你感兴趣的那种产品了。

[注解] be interested in 为固定搭配，意为"对……感兴趣"，所以用 interested。

75. [答案] completed

[译文] 上个月竣工的那座高楼是我们的新教学楼。

[注解] 本题考查过去分词作定语的用法。complete 的逻辑主语是 the tall building，二者之间是被动关系，又有 last month 这一时间状语表示是上个月完工的，所以填 completed。

76. [答案] B

[译文] 听说 Bob 升职了，朋友们都前来向他祝贺。

[注解] 本题考查非谓语动词作状语的用法。heard 是过去分词，表示被动或完成；hear 是动词原形，不能放在句首作状语；to hear 是动词不定式，表示将来，通常放在句首作目的状语；having heard 是现在分词主动式的完成时态，表示主动和完成（"听说"发生在"祝贺"之前），在此句做时间状语，符合题意。

77. [答案] playing

[译文] 正在那里拉小提琴的孩子们下周将登台表演。

[注解] 本题考查分词作定语的用法。play 的逻辑主语是 the children，用 playing 表示主动和正在进行。

第 5 章

1. [答案] C

[译文] 我毫不怀疑股票市场将会从经济危机中复苏过来。

[注解] 本题主要从句意上理解。I don't doubt 后面引导的是宾语从句，四个选项都可以引导宾语从句，但是根据句子意思，只能选答案 C。选项 if 意思是"是否"，what 和 which 与句子意思明显不相符合。

2. [答案] D
   [译文] 销售经理公布了消息，新产品三个月来在本地市场一直销售良好。
   [注解] 本题考查同位语从句。名词 news 后面的同位语从句一般不能由 whose, what, which 来引导，此外，这些连词引导的从句要在句子中充当一定的句子成分，如主语、宾语或定语等，而从句 the new product had been selling well in the local market for three months 中并不缺少这些句子成分，所以答案 A、B、C 都不正确。而 that 可以引导 news 后的同位语从句，说明 news 的具体内容，that 在从句中不充当任何句子成分。

3. [答案] B
   [译文] 没有证据能证明在不久的将来石油价格会下降。
   [注解] 本题考点是同位语从句中连接词的用法。that 引导的是同位语从句，而 which, where, as 均不符合题意。

4. [答案] C
   [译文] 你认为他让我们都参加会议的建议怎么样？
   [注解] 本题考查对同位语从句的掌握。同位语从句跟在某些名词的后面，用以说明该名词所表达的具体内容。名词后用 that 连接同位语从句，that 只起连接作用，不充当任何句子成分。

5. [答案] D
   [译文] 当她被邀请在会上发言时，她不知道该如何清楚地表达自己的想法。
   [注解] 本题考点是疑问词+不定式结构。疑问词 who, what, which, when, where 和 how 后加不定式构成一种不定式短语，可用来作主语、宾语、表语和双宾语。同时疑问词的选用要根据上下文的逻辑关系来定，通常 who 表示人，what 表示内容，which 表示选择，when 表示时间，where 表地点，how 表方式。

6. [答案] B
   [译文] 我们都为年销售量翻了一番这个消息感到兴奋。
   [注解] 本题考查了同位语从句。同位语从句多由 that 引导，that 只起连接作用，不充当任何语法成分。题中的分句部分是用来说明和解释主句中的 news 的，故用 that 来连接。

7. [答案] C
   [译文] 那儿有那么多的衣服，以至于我真的不知道该选哪一件。
   [注解] 根据题意，空格处缺少一个代词来代替 dress，综合四个答案只有 which 是代词。

8. [答案] B
   [译文] 她想知道草地上的那个孩子是谁家的。
   [注解] know 是及物动词，其后可接宾语从句，而空格后 child 是名词，显然空格

· 233 ·

处缺少一个引导词，并且在从句中要作 child 的定语，因此只有 whose 符合。

9. [答案]　　C

　　[译文]　　他从张小姐那里得到消息说，王教授第二天不能见他。

　　[注解]　　本题考查了 that 引导的同位语从句。that 只起连接作用，在从句中不充当任何句子成分。同位语从句的先行词通常为 fact，news，information，message 等。

10. [答案]　　D

　　[译文]　　无论谁触犯了法律，迟早都要受到惩罚的。

　　[注解]　　空格处缺少一个主语从句的引导词，B、C 两项不具备有这种功能，可首先排除。whoever 的意思为"无论谁，任何人"，相当于 anybody who 的意思。在这里恰好符合句意。

11. [答案]　　A

　　[译文]　　中国足球队赢得那场比赛的消息使我们大家欢欣鼓舞。

　　[注解]　　在同位语从句中，that 只起连接作用，不充当任何语法成分。

12. [答案]　　C

　　[译文]　　唤醒我的是从隔壁房间传来的某人吵闹的哭声。

　　[注解]　　本句缺少一个主语从句的引导词，并且这个引导词还要在从句中充当主语，因此选项 A 和 B 可以排除。因为 how 引导名词性从句时在从句中只能作状语；that 引导名词性从句时在从句中不充当任何成分。根据句中可知，what 符合句意，而 which 意义不符。

13. [答案]　　B

　　[译文]　　没有证据表明他曾在谋杀现场。

　　[注解]　　he was on the site of the murder 是同位语从句，说明 evidence 的内容，因此只能用关系词 that 引导。

14. [答案]　　B

　　[译文]　　我们调查了市场上的其他公司，看看他们是如何处理客户投诉的。

　　[注解]　　本句考察宾语从句，填入的连接词在从句中应表示方式，故选择 B。

15. [答案]　　A

　　[译文]　　请随时告诉我们你对节目的想法，使我们能从你的观点和经验中获益。

　　[注解]　　从空格前的 tell us 可知后面需要填入宾语，what you think about 表示"你所想的"，可用于宾语从句，此处正确。that 可用于宾语从句，可是不做宾语成分；if 表示"是否"，可用于宾语从句，但与句意不符；lest 表示"以免"，一般用于状语从句。

第 6 章

1. [答案]　　B

　　[译文]　　我设法放弃了我发现不可能继续经营的生意。

　　[注解]　　本题主要考查限制性定语从句的用法。根据句子结构，这里需要一个引导定语从句的连接词来修饰先行词 business，并在从句中作宾语。四个选项中只有连接

词 which 可以引导定语从句并修饰名词 business，因此，答案为 B。

2. [答案]　　B

[译文]　　我不得不再次离开生活了八年的北京。

[注解]　　本题考查非限制性定语从句的用法。题中 Beijing 是表示地点的先行词，在主句中起状语的作用。而选项 A、C、D 都是关系代词，另外，that 不能引导非限制性定语从句。因此只能用关系副词 where 来引导，并在定语从句中作状语。

3. [答案]　　A

[译文]　　这本书是为那些母语不是英语的学习者而设计的。

[注解]　　本题考查的是定语从句的关系词的选择问题，根据空格后面的名词 native languages 可知，这里应填一个表所属格关系的词，而只有 whose 有此用法，故本题正确答案为 A。

4. [答案]　　D

[译文]　　她很了解那个与她共事很久的年轻人。

[注解]　　本题考查由 whom 引导的定语从句，当 whom 在从句中作介词的宾语时，应将介词提前。又因 work with sb 为固定结构，故 D 项为正确答案。

5. [答案]　　B

[译文]　　假期我住的那个宾馆管理得相当差。

[注解]　　题中 the hotel 是表示地点的先行词，因此应用 where 引导的定语从句来修饰。the hotel where I stayed 相当于 the hotel at which I stayed 或者 the hotel I stayed at。stay 为不及物动词，应加介词 at，再加宾语，故其余三个选项均有语法错误。因此，答案应是 B。

6. [答案]　　D

[译文]　　这就是那台给我们带来诸多麻烦的显微镜。

[注解]　　本题考查的是定语从句，由"介词 + 关系代词"构成，而选项中，只有 with 能与 have trouble 连用，have trouble with 实为固定搭配，意为"有麻烦"。在本题中，实际上是把 with 提到关系代词前面了。故选 D 项。

7. [答案]　　D

[译文]　　正如往常的那样，三分之一的工人已经超额完成了生产任务。

[注解]　　as 引导非限制性定语从句通常放在句首或句尾，可译为"正如……"。另外，as 也可以和 such、same 连用引导定语从句。

8. [答案]　　C

[译文]　　琼斯先生过去的生活非常艰苦，现在事业非常成功。

[注解]　　本题考查定语从句中关系代词的用法，whose 表示"（某人）的"，是所有格，必须接名词，其本身有限定词的功能。A、B 两项均不能引导定语从句，whom 引导定语从句在从句中作宾语，也不合题意，故选 C 项。

9. [答案]　　A

[译文]　　我们系有很多藏书，其中很多都是英语书。

[注解]　　本题考查了非限制性定语从句。这种从句对所修饰的词没有限制意义的作

用，与主句关系不紧密，把它们拿掉，主句照样成立。它们和所修饰的词之间常加一个逗号。只有 who，whom，whose 和 which 等能引导这类从句。本题中 many of 意为"……中的许多"，many of which 引导的是非限制性定语从句。故 A 项为正确答案。

10. [答案]　C
    [译文]　移民们不得不在文化和生活上使自己适应他们迁入的新环境。
    [注解]　move into 是"迁入"的意思。

11. [答案]　D
    [译文]　杰克说，地铁建设将于十月完工，这使我们十分惊讶。
    [注解]　本句考察非限制性定语从句。非限制性定语从句用关系词 which 引导，在本句中，which 指前面 Jack 说的话，故 D 为正确答案。

12. [答案]　C
    [译文]　经理说，有两个原因导致我们去年的销量快速下滑。
    [注解]　reason 后面跟关系副词 why 引导的定语从句，表示原因，故选 C。

13. [答案]　C
    [译文]　事实上，人们长时间工作有不同的原因。
    [注解]　该句是定语从句，先行词 reason 加上关系副词 why 构成 the reason why...句式，表示"……的原因"。where 为关系副词，指地点，which 为关系代词，指物，how 不可用于定语从句。

14. [答案]　D
    [译文]　宽带连接的广泛存在使得网上购物更容易。
    [注解]　该句为非限制性定语从句，关系代词 which 指代 Broadband connections are widely available now 整句内容，因此答案选 D。

15. [答案]　B
    [译文]　除了经济上的考虑，人们长时间工作还有其他原因。
    [注解]　该句是定语从句，先行词 reason 加上关系副词 why 构成 the reason why...句式，表示"……的原因"。what 不可用于定语从句，when 为关系副词，指时间，where 为关系副词，指地点。

16. [答案]　B
    [译文]　我们为自己的校园感到非常骄傲，它是国内最漂亮的校园之一。
    [注解]　这是一个非限制性定语从句，此处的 which 作为关系代词修饰前面的 campus，因此选 B。

第 7 章

1. [答案]　A
   [译文]　万一你要给我打电话商量事情，请注意下个星期我不在波士顿。
   [注解]　本题主要考查对状语从句引导词的理解。in case 表示"万一，以免"，unless 表示"如果不，除非"，until 表示"到……为止"，so that 引导目的状语从句，

表示"以便，为了"。依据句子意思，此处只能选答案 A。

2. [答案]　A
   [译文]　当他回到办公室，我就会叫史密斯先生给你打电话。
   [注解]　本题主要考查对句子意思的理解和固定结构的掌握"一般将来时＋when＋一般现在时"，表示"到……，就会……"，表示将来的动作。故答案选 A。

3. [答案]　C
   [译文]　虽然他很年轻，但是他已经证明他是个能干的销售员。
   [注解]　本题主要考查固定结构。as 在句中作"虽然，尽管"讲，它引导的让步状语从句要用倒装语序。此句中，被倒装的部分是表语 young，答案选择 C。其他三个选项一方面和句意明显不相符合，另一方面引导的定语从句也不能用倒装语序，所以均应该排除。

4. [答案]　D
   [译文]　她没有参加昨天晚上的聚会，因为她不得不完成她的学期论文。
   [注解]　本题考查对主从句逻辑关系的理解。主句说她没有参加昨晚的聚会，从句说她要完成学期论文，显然是解释她不能参加昨晚的晚会的原因，因此应该选表示原因的 because。

5. [答案]　C
   [译文]　那个小偷一出现在街道拐弯处就被警察看到了。
   [注解]　本题考查的是词义辨析。not until "直到……才"；the moment "一……就……"，相当于 as soon as，when 引导的从句；其他可引导时间状语从句的词组有：each time，every time，the instance，the minute 等；as long as "只要"；only if "只要……"。根据句意 C 是正确答案。

6. [答案]　B
   [译文]　除非你年满 16 岁，否则你拿不到驾驶执照。
   [注解]　从句的连词要用假设含义的否定词，这样排除了 A、C、D 项逻辑含义不对。正确答案是 B"除非"。

7. [答案]　C
   [译文]　如果你有什么问题或需求的话，请在每个工作日的下午五点后与经理联系。
   [注解]　该句主、从句之间，没有因果关系，故不能选择 A。where 表示地点含义，但在该句中不需要有地点含义的词，所以，选 B 不对。though 有明确的词义，表示"虽然"，如果选 D，则句子逻辑不对。

8. [答案]　C
   [译文]　每次苏珊爬上高楼的楼顶时，她就会感到非常害怕。
   [注解]　选项 A，意思为"既然"，与句中其他词无法构成合乎逻辑的句子。选项 D，可以用来引导时间状语，意思为"自从"，此处意思不通。因此，选项 A、B、D 为错误答案。

9. [答案]　A

   [译文]　他出门时就会戴上太阳镜，这样无人会认出他。

   [注解]　本题考点是连词的用法。so that，以便，为的是；now that，既然；as though，好像；in case，以防，万一。本题最大的干扰项是 D 项，如果用 in case 则句意就变成了他希望人人都能认出他，与主句含义相违。根据题意，应该选 A。

10. [答案]　B

    [译文]　只要他还在进行这个项目，我就不介意他什么时候完成。

    [注解]　本题中四个选项均可引导状语从句，in case 意为"以防"，even if 意为"即使，尽管"，as long as 意为"只要"，as far as 意为"远到，直到，至于"。根据句意只有 B 项合适，故 B 项为正确答案。

11. [答案]　B

    [译文]　直到去年李雷在美国度假，他才见到了这位知名的美国教授。

    [注解]　"not... until"引导时间状语从句，是固定短语，表示"直到……才……"。其他选项 unless 意为"如果不，除非"，if 意为"如果"，whether 意为"是否"，均不符合句意。因此，应选 B 项。

12. [答案]　B

    [译文]　没有几家公司对我们所需要的软件感兴趣，因为这个市场太小了。

    [注解]　since 意为"因为，由于"，符合句意。so that 意为"因此"，as if 意为"好像，似乎"，although 意为"虽然"，均不符合句意。

13. [答案]　B

    [译文]　除非董事会所有成员一致同意，否则不可做出如此重大项目的决定。

    [注解]　if 表示"如果"，一般用于条件状语从句；unless 表示"除非"，一般用于条件状语从句；though 表示"尽管"，一般用于让步状语从句；as 表示"由于"，一般用于原因状语从句。联系上下文，故选 B。

14. [答案]　D

    [译文]　没有证据显示查尔斯犯了罪，所以他被释放了。

    [注解]　but 表示转折，for 表示原因，or 表示选择，so 表示结果，故选 D。

15. [答案]　A

    [译文]　一旦收到您的申请，我们会给您发送电子邮件确认。

    [注解]　once 表示"一旦……就……"，因此答案是 A。

第 8 章

1. [答案]　is

   [译文]　理查德博士偕夫人和三个孩子将于今天下午到达北京。

   [注解]　本题的考点为主谓一致的用法。当主语后面跟有 together with, with, as well as, no less than, along with, like, rather than, but, except, besides, including, in addition to 等引导词时，其谓语的单复数必须与这些词前面主语的单复数保持一致。本句中的主语是 Doctor Richard，所以谓语要用 is。

· 238 ·

2. [答案] knows

[译文] 无论职员还是经理，现在对该事故都一无所知。

[注解] 本题考点为主谓一致的用法。其考查的便是同学对于"就近原则"的掌握。由 neither... nor, not only... but also, either... or, or, nor 等连接的并列结构作主语，其后谓语动词的单复数形式通常按照"就近原则"处理，即靠近谓语动词的主语的单复数决定该谓语动词的单复数。故该题中谓语动词应与主语 manager 一致，为单数形式 knows。

3. [答案] D

[译文] 经理和他的顾问都同意参加这个世界博览会。

[注解] 本题考点为主谓一致的用法。其原因与历年真题解析题 1 是一样的，该句的谓语动词要跟 as well as 前面的主语的单复数保持一致，其前面的主语是 the manager，所以谓语动词要用单数，因而答案选择 D。

4. [答案] C

[译文] 商业和专业服务在黄页中列出。

[注解] 该句是简单句，缺少谓语，主语 services 和谓语动词 list 是被动关系，而 services 表示多种服务，用复数，因此应为 are listed。

5. [答案] B

[译文] 在大学学习期间，他认识了那位教授，并从他那里学到了很多。

[注解] while 表示"当……的时候"，本句完整结构为 while he was studying at college，主句和从句在主语一致的情况下，从句中的主语和 be 动词可以省略。

第 9 章

1. [答案] A

[译文] 只有当我们完成了所有的工作，才意识到已经太晚了，以至于赶不上回家的车。

[注解] 本题考查的知识点为倒装。only 引导的词组或句子放在句首作状语时，通常要用倒装结构，因此可以排除答案 C、D；又因为句中的时间状语从句用的过去完成时，那么主句的时态应该属于过去时的范畴，答案 B 也被排除，故答案为 A。

2. [答案] D

[译文] 直到前天他才同意在会议上做报告。

[注解] 本题考查的知识点为倒装。否定词 Not 放在句子的开头，主句要倒装，因此可以排除答案 A、C；又因为句子提到的时间状语为"前天"the day before yesterday，所以其时态应该属于过去时范畴，答案 B 也被排除，故答案为 D。

3. [答案] A

[译文] 直到昨天我才了解到有关那个即将完成的方案的内容。

[注解] 本题考查的知识点为时态及倒装。根据时间状语 not until yesterday，本句应该用过去时；又由于否定词在句首，所以句子要使用部分倒装，故答案为 A。

4. [答案]　D

　　[译文]　他习惯了坐飞机，不管什么情况下他都没有怕过。

　　[注解]　本题考查的知识点为倒装。表示否定意义的 on no occasion 位于第二并列分句的句首，因此要使用倒装语序，可以排除答案 A、B；再根据第一分句的意义和 ever 在句中的应用可知第二分句时态应为现在完成时，故答案为 D。

5. [答案]　D

　　[译文]　妈妈听到这个好消息后，激动得彻夜未眠。

　　[注解]　本题考查的知识点为部分倒装。以 so 开头的句子，形容词或副词会紧接其后，其句型通常使用部分倒装，其句子结构通常是系表结构，故将系动词前置；如果是主谓宾结构，就将助动词前置。故答案为 D。

6. [答案]　A

　　[译文]　学生们的音乐演奏声是如此之大以至于人们在街上都听得见。

　　[注解]　本题考查的知识点为倒装。当"so + 形容词/副词……that"结构位于句首时，表示强调，句子通常采用部分倒装形式；又根据 that 分句中的时态，可以推测出主句也用过去时态，故答案为 A。

7. [答案]　B

　　[译文]　如果上周五他动身，就已经到达巴黎了。

　　[注解]　本题考查的知识点为倒装及虚拟语气。该句是表示过去情况的虚拟条件句，省略 if 的条件从句需要将 had 提到句首，故答案为 B。

8. [答案]　D

　　[译文]　迪克因为忙，很少有时间去看电影，简也是一样。

　　[注解]　本题考查的知识点为倒装。前半句用 rarely 一词，可以知道后面的内容也是表示否定意义，即"……也一样不……"。在英语中，这种表示否定的结构，通常使用 neither 或 nor，且一般将 neither, nor 等置于句首来表示不同主语的同样动作的否定，此时，句子需采用倒装语序。故答案为 D。

9. [答案]　B

　　[译文]　他们一收完小麦，瓢泼大雨就从天而降。

　　[注解]　本题考查的知识点为倒装。当一句话由 no sooner...than 连接的两个分句组成时，no sooner 所在的分句需要倒装，因此可以排除答案 C 和 D；又从 than 所引导的分句可知该句是过去时态，因此前一分句要用过去时的范畴，且为过去完成时，故答案为 B。

10. [答案]　A

　　[译文]　直到河里的鱼儿全死光了，政府才意识到污染是多么的严重。

　　[注解]　本题考查的知识点为倒装。当 not until 放在句首时，句子的结构必须使用部分倒装的结构，因此可以排除 B 和 C 两个选项。由于"政府才意识到污染是多么的严重"这一动作发生在"鱼死"这个动作之后，所以"政府意识"这一动作应当用一般过去时。故答案为 A。

11. [答案]　B

[译文]　当我们匆忙赶到机场时才发现航班取消了。

[注解]　only 引出的从句置于句首时，主句要倒装，倒装形式为"助动词 + 主语 + 动词原形"，由从句中可以看到时态应为过去时。

12. [答案]　C

[译文]　直到昨天我才对新的广告活动有了一点了解。

[注解]　not until 引导的时间状语置于句首时，主句要倒装，倒装的形式是"助动词 + 主语 + 动词原形"；另外，时间状语 yesterday 提示本句要用过去时。

13. [答案]　D

[译文]　乔治一做完演讲，听众中的一位年轻女士就站起来表示抗议。

[注解]　该句为倒装句，hardly 置于句首，主句部分倒装，倒装形式是助动词置于主语之前。

14. [答案]　B

[译文]　我们一坐下，我就意识到把文件落在家里了。

[注解]　no sooner... than... 表示"一……就……"。从句 no sooner 后面的谓语要用部分倒装形式，sit down 的动作发生在主句 I realize 之前，提示使用过去完成时，表示"过去的过去"，故答案为 B。

15. [答案]　A

[译文]　只有真正了解你们的业务之后，我们才可以推荐合适的保险计划。

[注解]　only 置于句首，修饰状语 after we really understand your business，表示强调，主句使用倒装句，其形式为部分倒装，把助动词或情态动词放在主语之前；如果 only 放在句中，则不必倒装，语序是 We can recommended... only after we...。

16. [答案]　C

[译文]　他刚辞去一个小公司的工作，马上就得到了一家跨国大公司提供的职位。

[注解]　本句是 no sooner... than... 引导的倒装句，其形式是 No sooner had sb. done... than...。

第 10 章

1. [答案]　D

[译文]　就是因为想买一本词典，我昨天才进城了。

[注解]　本题考查对于强调句型的掌握。强调原因，使用的是"It was + 被强调成分 + that"这一固定的强调句型。因此选择 D。

2. [答案]　B

[译文]　直到出了车祸，我才认识到自己的粗心大意。

[注解]　本题考查对于强调句型的掌握。强调时间，使用的是"It was not until + 被强调成分 + that"这一强调时间状语从句的固定句型，表示"直到……才"。因此答案选择 B。

3. [答案] C
   [译文] 正是因为他在面试时的良好表现使他得到了这家大公司的工作。
   [注解] 本句考查强调句型 It is...that...。
4. [答案] A
   [译文] 我们正是在他们的伦敦分行开会讨论了这个问题。
   [注解] 强调句 It is...that... 强调地点，答案为 A。
5. [答案] D
   [译文] 正是在经济危机后不久，电子商务的销售开始增长。
   [注解] 强调句 It is...that... 强调时间状语 "soon after the economic crisis"，因此答案为 D。
6. [答案] B
   [译文] 直到昨天商业谈判才圆满结束。
   [注解] 本句考查强调句型 It is...that...。

第 11 章

1. [答案] solution
   [译文] 显然，核电绝不是解决能源危机的唯一办法。
   [注解] 此空格前为定冠词和形容词，因此需用名词。
2. [答案] believe
   [译文] 参加会议的人没有一个人相信这个新建议能顺利执行。
   [注解] 此空格前为情态动词，后跟宾语从句，因此需要谓语动词，而且用原形。
3. [答案] boring
   [译文] 课太乏味了，教室里很多学生都睡着了。
   [注解] 此空格前为系动词和副词，可推断需形容词，而且是主动意义。
4. [答案] effectively
   [译文] 政府努力寻找有效处理污染问题的方法。
   [注解] 此空格应该填状语，即副词。
5. [答案] applications
   [译文] Sandy 申请了很多管理职位，但都没有成功。
   [注解] 此空格前为介词，因此后跟名词。
6. [答案] cheerful
   [译文] 毕业生们在离校之前举行了一个愉快的告别晚会。
   [注解] 此空格前为不定冠词，空格后为名词，所以用形容词。
7. [答案] deeply
   [译文] 虽然他被她所说的深深地伤害了，但他什么也没说。
   [注解] 此空格在充当谓语的被动式中间，因此用副词。
8. [答案] investment
   [译文] 我不能确定我们是否能从投资中受益。
   [注解] 此空格前为定冠词，所以用名词。

附录 B "实战演练"参考答案

9. [答案] national
   [译文] 这个机构发起了一场全国性的反对在公众场合吸烟的运动。
   [注解] 此空格前为不定冠词，空格后为名词，所以用形容词。

10. [答案] directly
    [译文] 参加培训课程的申请应直接送到报名处。
    [注解] 此空格需用副词。

11. [答案] entirely
    [译文] 经理直到这个星期才完全意识到酒店供热系统的问题。
    [注解] 此空格在系动词和形容词之间，因此用副词。

12. [答案] difference
    [译文] 恐怕在他们看来没有分别。
    [注解] much 后接名词。

13. [答案] employee
    [译文] 我肯定才被录用的秘书将会证明是个高效的雇员。
    [注解] 形容词 efficient 修饰名词。

14. [答案] performance
    [译文] 我听说这个音乐组合将赴香港进行为期三天的表演。
    [注解] three-day 为形容词，因此后接名词。

15. [答案] extremely
    [译文] 对这个地区的农民来说，洪水之后的生活极其艰难。
    [注解] 此空格在系动词和形容词之间，因此用副词。

16. [答案] fasten
    [译文] 在航班起飞之前，所有的乘客被要求系紧安全带。
    [注解] to 为不定式符号，空格处应为动词原形，而形容词 + en 构成动词。

17. [答案] appointment
    [译文] 我不能和你一起去购物，因为我和牙医今天下午约好了。
    [注解] 不定冠词 an 后应该接名词，而动词 + ment 即可变为名词。

18. [答案] was questioned
    [译文] 这个父亲想知道为什么他儿子上周被警察询问。
    [注解] 此空格应该在从句中充当谓语，而 question 可直接转化为动词，且根据句子要求，应该用被动语态。

19. [答案] settlement
    [译文] 在罢工解决之后，火车服务现在恢复正常。
    [注解] 定冠词后应该接名词。

20. [答案] widen
    [译文] 我们应该多读、多看，以便扩展视野。
    [注解] to 为不定式符号，空格处应为动词原形，而形容词 + en 构成动词。

· 243 ·

21. ［答案］　economic
　　［译文］　有些专家建议我们应放慢经济发展的速度。
　　［注解］　此空格前为定冠词，空格后为名词，所以用形容词，意思为"经济的"。
22. ［答案］　additional
　　［译文］　做第二职业赚更多的钱也意味着你得付额外的所得税。
　　［注解］　此空格前为动词，空格后为名词，所以用形容词。而名词＋al 可变为形容词。
23. ［答案］　equipment
　　［译文］　现在不缺原材料，但我们需要性能可靠的设备。
　　［注解］　形容词后用名词，而形容词＋en 构成动词。
24. ［答案］　successful
　　［译文］　在罢工成功解决后，火车服务恢复正常。
　　［注解］　此空格前为定冠词，空格后为名词，所以用形容词，而名词＋ful 可变成形容词。
25. ［答案］　internationally
　　［译文］　如果一个公司想把产品销往全世界，就应该先做一个市场调查。
　　［注解］　此空格需填副词。
26. ［答案］　reasonable
　　［译文］　父母为孩子付教育费用是合理的。
　　［注解］　此空格前为系动词，因此此处应为形容词，而动词＋able 可变为形容词。
27. ［答案］　proposal
　　［译文］　会议上，约翰·史密斯提了一个建议。
　　［注解］　此空格前为不定冠词，所以空格处用名词，propose 为动词，加上后缀-al 后即可变为名词。
28. ［答案］　eagerly
　　［译文］　这是一个漫长的冬季，我们急切地等待春天的到来。
　　［注解］　此空格在谓语中间，因此只能充当状语，即用副词。
29. ［答案］　strength
　　［译文］　他们完全认识到了联盟的力量和影响。
　　［注解］　此空格前为形容词，因此此处须用名词。
30. ［答案］　receptionist
　　［译文］　我姐姐最近得到一个酒店接待员的工作。
　　［注解］　reception 为名词，意思为"接待"（抽象名词），而空格处需名词，且意思应为"接待员"。
31. ［答案］　objection
　　［译文］　如果没人反对，我们开始下一个议题。
　　［注解］　no 后只能用名词，而以字母 t 结尾的动词＋ion 即可变成名词。

32. [答案] response
    [译文] 到目前为止，还没有对你的计划的正面回应。
    [注解] 此空前为形容词，后接名词。
33. [答案] costly
    [译文] 在这个地方买房是很花钱的事。
    [注解] 此空格前为不定冠词，空格后为名词，所以用形容词。
34. [答案] golden
    [译文] 这个商人失去了赚大钱的机会。
    [注解] 此空格前为不定冠词，空格后为名词，所以用形容词。
35. [答案] protection
    [译文] 你应该意识到，这种稀有的鸟应该受到人类保护。
    [注解] 此空格处需用名词，而以字母 t 结尾的动词 + ion 即可变成名词。
36. [答案] permission
    [译文] 你得到当局开业的许可了吗？
    [注解] 此空格处需用名词，而以字母 t 结尾的动词 + tion/sion 即可变成名词。
37. [答案] payment
    [译文] 如今，购物使用电子支付比现金或支票更方便。
    [注解] 填入的单词与 electronic 构成句子的主语，因此应该是名词。
38. [答案] growth
    [译文] 网上购物的发展使消费者行为发生了根本变化。
    [注解] 定冠词后接名词。
39. [答案] responsibility
    [译文] 录用新员工是人力资源部的职责。
    [注解] 定冠词后接名词。
40. [答案] education
    [译文] 我一直兼职赚钱继续学业。
    [注解] 所有格后接名词。
41. [答案] comfortable
    [译文] 一半以上的员工说他们和上司说话时感到不自在。
    [注解] 连系动词后接形容词。
42. [答案] harmful
    [译文] 各种水污染对人和动物的健康都有危害。
    [注解] 连系动词后接形容词。
43. [答案] entirely
    [译文] 如果给我们机会来经营你们的产品，结果完全会令人满意。
    [注解] satisfactory 是形容词，须用副词来修饰。

44. [答案] importance
    [译文] 经理强调了制定公司长期战略的重要性。
    [注解] 定冠词后接名词。
45. [答案] employers
    [译文] 在家上班不仅对雇员，而且对雇主都很灵活、有益。
    [注解] not only... but also 强调并列关系。
46. [答案] equipment
    [译文] 地方政府决定对农村医院投入更多资金。
    [注解] 定冠词后接名词。
47. [答案] worse
    [译文] 我试图自己修电脑，但把电脑弄得比我想象的还要糟。
    [注解] than 前应为比较级。
48. [答案] achievement
    [译文] 赢得三块金牌是到目前为止他取得的最卓越的成绩了。
    [注解] remarkable 为形容词，后接名词。
49. [答案] effectively
    [译文] 为有效处理频发的火车事故，设立了一个特别委员会。
    [注解] 修饰动词用副词。
50. [答案] required
    [译文] 除必修课外，还有一些可供个人选择的其他课程。
    [注解] required 为形容词，修饰 courses。
51. [答案] successful
    [译文] 如果想有生之年成功，就应该诚实、自信。
    [注解] 表语要求形容词，名词 success + ful 构成形容词。
52. [答案] suggestion
    [译文] 那位工程师在会上提了一个改善公共交通系统的建议。
    [注解] 冠词后接名词。
53. [答案] pleased
    [译文] 很高兴通知你，你获得了一等奖。
    [注解] 表语要求形容词，动词 + ed 可构成形容词。
54. [答案] helpful
    [译文] 专家为这个项目提出了一条有益的建议。
    [注解] 形容词作定语。
55. [答案] published
    [译文] 根据昨天发表的报告，越来越多的年轻人参与到社区活动中。
    [注解] 形容词作后置定语。

56. [答案] contribution
    [译文] 经理在讲话中向对公司做出贡献的员工表示感谢。
    [注解] 所有格后接名词。
57. [答案] disappointment
    [译文] 令她失望的是，她申请工作遭到拒绝。
    [注解] 所有格后接名词。
58. [答案] particularly
    [译文] 在某些情况下，通过眼神交流似乎尤其重要。
    [注解] particularly 修饰形容词 important。
59. [答案] additional
    [译文] 由于更多客户要参加会议，我们要额外多准备一些椅子。
    [注解] 形容词作定语。
60. [答案] independence
    [译文] 这些公寓让老年人保持独立性，同时提供医疗护理。
    [注解] 所有格后接名词。
61. [答案] directly
    [译文] 我们希望把所有直接卷入这次冲突的各方召集起来。
    [注解] 修饰动词用副词。
62. [答案] active
    [译文] 我们应继续给予联合国充分而积极的支持。
    [注解] 形容词作定语，修饰 support。
63. [答案] management
    [译文] 制定预算是任何机构管理控制过程中的一个重要部分。
    [注解] 名词修饰名词。
64. [答案] application
    [译文] 我们很高兴通知您，您的会员资格申请已被接受。
    [注解] 所有格后接名词。
65. [答案] suitable
    [译文] 公司提供多种适合员工目标、背景和才能的岗位。
    [注解] 形容词作后置定语修饰 roles。
66. [答案] personal
    [译文] 我们竭尽全力确保交易和您的个人信息安全。
    [注解] 形容词作定语，修饰 information。

附录 C "专项练习"参考答案

第 1 章

1. efficiency
2. skillful
3. electricity
4. To serve
5. motivation
6. enlarge
7. qualified
8. plays
9. thoughtful
10. confused
11. relaxation
12. has been reading
13. to become
14. survivors
15. consideration
16. impossible
17. is
18. exciting
19. anxiety
20. sense
21. absence
22. distance
23. selfless
24. fluently
25. childlike
26. expressions
27. heavily
28. dangerous
29. farther
30. thankful
31. receptionist
32. musical
33. modernize
34. application

第 2 章

1. C   2. C   3. C   4. B   5. A   6. D   7. C   8. C   9. A   10. A
11. B   12. A   13. A   14. B   15. B   16. D   17. B   18. B   19. C   20. A
21. D   22. C   23. D   24. B   25. D   26. D   27. B   28. D   29. D   30. D
31. D   32. C   33 B   34. C   35. C   36. D   37. D   38. B   39. C   40. C
41. C   42. B   43. B   44. C   45. B   46. D   47. B   48. D   49. A   50. D
51. C   52. A   53. A   54. C   55. A   56. B   57. A   58. A   59. D   60. A

第 3 章

1. B   2. C   3. A   4. A   5. D   6. C   7. C   8. D   9. A   10. D
11. C   12. C   13. D   14. B   15. A   16. B   17. C   18. B   19. C   20. C
21. D   22. C   23. D   24. D   25. C   26. C   27. D   28. C   29. B   30. C
31. C   32. C   33. D   34. B   35. C   36. C   37. D   38. C   39. A   40. C
41. B   42. D   43. A   44. C   45. A   46. D   47. C   48. C   49. B   50. B

第 4 章

I . 1. Reading   2. to offer   3. to be invited   4. studying
5. collecting   6. to operate   7. amused, amused, amusing
8. holding   9. setting   10. to set   11. considered

· 248 ·

附录 C 专项练习参考答案

12. to be studying   13. to have been treated   14. making, being made
15. live, living   16. smoking   17. being invited   18. to do
19. getting   20. seeing   21. to post   22. reading
23. finishing   24. admit   25. to admit   26. repairing(to be repaired)
27. to repair   28. heard   29. hear   30. to learn
31. playing   32. play   33. decorated   34. decorate
35. to do   36. covered   37. being sung   38. informed
39. moving   40. to have translated   41. to have been translated
42. stolen   43. burning   44. To improve   45. Study
46. Studying   47. Seen   48. Seeing   49. to have given
50. to hear   51. to be invited 52. to find   53. Not having completed
54. looking   55. being   56. was   57. to do, to live
58. built   59. to be built   60. being built

Ⅱ. 1. B   2. B   3. B   4. A   5. D   6. A   7. C   8. B   9. C   10. A
11. D   12. C   13. A   14. C   15. A   16. B   17. D   18. A   19. C   20. A
21. B   22. D   23. D   24. A   25. B   26. D   27. A   28. C   29. A   30. B
31. A   32. C   33. C   34. B   35. A   36. B   37. D   38. C   39. D   40. B

第 5 章

1. A   2. A   3. B   4. C   5. A   6. C   7. C   8. B   9. C   10. B
11. A.   12. D   13. C   14. B   15. B   16. C   17. C   18. A   19. C   20. D
21. A   22. C   23. C   24. A   25. D   26. D   27. C   28. A   29. C   30. D
31. B   32. A   33. C   34. C   35. B   36. C   37. B   38. C   39. C   40. A
41. B   42. A   43. B   44. D   45. C   46. A   47. D   48. A   49. B   50. D

第 6 章

1. D   2. B   3. D   4. D   5. A   6. C   7. C   8. A   9. B   10. A
11. C   12. A   13. D   14. C   15. D   16. B   17. B   18. C   19. A   20. B
21. B   22. C   23. D   24. C   25. A   26. B   27. A   28. C   29. B   30. C
31. D   32. B   33. A   34. B   35. A   36. C   37. B   38. D   39. C   40. B
41. C   42. D   43. A   44. D   45. D   46. C   47. B   48. B   49. C   50. B
51. D   52. A   53. B   54. A   55. C   56. D   57. B   58. B   59. C   60. B
61. D   62. C   63. A   64. C   65. B   66. D   67. B   68. B   69. C   70. C
71. A   72. D   73. B   74. B   75. B   76. C   77. D   78. C   79. C   80. A
81. B   82. C   83. D   84. B   85. D

第 7 章

1. C   2. A   3. A   4. B   5. D   6. A   7. C   8. D   9. D   10. D

11. C	12. B	13. B	14. B	15. C	16. A	17. B	18. D	19. D	20. C
21 B	22. D	23. B	24. D	25. D	26. B	27. C	28. D	29. B	30. D
31. D	32. B	33. C	34. C	35. B	36. A	37. D	38. A	39. D	40. A

第 8 章

1. is	2. is	3. is	4. is	5. is	6. is
7. shows	8. has	9. is	10. is	11. rot	12. has
13. am	14. is	15. was	16. has	17. is	18. has
19. is	20. have	21. was	22. makes	23. want	24. attends
25. is worked	26. is	27. learns	28. races	29. is	30. doesn't
31. was	32. seems	33. have	34. equals	35. are	36. has
37. goes	38. is	39. is	40. have		

第 9 章

1. B	2. D	3. A	4. A	5. D	6. A	7. B	8. C	9. A	10. C
11. D	12. D	13. B	14. A	15. D	16. B	17. A	18. A	19. C	20. A
21. A	22. A	23. C	24. B	25. A	26. A	27. B	28. A	29. A	30. C
31. B	32. C	33. D	34. B	35. C	36. D	37. A	38. C	39. B	40. A
41. C	42. A	43. D	44. C	45. A	46. B	47. A	48. B	49. C	50. A
51. A	52. C	53. B	54. A	55. B	56. C	57. B	58. A	59. D	60. D
61. A	62. B	63. A	64. D	65. A	66. C	67. B	68. B	69. C	70. D

第 10 章

1. D	2. B	3. A	4. C	5. A	6. A	7. C	8. A	9. C	10. A
11. B	12. C	13. D	14. A	15. D	16. C	17. C	18. A	19. C	20. D
21. A	22. C	23. D	24. A	25. B	26. A	27. B	28. C	29. B	30. D
31. D	32. D	33. C	34. D	35. A	36. D	37. B	38. B	39. B	40. A
41. A	42. A	43. C	44. D	45. C	46. A	47. B	48. B	49. A	50. C

第 11 章

Ⅰ. 1. B	2. D	3. A	4. C	5. B	6. C	7. B	8. D	9. C	10. B
11. A	12. C	13. D	14. C	15. B	16. B	17. A	18. A	19. A	20. B
21. C	22. B	23. B	24. C	25. A	26. D	27. A	28. D	29. B	30. A
31. D	32. A	33. C	34. C	35. B					

Ⅱ.
1. accommodation	2. acceptance	3. addition	4. additional
5. Action	6. actual	7. advanced	8. allowance
9. amazement	10. analysis	11. anxious	12. appetizing
13. appearance	14. approval	15. arrival	16. artist
17. assistance	18. attendance	19. awareness	20. behavior
21. boundless	22. Careless	23. central	24. challenging
25. childhood	26. classify	27. colorful	28. collection
29. complaint	30. Confidence	31. consequently	32. considerable
33. considerate	34. consideration	35. container	36. curiosity
37. deadly	38. decision	39. defense	40. definition
41. delivery	42. independent	43. depth	44. dirt
45. discovery	46. distant	47. eastern	48. economical
49. effective	50. efficiency	51. energetic	52. environmental
53. evident	54. exception	55. expectation	56. explanation
57. Failure	58. faithful	59. flexibility	60. flight
61. global	62. growth	63. guidance	64. hatred
65. height	66. Honesty	67. illegal	68. increase
69. invitations	70. judge	71. knowledge	72. length
73. longing	74. loosens loosened, loosed, looses		75. loss
76. magical, magic	77. majority	78. monthly	79. motherly
80. noisy	81. northern	82. occasionally	83. original
84. partly	85. patience	86. poems	87. possibility
88. presence	89. priority	90. privacy	91. products
92. proof	93. proposal	94. qualification	95. reasonable
96. reference	97. refusal	98. reliable	99. reservation
100. risky	101. safety	102. scholarships	103. scientific
104. shortage	105. Shortly	106. simplify	107. sleepy
108. society	109. solution	110. specialist	111. specifically
112. Speech	113. successful	114. success	115. talktive
116. technician	117. threatened	118. variety	119. various
120. weight			

参 考 书 目

[1] 王建军．各个击破语法[M]．延边：延边人民出版社，2006．
[2] 李俊峰，汪家扬．大学英语语法讲座和练习[M]．北京：兵器工业出版社，1997．
[3] 李晓莉，罗东山．实用英语语法[M]．武汉：华中科技大学出版社，2007．
[4] 王善芝．简明英语语法讲座[M]．北京：国防工业出版社，2007．
[5] 张福元．英语语法精讲与测试[M]．上海：华东理工大学出版社，2008．
[6] 张向阳．实用大学英语语法教程[M]．南京：东南大学出版社，2008．
[7] 田夕伟，杨春霞．高职高专英语语法教程[M]．北京：科学出版社，2008．
[8] 张金正．大学英语语法42讲[M]．北京：国防工业出版社，2007．
[9] 章振邦．新编英语语法教程[M]．上海：上海外语教育出版社，1992．
[10] 何庆机．大学英语语法教程[M]．上海：东华大学出版社，2006．
[11] 张道真．实用英语语法[M]．北京：商务印书馆，1995．
[12] 张鑫友，许峰．大学英语语法[M]．武汉：湖北人民出版社，2001．
[13] （美）托马斯·艾略特·伯利．英语用法最常见错误[M]．山东：山东科学技术出版社，1982．
[14] 王发明．高等学校英语应用能力考试（A级）词汇必备[M]．北京：外文出版社，2008．